With the compliments
of the
Canada Council

Avec les hommages
du
Conseil des Arts du Canada

THE FOUNDING OF CANADA

Beginnings to 1815

THE
FOUNDING
OF
CANADA

Beginnings to 1815

Third Printing

By

STANLEY B. RYERSON

PROGRESS BOOKS
TORONTO CANADA
1972

ISBN 0-919396-04-6 (Clothbound)
ISBN 0-919396-15-1 (Paperback)

Progress Books, 487 Adelaide St. West, Toronto 133, Canada.
Printed and bound in Canada.

The text of this book was typeset 11 on 13 Baskerville by Eveready
Printers Ltd., Toronto, and printed offset on Kruger Workbook.

Contents

MAPS

ILLUSTRATIONS

Foreword

Canadians, approaching the 100th anniversary of Confederation, face some singularly vital questions. One has to do with the relations between French and English-speaking Canada: can the arrangement of 1867 continue, without radical modification, into a second century? Another, looming larger still, involves our relations with the United States: can we survive as an independent country, in face of pressures for absorption—cultural, economic, and above all, military? These questions confront us in a setting charged with the overriding issue of human survival in the thermonuclear age. National equality, Canadian independence, peace, are inseparably interwoven.

Can an understanding of the historic roots of our present problems help us in the search for answers, for a sense of direction? I believe it can.

The Canada of today, like the rest of our world, is the product of driving-forces, of an evolution, that can be studied and understood: that is the approach taken in the present outline-sketch. Considered as fundamental are the actual, living *relationships of people at work,* their slowly extending mastery of the forces of nature, the conflicts of social structure arising from relationships of property. The struggles and ideas of people are what make history. They operate, not in a vacuum but in and upon a specific setting, a given social system. This is what Marx described as the standpoint which views "the evolution of the economic formation of society as a process of natural history.". . .

What I have attempted here (and in a sequel that is in preparation, on the period 1815 to 1871) is no more than a preliminary breaking of ground, suggesting a line of approach to a re-interpretation of this country's history. I trust that this study may make some contribution to the wide-ranging debate about the nature of Canadian reality, the forces that have shaped our past and present, our responsibilities toward tomorrow.

S.B.R.

Toronto
November
1962

NOTE ON THIS EDITION

Apart from correction of some errors of detail, and the adding of supplementary notes to several chapters, this Edition differs from the first in that the final chapter, "Outcome of the War," is largely new (it was first published in the Summer 1962 issue of *The Marxist Quarterly*). A brief comment on Marxism and Canadian history-writing, previously included in the *Foreword*, now constitutes a *Postscript*, followed by acknowledgment of my indebtedness to friends, co-workers and researchers for invaluable assistance in this project.

FOOTNOTES AND REFERENCE NOTES

A satisfactory solution of this problem has yet to be found; so I have adopted the unsatisfactory one of relegating source-references to the back of the book, while retaining footnotes mainly for comment on or polemic with contemporary authorities.

I

Bedrock of Canada. Beginnings of Life. "Labor Created Man."

THREE OCEANS BORDER OUR COUNTRY, WITH LAND BOUN-
daries to the south and northwest. In all, they encompass
close to four million square miles of territory. Age-long
processes shaped this North American land mass. Our
coasts and watercourses, the mountains, lakes and plains
have a history of their own. Long before the coming of
man, the surface of this land was being fashioned: in part
by the slow weathering process of wind and water, frost
and snow; in part by convulsive, shattering upheavals
born of mighty shifts or volcanic action from the depths
below. About three billion years ago there took shape the
mighty arc of rock that is the Canadian Shield. One of the
oldest formations in the world, it underlies our Arctic
islands and, on the mainland, sweeps westward in a wide
half-circle around Hudson Bay, from Labrador to the
mouth of the Mackenzie. This, Canada's massive cornerstone, is the ancient core of the continent.

Much later, a series of earth-shaking upheavals—named
by geologists the Appalachian and the Laramide Revolutions—formed our mountainous eastern and western ram-
parts.

The Shield itself is the product of a series of geological revolutions—mighty subterranean thrusts that lifted
up masses of granite and sedimentary rock to make great
mountain ranges. These in the course of millions of years
were worn down into low, rounded hills, and later scraped
bare by the glaciers of the Ice Age.

The era during which the Shield took shape is known as the Precambrian. Its upthrusts of molten crystalline rock brought into being the gold and silver deposits at Porcupine, Kirkland Lake and Cobalt, Ontario, and the copper and nickel ores of Sudbury and those of Coppermine in the North West Territories. They brought, also, the iron deposits of Steep Rock, Michipicoten, Marmora, Ungava, Labrador.

The Precambrian era goes far back beyond the first beginnings of life. Only its later formations, dating back some six hundred million years, hold fossil traces of some of the earliest living organisms.

The eras that followed the Precambrian are known as those of Ancient, Middle and Recent Life.*

In the first of these life evolved from its early marine beginnings to the first appearance of land plants and, in the animal world, of fishes, amphibians and reptiles. During part of this era, which lasted some four hundred million years, the Canadian Shield was linked by land, via Greenland, with what now is Europe. Where now the Rockies and Appalachians stand, the sea filled two great troughs; in these, beds of sediment were laid down; much later they were twisted, folded and hoisted up into great mountain ranges. At one point the sea-floor in the eastern trench was slowly lifted, emerging as a swampy plain. Its luxuriant vegetation in time was submerged, compressed and transformed into the coal deposits of Nova Scotia.

At the close of the era, enormous pressure built up from the side of the Atlantic sea-bed, forcing up the eastern edge of the continent and, with much crumpling of strata, forming the ranges of the Appalachians—the Shickshocks, Green Mountains, Alleghenies. The Gaspé copper deposits and the iron ores of Wabana, Newfoundland,

---

*Paleozoic, Mesozoic, Cenozoic.

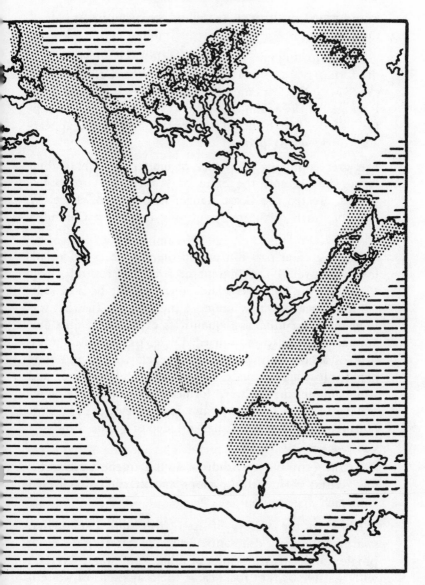

North America in the Era of Ancient Life.
(Shaded areas: water. White: land)

were formed in this era, as well as the bituminous coal of the Maritimes.

The following era, that of "Middle Life," opened with the forming of the Coast Range of British Columbia and closed with the Laramide Revolution which fashioned the Rockies. In the realm of life it was the age of great reptiles, of the first birds and mammals, and of the appearance of flowering plants.

A great uplifting of a ridge of molten rock, extending from what is now the State of Washington up to the Yukon, created the Coast Range; its ore deposits are the basis of much of the metal mining in British Columbia today.

In the greater part of this and the preceding era a shallow sea covered the present area of the central Great Plains: on its floor were laid down the flat beds of sedimentary rock that now underlie the Prairies. In what was then undersea mud vast quantities of marine plants and animal organisms were buried. Under the mounting pressure of accumulating sediment the clay, sand and lime deposits turned to shale, sandstone and limestone; and from organic matter were formed the great pools of oil and natural gas of Alberta and Saskatchewan. (The Fort Norman and Turner Valley oil deposits date from the close of the preceding era.)

As the central sea withdrew, it left to the westward a low coastal plain, with swamps and marshlands covered with rich vegetation.

Here, in the valleys of Red Deer and Drumheller, swarmed the giant dinosaurs. From the decaying debris of jungle forests, turned into peat-bogs and then overlaid with massive beds of rock, came the coal seams of western Alberta and eastern British Columbia, typified by those at Drumheller and the Crow's Nest Pass.

Meanwhile, in the great sea-trough that separated the western plain from the Coast Range, enormously thick beds of sediment had been laid down. As their weight increased conflicting pressures were set up involving the adjoining land masses and the ocean floor of the Pacific. This process came to a head with a mighty series of thrusts that hoisted the trough-beds upward and eastward. The result was the series of mountain chains extending through the Mackenzie and Franklin ranges, the Rockies and right down through the Andes to Cape Horn. This was the Laramide Revolution. (Somewhat later, on the other side of the earth, a similar upheaval gave birth to the Alps, Carpathians and Himalayas.)

The latest of the great eras of geological time is that of "Recent Life."

The great reptiles of the preceding era had been wiped out, perhaps because the Laramide upheaval brought changes in climate and vegetation that affected their food supply. The new era witnessed a remarkable evolution of mammals of many and varied types. Deer, bison and musk-ox, camel, rhinoceros, mastodon (fore-runner of the elephant) and a prehistoric form of horse, roamed over North America. Lemurs and other small monkeys were present on this side of the world; but it was in Asia, not in the Americas, that the man-like (anthropoid) apes appeared—including those that were the precursors of man.

In the course of hundreds of thousands of years, some of the anthropoid apes acquired an erect posture and, with it, the use of the forepaws as *hands*. By learning to make *tools*, these "pre-men" set themselves apart from other animals: instead of simply grazing and gathering sustenance from nature as it was, they began to work on nature, use it for their purposes, and thereby to transform it. In the course of working together, they created *speech*.

With the use of the hand, labor and speech, the human brain was gradually perfected: Man emerged.

"Labor," says Frederick Engels, the co-founder with Karl Marx of scientific socialism, *"begins with the making of tools."* And further: *"Labor . . . is the primary basic condition for all human existence, and this to such an extent that, in a sense, we have to say: labor created man himself."*

Slowly, man gained a measure of mastery over nature—and with each advance his horizons widened. At the same time, as Engels points out, "the development of labor necessarily helped to bring the members of society closer together by multiplying cases of mutual support, joint activity, and by making clear the advantage of this joint activity to each individual."

Thus, in struggle with the forces of nature, human society was taking shape. Man was from the first a social being.

The "first great victory of mankind over nature" was the discovery that friction can be made to produce fire. This gigantic advance, commemorated in legends (the story of Prometheus defying the gods by giving man the gift of fire is one of many), was the starting point of man's technology: "the first instance of men pressing a non-living force of nature into their service."

This great discovery occurred in the Old World, before man came to this continent.

In the latter part of the era of Recent Life there occurred the so-called Ice Age: during a period of a million years or so, huge continental glaciers, under pressure of mountainous accumulations of ice, fanned out from four main centres—the western mountains, Keewatin (west of Hudson Bay), Labrador and Greenland. At four different times the ice sheets spread, covering an area

greater than that of Canada today. In long intervals of
warmer climate, they melted at the edges and shrank
back. (The most recent withdrawal of the ice sheet began
only some 20,000 years ago; its vestiges are today's glaciers, the zone of permafrost, the polar ice-cap in the
Arctic and Antarctica.) The great glaciers in their inva-
sions scraped the Shield bare and dumped its soil in what
are now the fertile St. Lawrence drainage basin and the
western Prairies. They piled up great drifts of broken rock,
blocked old water courses, and left behind innumerable
new rivers and lakes. Southern Manitoba was for a time
covered by what geologists have called "Lake Agassiz,"
successors to which are Lakes Winnipeg, Winnipegosis
and Manitoba. "Lake Ojibwa" occupied what is now the
Northern Ontario clay belt. The fore-runner of the three
upper Great Lakes was one, "Lake Algonquin," and of
Lake Ontario, "Lake Iroquois," which at one time
emptied into the Hudson River, and at another opened
directly on the incoming waters of the Atlantic.*

Of the work of the ice sheets, the leading Canadian geol-
ogist A. P. Coleman has written: "Canada is not only the
oldest, but also the youngest, country in the world, since
its present surface, its lakes and rivers and its scenery,
have been profoundly modified and impressed by events
in the latest part of geological time. . . . A very ancient
land surface has been completely renovated. . . . In the
north the bare rocky hills show the scouring, polishing
and striations made by advancing ice; while toward the
south there are gently undulating stretches of boulder
clay making excellent farms. . . . The rejuvenating work
of the ice sheets [has provided] rich soil, easily harnessed
water power, and a great chain of lakes for inland communication."

---

*Recent researches indicate that the inland waters met the sea near
the present site of Prescott.

NORTHERN
ARCTIC BELT

ARCTIC ARCHIPELAGO

ARCTIC CIRCLE

CORDILLERAN REGION

GREAT PLAINS

CANADIAN SHIELD

HUDSON BAY

LOWLAND

CANADIAN SHIELD

INTERIOR LOWLANDS

APPALACHIAN REG

Main divisions of the present Canadian land mass.

Thus was the great land mass of Canada fashioned through the slow ages of geological time. Between the Western Cordillera and the Shield, and between the Shield and the Appalachians, ran two of the three main drainage and irrigation systems of the continent: the Great Lakes-St. Lawrence system and that of the Arctic and Hudson Bay (the third being that of the Mississippi). Forest and fertile plain and valley, coal and gas and oil and uranium, non-ferrous metals and iron ore—from coast to coast it was a vast storehouse of resources, energy, potential.

But it was to a still-unknown land, in whose forests and plains roamed the mammoth and the mastodon, that Man came, crossing over to the Americas from what is now Siberia during the slow withdrawal of the last ice sheets.*

MAN'S ENTRY INTO
THIS HEMISPHERE

---

*The generally prevailing view is the one stated here—that the Americas were originally peopled through migration from North-East Asia. A number of other theories have been advanced, however. Paul Rivet, of the Institute of Ethnology of the University of Paris, argues strongly in *Les Origines de l'Homme Américain* (1943) for a threefold series of migrations: from Asia via the Bering route (the earliest); from Australia, around the rim of the Antarctic area; and from the Melanesian islands of the Pacific.

Another hypothesis, of "dual entry from east and west into this continent" is advanced by F. Ridley ("Transatlantic Contacts of Primitive Man: Eastern Canada and Northwestern Russia". 1960). While accepting the theory of migration via Bering Strait, Ridley points to a discontinuity in certain types of stone tools and pottery extending from the Lake Baikal area in Siberia to eastern Ontario (a distance of some 6,000 miles); and notes, in contrast, the presence of striking similarities in polished stone and ground slate implements, in the use of red ochre in burials, and in decorative techniques in pottery, as between cultures of the St. Lawrence Valley and of northwestern Europe in the period of 500 to 1000 B.C. He concludes: "On the possibility of passage across the north Atlantic: It is 500 miles from Europe to Iceland and 200 miles from Iceland to Greenland. Passage from Greenland to Labrador was no insurmountable problem since archaeology and history advise of these territories being in possession of the Canadian Eskimo."

II

First Dwellers in Our Land. Ancient Communal Society

THE WRITTEN RECORD OF OUR COUNTRY'S HISTORY covers less than five centuries. Before that there were more than two hundred centuries of human habitation, struggle and achievements. The bare outline of this "prehistory" is gradually taking shape as archaeologists piece together the mute, scattered bits of evidence of ancient camp-sites and primitive settlements. This information is correlated, in turn, with what is known of the material culture and social life of the Indian and Arctic peoples in recent times. The piecing togther of a composite picture of our most distant past is itself an evolving process. New archaeological discoveries are being made all the time, adding to our knowledge and often modifying previous assumptions. So the picture we possess at present is incomplete, and subject to amendment.

Man came to North America from Asia, probably during the latter stages of the most recent glacial period. The great ice sheet then overlay most of the northern half of the continent, except for western Alaska and the Klondike valley. A narrow neck of land connected easternmost Siberia and the western tip of Alaska: over it, some time between twenty and forty thousand years ago, primitive Stone-Age hunting peoples entered this continent. Likely they were pursuing the reindeer and bison, mammoth and mastodon that had long been crossing over by this same land-bridge. Later, the sea level rose and submerged the connecting isthmus: thereafter, migrants from Asia must

have used dug-out canoes or kayaks made of skins to traverse the 40 to 50-mile-wide Bering Strait with its "step-
ping-stones," the islands of Big and Little Diomede.*

Apparently there were successive waves of migration,
spread over thousands of years. The newcomers, moving
slowly from one hunting area to another, gradually fanned
out over the continent. (In time, some reached South
America: its southern tip was inhabited at least eight or
nine thousand years ago.)

The last glacial period was marked by intervals of advance and retreat. Intermittently, the ice sheet spread
south of our present border, then shrank back. It was during these intervals of retreat of the ice that the peoples
who had crossed over from Asia fanned out over the continent. The last southward thrust of the ice sheet began
about twenty thousand years ago, and lasted ten thousand
years. When it was over, the prehistoric mammoth and
mastodon had vanished and the large inland seas that
were the forerunners of the Great Lakes lay along the
southern edge of the ice-scraped Laurentian Shield.

The Stone Age hunters who were the first inhabitants
of North America represented, with their Amerindian
descendants,** a distinct ethnic type. While closest to the
Mongol peoples, in all likelihood they stemmed from an
East Asian stock that was the common ancestor of them
both. (The Eskimo, or Inuit, who may have come later,
are more closely related to the Mongol peoples.)

So long ago did the migrations take place that, despite
the physical resemblances, there has been found so far no
convincing trace of kinship between any Asian tongue
and the hundred and twenty or so languages of the native

---

*See Note, p. 9.
**The name "Indian" was given in error by Columbus, who thought
he had reached the approaches to India. The geography was straighten-
ed out later, but the name remains.

peoples of the Americas.* But there were marked cultural resemblances as between the Chukchi, Koryak and other Eastern Siberian groups, and the native inhabitants of the Canadian Arctic and North Pacific regions. Their tents and canoes were of similar construction, as were their baskets and other containers; there are also marked resemblances in folklore—as in the prevalence of myths whose central figure is the Raven.

The material culture of the first dwellers in this land belonged to the latter part of the period known as the Old Stone Age.** They made tools of chipped stone, wood and bone, and knew the use of fire. They clothed themselves with skins, and made dwellings of bark or hides stretched over tree-poles, or out of snow—depending on the place or the season. Their only domestic animal was the dog.

During the twenty or thirty centuries that preceded the European "discovery" of North America, the peoples inhabiting this continent passed through a number of distinct phases of Stone Age development. The artifacts (man-made objects) that have been found in long-buried camp-sites, settlements and burial grounds bear witness to a slow but definite progression in technique.

In 1951 a Canadian archaeologist, Thomas Lee, discovered a camp-site that is one of the oldest on the continent. It stood "on a wooded hilltop overlooking Sheguiandah Bay on Manitoulin Island." There he found artifacts in a bed of peat; carbon-dating showed them to be more

---

*A possible exception is the Athapaskan Indian language, but this is uncertain. In any case, the extent of the "break" with the languages of Asia may be due to the greater fluidity of those forms of speech that are not "held" or fixed in a written language.

**Old Stone Age: *Paleolithic*. New Stone Age: *Neolithic*. (In the Eastern Hemisphere the age following the Neolithic was that of Bronze, followed in turn by that of Iron.) See Table, p. 18.

than 9,000 years old.* But underlying them, imbedded in boulder clay, were stone tools of vastly greater antiquity—which provided *"strong indications that man was present before the last ice sheet advanced over the area."* These ancient people quarried quartzite from the ridges of Manitoulin. With it they made projectile points (arrow and spear-heads) which they used in hunting the wooly mammoth.

If Lee's estimate of the age of the older, boulder-clay relics were to be confirmed, it could mean that man had come to this continent far earlier than had been believed hitherto.

On the western prairie, fluted stone arrow points (of the type known as "Folsom") have been found: they may be between ten and twenty thousand years old. Northeast of Winnipeg, at Whiteshell, there are the encampment-sites of a hunting people; they left behind—perhaps 10,000 years ago—weapons and tools of stone and bone, and heaps of discarded clam-shells.

Sometimes these "Paleo-Indian" peoples fashioned their stone artifacts in large quantities at a quarry-site. This was the case on Manitoulin, and similar ancient "tool works" have been found in Quebec, near Tadoussac and at the south end of Lake Mistassini.

The next phase of ancient Indian history is the "Archaic," also known as "Laurentian"; it flourished north of the St. Lawrence some five or six thousand years ago. The double-edged knives and spear-heads of ground slate of the Laurentian hunting people reflected a new level of technical skill. They used the atlatl or spear-thrower, the gouge, and a moon-shaped cutting tool like the Eskimo

---

*Carbon-dating: a method (discovered in 1949), based on the known rate of disintegration of radioactive carbon (C14), which makes it possible to establish the age of organic matter—vegetation, fossils, bones. A process developed at the University of Manitoba (1953) measures the age of such materials dating as far back as forty to fifty thousand years. See Note at end of Chapter.

ulo or "woman's knife." They made beautifully carved ornaments of banded slate.

Around this time, a people of the Lake Superior area were mining and working copper. Smelting was unknown, but they tempered the beaten metal by heating and cooling it. Through trade, the products of these early metallurgists were spread over a wide area.

More recent than the Laurentian culture is that of the "Woodland" period. It is marked by the introduction of pottery, weaving and agriculture. These epoch-making developments mark the arrival of the New Stone (Neolithic) Age. Out of the Woodland culture there later developed the Iroquoian and Algonkian cultures.

Agriculture seems to have been developed in the New World independently of its appearance in the Old. Corn was being grown in New Mexico four thousand years ago.* Its cultivation probably spread northeastward via the Mississippi and Ohio valleys and reached southwestern Ontario at least three thousand years ago. (Some of the Laurentian people appear to have ground corn; but its extensive cultivation belongs to the Woodland period.)

The oldest pottery discovered in the northeastern part of the continent dates back perhaps three thousand years. There are strong suggestions of possible connection with Siberian work of a similar or earlier period; but what may have been the path that such cultural influence followed remains unclear.

The earliest centre of the ancient Iroquoian culture seems to have been in southern Ontario. Whereas the earlier Woodland people camped at waterside sites by the

---

*Traces of agricultural activity dating back some eight thousand years have been discovered recently in Mexico. The cultivation of maize in what are now Guatemala, Mexico and Peru provided the foundation for the highly-developed Maya, Aztec and Inca civilizations that flourished there in the early centuries of the present era.

streams or lakes, the Iroquoians tended to settle inland, on ground suitable for raising crops of corn. The Iroquoian culture spread from southern Ontario into the area of western New York State. It may have been in existence for over a thousand years before the Europeans came.

At that time, it was mainly the Iroquoians who practised agriculture; most of the Algonkian and other peoples still remained at the hunting and food-gathering stage of development.

The arts of making pottery with fired clay, of weaving and of cultivating edible plants—all were most probably the work of woman. She had made baskets, and now clay pots; she wove rushes into mats and garments; from gathering roots and berries, she learned to plant and nurture the seeds of beans and squash and corn. Her role as the first agriculturist may well have had something to do with her authority as head of the house in the Iroquoian tribal farming community. Thus, the eminent Canadian anthropologist Diamond Jenness speaks of "the important place that agriculture held in their economic life, and the distribution of labor . . . leaving the entire cultivation of the fields and the acquisition of the greater part of the food supply to the women."

The structure of society that prevailed among the earliest inhabitants of what now is Canada was the social system that existed in all other early communities: *primitive-communal society*.

Primitive-communal society is based on *common ownership* of hunting or fishing grounds, communal dwellings, food-stores. Individual property is limited to articles of personal use. At this level of technique, with productive powers at a rudimentary level, the struggle for a bare minimum of subsistence took up nearly all of people's time and energies. Under these conditions, mutual aid and the sharing in common of food and shelter were a law of survival. Because there could be no question of any regular provision of a surplus of food or other necessities, there was no place for a leisure class living off the surplus produce of others.

At this stage, the division of society into classes has not yet taken place: instead of a cleavage within society, as between groups whose relationship to the means of production sets them in opposition to each other (slaves and slave-owners, feudal landowners and serfs, capitalists and wage-workers)—here the community is united, sharing on an equal footing in the struggle for survival.

In the absence of class-division, the *state* as a separate machinery of force for maintaining class rule does not yet exist. Moral pressure, public opinion, the weight of tradition and taboo, take the place of police and prisons.

Only in one area, at the time of the Europeans' coming, was this primitive-communal society beginning to break up and give way to a social structure based on slavery: on the Pacific Coast. Everywhere else the primitive-communal system was still flourishing.

And it was the startling fact of the existence of this form of society that evoked the wondering comment of practically every European "discoverer" of the New World. To cite only a few:

"It appeared to us that they had no laws [and] live in complete liberty" (Giovanni Verrazzano, 1524).

"These people live as it were in community of goods" (Jacques Cartier, 1534). ,

"There is no government among the Savages" (Samuel de Champlain, 1633).

"The Savages are utter strangers to distinctions of Property, for what belongs to one is equally another's" (Baron de La Hontan, 1702) .

Distribution of Indian and Arctic peoples.

Such, in briefest outline, is the record of antiquity of the first dwellers in our land.

When the European invaders first reached these shores there were more than fifty tribes in what now is Canada, with a population of perhaps a quarter of a million. They spoke eleven main languages, with many variations of dialect. The major language groupings were: the Inuit or Eskimo people inhabiting the northern fringe of the continent above the tree-line, from Alaska to Labrador and Newfoundland; and to the south, the "Indians": Algonkian, Athapaskan, Iroquoian and Pacific Coast peoples. The Athapaskan inhabited an area that included the

Yukon and British Columbia interior and the northwestern prairie. The Algonkian tribes hunted and fished from the Prairies to Newfoundland; the Iroquoian lived in agricultural settlements in southern Ontario, and south of Lakes Erie and Ontario, as far east as the Richelieu. (From about 1300-1500 A.D. they also occupied the St. Lawrence valley as far east as the Gulf.)

These peoples were the first among the "founders of Canada." Their labor created a material culture that flourished for centuries before the Europeans invaded North America. And when the European traders came, it was on the labor of the native peoples that they built their fortunes.

STAGES OF PREHISTORY
(A rough estimate, for Eastern Canada)

Period	Techniques	Years Ago
Paleo-Indian	Chipped stone points Quartzite quarries	12,000 - 7,000
Archaic or Laurentian	Ground, polished stone tools Lake Superior copper working	7,000 - 2,500
Woodland	Pottery; burial mounds; trade; agricultural beginnings	2,500 - 1,100

Pre-Algonkian, pre-Iroquoian cultures

III

Stone Age People of the Arctic

LIKE THE "INDIANS," THE ARCTIC PEOPLE HAVE HAD A name foisted on them that is none of their own choosing. Of the name "Eskimo" George Heriot wrote in 1807 in his *Travels through the Canadas*: "Their name is said to be derived from a word in the Abenaki* language . . . [meaning] an eater of raw flesh; they being the only people in North America who use their food in this state." (This was in any case wildly inaccurate, since the "Eskimo" generally cooked their meat.) Their own name for themselves is "Inuit," meaning "the people."

The forebears of the modern Eskimo or Inuit may have been the last group to migrate to North America from Asia. (Some ethnologists, however, believe the Athapaskan people were the last to come.)

In any event, relics have been found of Stone Age Arctic cultures dating back more than 4,000 years. In 1954 a 3,000-year-old village with vestiges of 208 dwellings was discovered at Isloolik, on the shore of Foxe Basin, in northern Melville Peninsula. The earliest northern culture is that known as the Sarqaq. Its remains, found in the eastern Arctic, include burins (a chisel-edged cutting tool) and tiny flint blades, saucer-shaped soapstone lamps, triangular arrow heads.

The following stage was that of the Dorset people—so named from the prehistoric settlements discovered by

---

*The Abenaki: an Algonkian Indian group, inhabiting the Maritimes. It was here that the Jesuit Biard in 1611 first recorded the name "Eskimo." Later it was encountered among the Crees (also an Algonkian people).

Jenness at Cape Dorset on Baffin Island. Their distinctive harpoon heads, stone dwellings and burial places have been discovered as far up as the northernmost part of Ellesmere Island.

Later came the Thule culture: its turf-roofed square stone dwellings have been found from Coronation Gulf to Labrador and Greenland.* It came to an end several generations before the period of European discovery.

The settlements of the present-day Eskimo people extend in a great arc from Eastern Siberia to Greenland. There are two conflicting views as to the origin of their Arctic culture. One situates it in North America, the other in Siberia.

The Danish authority Kaj Birket-Smith has interpreted the successive phases of Eskimo cultural development as steps in a gradual adaptation to life by the Arctic seas. At first, the forerunners of the Eskimo were inland hunters and fishermen. Then, about 4,000 years ago, they moved out to the shores of the Arctic Ocean, and created an economy based on the seal-hunt (the Sarqaq and Dorset cultures). Between 1000 and 1500 A.D. there was a further adapation to the sea, and the whale-hunt became a central feature of Arctic life (this paralleled the period of the Thule culture).

Finally, in historic times, there took place a new migration seaward of inland caribou-hunting tribes who till then had remained in the interior Barren Lands west of Hudson Bay. The cause of this movement to the seacoast may have been pressure on the part of Athapascan Indian tribes moving up from the south. The death by starvation in the late 1940's of nearly all the survivors of the 800-strong Ihalmiut people—the Barren Lands caribou hunters—marked the last tragic chapter in this phase.

---

*The names Sarqaq and Thule come from districts so named in West and Northwest Greenland.

(A burning indictment of the criminal indifference and neglect of the white authorities, responsible for this extermination of a defenseless people, is contained in Farley Mowat's *People of the Deer* and *The Desperate People*.)

As against the theory of inland North American origin of Eskimo culture, there are strong indications that its birthplace was in the coastal areas of the Bering Sea. Here, on the shores of the Chukotsk Peninsula (the northeastern tip of Siberia), live some 1200 Eskimos, descendants of an ancient Bering Sea people. Archaeological finds link the Old Bering culture with those of the very early Siberian Stone Age.

The hypothesis that the Eskimo are descended from an ancient Bering Sea people, hunters of sea-mammals, who later spread to the Arctic and sub-Arctic regions of North America, is supported by Diamond Jenness, as well as by Soviet anthropologists. (If correct, this theory would imply that the inland Caribou Eskimo had branched off from the coastal people, rather than the other way round.)

In the course of centuries the Inuit, patiently struggling with the most formidable obstacles and hardships, successfully created on the Arctic sea-coasts a unique Stone Age culture. Hunters of the great sea-mammals—the ringed and barbed seal, the walrus, the whale—they made full use of their quarry: it yielded them "food, blubber for lamps, skin for clothing, boat coverings, harpoon floats and the thongs, and to some extent the sinews for sewing thread, as well as bones and ivory for implements."

For land transport they devised the sledge, built on runners and drawn by dogs or people. On water they used the light hunting canoe or *kayak*, made of skins, and as a transport vessel the larger *umiak* or "women's boat." Their chief weapon in the hunt was the harpoon, made with a shaft of wood or bone, and a detachable head of

Umiak (women's boat), Kayak (men's canoe).
An 18th-century engraving.

sharpened bone or flint, fastened with a line of seal thong. There was a limited use of copper (beaten "cold," not smelted) among the Copper Eskimo of the west-central Arctic.

Concerning some of the technical achievements of the Inuit, Dr. John Rae, explorer and scientist, wrote a century ago:

"The goggles which they have invented to protect their eyes from the glare of the snow, with its narrow slit, to admit only a small amount of light, the blackened inner surface, and the peak (like that of a cap) to keep the sun off, are all perfect. The Eskimo's mode of building his snow-hut—only about six inches thick in the wall—would puzzle an architect or an engineer, until he saw how it was done. The bed-place in his snow-hut is raised above the level of the top of the low door, so that those sitting or lying on it are out of the draught, and in the upper or warmer air of the interior. . . .

"Their iced sledge runners enable them to haul a double load. The Eskimo kayak is as perfect a model for speed as the most perfect racing boat, . . . with sufficient breadth to carry a seal on deck if required. The Eskimo is the only canoeman known who can capsize his canoe and, without leaving his place, right her again. His salmon spear is the most perfect I have ever seen; and his harpoon is so formed that it cannot possibly 'draw', as the whalers say; the line may break, but the harpoon head is a fixture."

The society of the Inuit was a primitive-communal one. In the arduous conditions of the Arctic, we are told,* they "combined . . . to wrest a precarious livelihood from the frozen sea by united effort. Food [was] common to all . . . [in] the tribal bands each man toiled for all, and shared his food in common." "Trapping grounds and hunting fields are the property of all. . . . The spoils of the chase do not exclusively belong to the hunter who secured them." They were shared according to definite rules, depending on participation in the common effort.

Reflecting these relationships of common labor and communal property were definite standards of morality. "The first great unwritten law is that no one may without reason avoid the struggle for food and clothing. He who does is not allowed to starve; but he is despised and looked down on by everybody." . . . "They would have killed without compunction any fellow countryman who attempted to hoard food while they were starving."

In this society there were no class divisions, and no

---

*Jenness, Birket-Smith and other authorities. See Reference Notes.

state. "The Eskimo recognize no chiefs among themselves, considering every man the equal of every other. . . ." Or again: "There is no state . . . no government . . . no rank or class."

Birket-Smith writes: "Among the Eskimos there is no state which makes use of their strength, no government to restrict their liberty of action." And of Eskimo society: "Here is no social tension to threaten its destruction, no cleavage between the individual and the whole, no cry for justice against a privileged brutality."

The sexes had "almost equal status"; in the hunt, "both men and women contributed to the discussion that decided the tactics to be employed."

Diamond Jenness gives a striking example of the gulf in outlook and attitude between 20th-century imperialism and primitive-communal society:

When the news of World War I reached Coronation Gulf, "Ickpuck would not believe our western natives when they told him that the white men were killing each other like caribou. . . . He pondered the matter for some days. . . . Certainly, white men who deliberately used their extraordinary knowledge and powers for the wholesale massacre of each other were strangely unnatural and inhuman."

The Inuit possessed a mythology that reflected their dependence on the forces of nature, which they believed were good or evil spirits. In their art, particularly in carvings of soapstone, ivory and bone, they achieved a high level of mastery.

The achievements of the Arctic people bear witness to man's powers of adaptation—and his creativeness. With nothing but a Stone Age technique, "the Eskimo brought into being, under the severe conditions of the Arctic, a specialized culture that enabled him to make excellent use of the resources of the North, overcoming difficulties that until quite recent times proved insuperable for Europeans, despite the superior technique at their disposal."

Neither John Rae, a century ago, nor present-day North American or Scandinavian students of the Arctic, would disagree with this estimate of the Eskimo, expressed by Soviet ethnographers in a recent study of the peoples of the Americas.

Eskimo dancing.

IV

Hunters, Food-gatherers, Agriculturists

THE INUIT DWELT NORTH OF THE TREE LINE, THE INDIAN peoples to the south of it. At the time of the coming of the Europeans, there were four main language groupings among the Indian peoples living between the Yukon and Newfoundland, and six among those on the Pacific Coast and its mountain hinterland.* In terms of the regions they inhabited and their mode of life, on the one hand, and of language groups on the other, the Indians east of the Rockies were divided as follows:

Hunting Peoples of the Mackenzie Yukon River Basins (some also in the Cordillera)	Athapaskan
Hunting Peoples of the Plains	Algonkian and Siouan
Hunting Peoples of the Eastern Woodlands	Algonkian
Agricultural Peoples of the Eastern Woodlands	Iroquoian

All these peoples were at one stage or another of Stone Age existence. The bow and arrow and spear, the stone club, knife, adze, axe, and scraper, the bone fish-hook, were their common implements of survival. Some knew the art of weaving, some that of pottery as well. Only the Iroquoians, more advanced, were tillers of the

---

*The peoples of the Pacific Coast we shall deal with separately in the next chapter.

soil; though a few neighboring Algonkian groups had learned something of tillage from them. The form of society was in all cases the primitive-communal clan system.

The *Athapaskans,* whose hunting grounds extended from the Yukon to southwest of present-day Edmonton, and eastward to the site of Fort Churchill, may have been the latest immigrants from Eastern Siberia. (It has been claimed—rather inconclusively—that their language bears traces of relationship with the Chinese-Tibetan-Siamese language group.) The most numerous Athapaskan tribe were the Chipewyan, who hunted north of the Churchill River to beyond the edge of the Barren Lands, pressing the Eskimo northward. Northwest of them were the Yellowknife, Dogrib, Hare and Kutchin; west and southwest, the Slave, the Beaver, Sekani, and other tribes—some of whom, like the Chilcotin, Carrier and Tahltan, crossed the Rockies to the valley of the upper Fraser, the Babine Lake district, and the valley of the Stikine. The main Athapaskan territory, however, was in the valleys of the Mackenzie and the Yukon.

Nomadic hunters, the Athapaskan peoples used stone projectile (arrow and spear) points and knives and adzes; but they made much use of wood, bone and antler for their implements and utensils. The Yellowknife, northeast of Great Slave and Great Bear Lakes, appear to have learned from the Eskimo something of the uses of copper. Through them, a few copper implements may have spread to other tribes to the south and east.

The fishing and hunting Kutchin of the Yukon also were in contact with the Eskimo to the north, as well as with the Pacific Coast Tlinkit to the south. Eskimo influence is seen in their compound bow (three pieces of wood, jointed and lashed with sinew), in the use of the sled (rather than the toboggan) and in the form of their flat-bottomed canoe (resembling the umiak). The position of women among them was one of drudgery and inferiority (the men, however, did the cooking).

To the south of the Athapaskans lived the *Plains Indians*: hunters of the buffalo. Most of the Plains tribes belonged to the Algonkian language group: the Gros Ventre, Piegan, Blood, Blackfoot and Cree. But the Assiniboine ("people who cook with hot stones") were a branch of the Sioux. After living for some time in the Lake of the Woods area, they had moved into the Western prairie. The Blackfoot were the strongest of the Plains tribes.

All were hunters, with bow and arrow and spear. Their tipis were made of buffalo hide spread over a conical frame of three or four tree-poles. They harnessed dogs as draft-animals, to draw the *travois*, a device made of trailing poles held together with webbing.

The buffalo hunt of the Plains people was a highly organized operation, requiring the disciplined participation of the community. Originally carried out on foot, with bow and arrow and spear, its range was vastly extended in the 18th century with the introduction of the horse (which spread northwest from Spanish Mexico)— and, later, of firearms. Alexander Henry, the fur trader, described the building of the "pound" into which the buffalo were herded for the kill: "Trees are cut down (with stone tools), laid upon one another, and interwoven with branches and green twigs . . ." Two lines or "ranges" of pointed stakes converge toward the entrance to the enclosure. "Young men are usually sent out to collect and bring in the buffalo—a tedious task which requires great patience, for the herd must be started by slow degrees. This is done by setting fire to dung or grass. Three young men will bring in a herd from a great distance. . . . Having come in sight of the ranges, they generally drive the herd faster, until it begins to enter the ranges, where a swift-footed person has been stationed with a buffalo robe over his head to imitate that animal. . . . When he sees buffaloes approaching, he moves slowly toward the pound, until they appear to follow him; then he sets off at full speed imitating a buffalo as well as he can, with the herd after him. The young men in the rear now . . . drive the herd on with all possible speed. . . . Every man, woman and child runs to the ranges that lead to the pound to prevent the buffalo from taking a wrong direction. . . . When the buffalo have been thus directed to the entrance of the pound the Indian who leads them rushes into it and out at the other side, either by jumping over the inclosure or creeping through an opening left for that purpose. The buffalo tumble in pell-mell at his heels, almost exhausted, but keep moving around the inclosure from east to west, and never in a direction against the sun. . . . The buffalo being caught, the men assemble at the inclosure, armed with bows and arrows; every arrow has a particular mark of the owner, and they fly until the whole herd is killed."

The *Algonkian* peoples ranged over a vast expanse of territory, from the foothills of the Rockies to Cape Breton. The transition from the life of the Plains hunters to that of the Eastern Woodlands was bridged by the Cree, one part of whom lived on the Prairie, another in the forest and muskeg country of the Laurentian Shield. The most numerous Algonkian tribe was the Ojibwa,* others were the Algonquin, Montagnais, Naskapi, Micmac, Malecite.

Possibly related to the Algonkian were the now extinct Beothuk of Newfoundland. Their triangular stone arrow-points and polished stone adzes, and lack of pottery, sug-

---

*Also called Chippewa: the meaning of the original name is "people whose moccasins have puckered seams."

gest an ancient or "paleo-Algonkian" strain. They were established in Newfoundland before the prehistoric Dorset people reached the island and mingled with them. The last surviving Beothuk, named Nancy Shawanahdit, died in 1829: her entire people had been exterminated by the Europeans. "There can be no doubt," says Prowse, the 19th century historian of Newfoundland, "that the settlers hunted them like wolves, and shot them in cold blood whenever they encountered them."

The Algonkian of the Eastern Woodlands were hunters and food-gatherers. Only in a few instances had any of them made a start at crop-raising: as did some of the Ottawas, living next to the agricultural Huron-Iroquois; and possibly the Micmac of Nova Scotia (although they were no longer practising it when the Europeans came).

Thus the Algonkian peoples had not reached the stage—which comes with agriculture—of establishing permanent settlements. Their dwellings were either the conical tipi, covered with bark or caribou hides, or the dome-shaped wigwam of the Ojibwa. Either type was easy to put up and transport from one camp-site to another.

Their tools and weapons were of stone, wood and bone. They used snowshoes, and had developed in the birch-bark canoe a superb means of transport. Overlying a frame of cedar, the birch bark was sewn with a thread made of cedar root, and the seams were caulked with pine pitch.

For clothing, the Woodland Cree and Naskapi made garments of rabbit or caribou fur. The Ojibwa and Algonquin made clothes of deerskin: they prepared the hides by scraping them with a stone knife and then rubbing them with the brains of the animal. The skins were sewn together with sinew.

There was some weaving (among the Ojibwa especially); and pottery-making, of a rather elementary type. Decorative work was done widely, as in ornamenting caribou or deer-skin clothing with stamped-on designs (the stamp being made of bone), or with embroidery; and in the sewing of dyed porcupine quills on to birch-bark baskets. Paintings on smooth rock surfaces of human and animal figures have been discovered at the water's edge in the Lake Superior and Lake of the Woods areas; they were done for the most part in red ochre, with the artist apparently working while seated in his canoe.

In the spring the Ojibwa tapped the maple for the run of syrup; they boiled it, to make sugar, by dropping heated stones into the birch-bark containers that served as buckets. They were also gatherers of wild rice. David Thompson the explorer described the process, which took place in September: While one man paddled, the rice-gatherer, seated in the canoe, "with a hand on each side, seizes the stalks and knocks the ears of the rice against the inside of the canoe . . . until the canoe is full . . . the women assist in unloading. A canoe may hold from 10 to 12 bushels . . . so plentiful is the rice, an industrious man may fill his canoe three times in a day." The women dried the rice, spreading it on a scaffolding built over a gentle fire; it was then ground with an oaken mortar and pestle.

Here, as among the other Algonkian tribes, the only division of labor was that between the women and the men. Real social division of labor, based on differing types of productive activity, comes only with the emergence of agriculture. Yet the seeds of it are present earlier: there are rare, scattered instances of specialized production, as in the prehistoric "tool works" where quantities of stone and flint arrow-heads and knives were produced; and in the primitive copper-mining that was carried on in the Lake Superior area—presumably by some Algonkian or pre-Algonkian people.

The *Iroquoian* peoples comprised a distinct language and cultural grouping. They lived in what is now southwestern Ontario and northern New York, as far east as the Richelieu-Hudson river valleys. Between the Detroit River, Georgian Bay and Lake Simcoe were the Neutral and Tobacco "nations" and the Hurons; south of Lake Ontario, the "Five Nations" confederacy: from west to east, the Seneca, Cayuga, Onondaga, Oneida, Mohawk. It was these five whom the French called "Iroquois," from an Algonkian word meaning "real adders"; their own name for themselves was Ho-de-no-sau-nee or "People of the Long House." The term Iroquoian as now used embraces the kindred peoples in Ontario as well as the members of the confederacy.

As distinct from the Algonkian, Athapaskan and Pacific Coast peoples, the Iroquoians were agriculturists. This stride towards civilization had meant far-reaching changes in their mode of life. Instead of living as nomads, they dwelt in settled communities. Instead of the hunter's temporary forest encampment they built large villages, oval-shaped and ringed with palisades; and the "long house" in place of the wigwam. Whereas the hunting peoples pitched their camps close to the running streams, the Iroquoian settlements were generally established well inland, in forest clearings.

When the French explorer Champlain first visited the Hurons near Georgian Bay in 1615, they were living in eighteen separate village settlements. As the Jesuit *Relations* described them: "Their dwellings were bark cabins, clustered within stoutly palisaded walls, and near each fortified town were fields of corn, beans, pumpkin and tobacco. Agricultural in habit, keen traders, and in the main sedentary, [the Hurons] made short hunting and fishing excursions, and laid up stores for the winter."

Indian women at work.
(*From Du Creux,* History of Canada, *1664*)

Using a crude digging-stick or hoe tipped with bone or shell, the Iroquoians raised beans, squash, pumpkin, corn and sunflowers (whose seeds provided a vegetable oil for cooking). Periodically the fields were divided into allotments assigned for working purposes to different families. When the fertility of the soil was exhausted (and they had no knowledge of how to restore it), the whole village would move to a new location. Once more there would begin the laborious work of making a clearing in the woods. In felling trees, the work of the crude stone axe was supplemented by charring the base of the tree-trunk. Clearing the land was the men's job; once it was done,

the women took over the work of planting and harvesting the crop.

The cultivation of crops began to make possible for
the first time the production (and storage) of a *surplus*
of foodstuffs. This in turn led to trade by barter. The
Hurons exchanged corn for skins, the "Tobacco Nation"
traded their staple—and a fairly wide trading network had
grown up prior to the European invasion.

Communal ownership still prevailed, however.

The land was held in common by the tribe. (The Indians' attitude to the land was once stated by the Shawnee
leader Tecumseh, negotiating with the United States government: "Sell land! As well sell air and water. The
Great Spirit gave them in common to all.")

On a basis of agricultural production, the Iroquoians
developed to its most mature point the tribal and clan
organization which was common to the Indian peoples.*
Its unit was the clan, a kinship group claiming a common
ancestor. Descent was traced on the woman's side of the
family: in other words, it was a *matrilineal* society. Children belonged to the clan of their mother; marriage between members of the same clan was forbidden.

The position of women in the matrilineal clan was
greatly enhanced by their role in agriculture and the

---

*The first scientific study of Iroquoian society was made by Lewis
H. Morgan (1818-81), in *The League of the Iroquois* (1855). In his
Ancient Society (1877) he showed the universal character of the course
of development of primitive society, the role of kinship and later of
property, the transition from the matrilineal to patrilineal family. His
findings were an independent confirmation of the materialist conception of history; Frederick Engels drew on them for his *Origin of the
Family, Private Property and the State.* Morgan visited Fort Garry,
N.W.T., in 1861.

Engels pointed out that Morgan was the first to attempt "to introduce a definite order into the history of primitive man." However,
Morgan's classification—"savagery" and "barbarism," with lower,
middle and higher stages of each—is no longer accepted by Marxists.
Division into ages of Stone (Paleolithic and Neolithic) and Metals
(Bronze and Iron) corresponds more closely to the development of the
productive forces, as against Morgan's categories of "levels of culture."

household economy. The women of each clan chose one of their number as "matron," to be head of the house (or houses) occupied by the families of her clan. "The women," writes Jenness, "were . . . the real guardians of all the names and traditions of a clan. Moreover, it was the women who controlled the long bark cabins that sheltered up to twenty individual families. Every cabin recognized some elderly female as its ruler."

Each clan bore a name which it alone in the tribe was entitled to use—usually that of some living creature, believed to be its original ancestor: this was its *totem.* An individual's name indicated the clan to which he or she belonged. The members of the clan were bound by strong bonds of solidarity and mutual assistance. An injury to one member by an outsider obligated the whole clan to avenge him.

Each clan had its own council, the democratic governing body of all adults, male and female. This council elected (and deposed) the sachems and war chiefs, who were nominated by the head woman or matron. Among tribes with several clans, the next level of organization was the phratry, or brotherhood, although in some of the weaker tribes this was lacking. Two or more phratries composed the tribe. Characteristic of the tribe was the possession of a commonly held land area, a common spoken language or dialect, common religious views. The tribal council consisted of the sachems or war chiefs elected by the individual clans. The council sat in public session, attended by other members of the tribe, who had the right to join in the discussion. Among the Iroquois, all decisions were reached unanimously.

Probably about the year 1570,* the five Iroquoian tribes (Seneca, Cayuga, Onondaga, Oneida and Mohawk) united in a confederacy that has endured for hundreds of

---

*Some authorities believe the date was considerably earlier.

years: the "League of the Long House." About 1720 these five were joined by a sixth, the Tuscarora. The purpose of the League was to renounce mutual warfare, while presenting a united front against outside marauders. Its founder was the legendary Deganawida, who, it was said, was of virgin birth; his mother guided him, and the wizard Hiawatha was his speechmaker. The pledge of the confederacy ran as follows: "I, Deganawida, and the Confederated Chiefs, now uproot the tallest pine tree, and into the cavity thereby made we cast all weapons of war. Into the depth of the earth, deep down into the under-earth currents of water flowing to unknown regions, we cast all weapons of strife. We bury them from sight and we plant again the tree. Thus shall the Great Peace be established." (This dream of the Great Peace was later drowned in the bloody wars fomented by the rival European trading powers.)

The tribal-military organization of the Iroquois foreshadows the eventual appearance—with the coming of class society—of the state. But as yet this did not exist: there was no separate, permanent machinery of "bodies of armed men and prisons." The war chiefs held office only for the duration of hostilities; the military force was the armed community. "There were no strata in society," writes Jenness regarding the Iroquois; and with respect to the hunting peoples he says: "In the absence of chiefs and of any legislative or executive body within the tribes or bands, law and order depended solely on the strength of public opinion."

East of the Rockies, Indian primitive-communal society never reached the point of break-up into a class society as a result of its own economic development. Its normal evolution was cut short by European conquest—which disrupted tribal society and sought to impose in its place the pattern of capitalist class relationships.

From Communal Society to Slave-ownership on the Pacific Coast

To the west, the Rockies not only formed a geographical barrier: they marked a Great Divide in historical development, as between the Indian tribes living to the east and those inhabiting the Pacific Coast. Here, on the off-shore islands and at the mainland river-mouths, were the villages of a people who—before the Europeans came—had embarked upon a new era in human history: that of *class society*.

The main language-groupings of the Coast peoples were:
—the Haida: Queen Charlotte Islands;
—the Nootka: western Vancouver Island;
and, from north to south on the mainland:
—the Tlinkit of the southern Alaska Panhandle;
—the Tsimshian of the Nass and Skeen River valleys;
—the Bella Coola;
—the Kwakiutl;
—the Coast Salish.

The last two had spread from the mainland to the northern and eastern parts of Vancouver Island as well.

Two cultures had met and mingled on the Coast. The older was based on the fishery and the hunting of sea-mammals. Its people had made their way south from Alaska and the Aleutians. Their ancient camp-sites on the lower Fraser and southeast Vancouver Island are the oldest yet discovered in the coastal area. One discovered near Yale is estimated to be 8,000 years old; another on Burrard Inlet goes back 2,400 years or so. The patterns of their artifacts suggest a relationship with the Arctic peoples (Aleutian or Eskimo).

Another culture was brought later to the coast from the interior mainland. It was based on woodworking: a village at Marpole on the lower Fraser (about 1,950 years old) contained well built cedar long-houses, made with polished stone adzes and hammers. The Coast Salish, Bella Coola and Tsimshian all came to the coast from the interior; the others, most likely, are descended from the ancient maritime peoples.

By the time that Russian, Spanish and English navigators first explored the Pacific Coast (from 1741 onward) its inhabitants had already achieved a high level of material culture. The reason for this was the extraordinary productivity of their main economic activity: the fishery. The abundance of salmon, herring, halibut and other fish —including the oil-rich oolakan—enabled the Coast tribes to secure more than enough for their immediate needs. Enjoying a mild climate, and with an abundant supply of the soft straight-grained cedar at hand, they were able to create a material culture more advanced than any other north of Mexico.

With their food-supply assured, the Coast peoples had more time to improve their stone tools, to develop woodworking, to specialize in production and barter their surplus products. The canoes of the Haida, the wooden dishes and utensils of the Kwakiutl, the wool woven by the Tsimshian, were exchanged—as well as fish-oil, furs and jade (used to make cutting-tools).

If the Iroquoian bark-covered "long house" represented an advance over the forest wigwam, the Coast Indians' great houses of cedar logs and planks bespoke a still higher level of technical achievement. Still using only the stone axe or adze, these people felled giant cedars, cut logs and, with wooden or antler wedges and a stone maul, split them into planks; and without the use of wheel or pulley raised heavy log beams into place, fitting together the woodwork of buildings sometimes several hundred feet in length, without the use of a nail. For furniture and storage bins they used great cedar chests, made by bending a plank into four sides, dowelling the fourth corner, morticing in a bottom, and providing it with a separate lid. Dugout canoes they made of cedar or other timber, up to sixty feet in length. Of the art of pottery they were wholly ignorant; basketwork and bark receptacles took its place. The Nootka of the west coast of Vancouver Island and the Coast Salish around the mouth of the Fraser were particularly skilful in making baskets; and the latter wove blankets, adorned with geometric patterns, from the hair of the mountain goat and the dog, mixed with bits of cedar bark.

Some time prior to the Europeans' coming, the old communal-clan organization of the West Coast Indians began to break up.

Primitive-communal society had been based on a sharing of meagre resources, on an undeveloped technique. But with a productivity of labor such as grew up on the Coast, private property arose; and the existence of private property disrupted the communal-clan system. Where individual families could by themselves produce more than enough for their needs, common co-operative labor was no longer the condition for survival.

True, the community was still organized on the old kinship lines: groups of related families occupying each "long house," groups of houses comprising the village, embracing several clans. Hunting and fishing grounds, berry-picking tracts, and housing were traditionally the common property of the clan. The oldest descendant of the clan's "group ancestor" was clan chieftain: organizer of its economic activity, custodian of clan property. But from being *custodians,* the chiefs were becoming private *proprietors.* Violating the ancient relationships of the communal-clan society, they took unto themselves the best fishing-grounds, the best of the produce. They traded the surplus goods—at first as clan representatives, then as outright owners. By degrees, they reduced the other clan members to a condition of dependency.

The wealth that the chiefs accumulated could not, at that level of economic development, be "invested." It could only be hoarded—or displayed. Hence the institution of the ceremonial potlatch: by giving away great quantities of presents, the chiefs strove to outdo one another in munificence—and thereby heighten their own prestige in the community.

Accompanying the emergence of private property was a gradual transition, within the kinship group, from tracing descent through the mother (matrilineal kinship) to tracing it through the father (patrilineal). While among the northern Tlinkit, Haida and Tsimshian the matrilineal system still prevailed, the Kwakiutl were in transition to patrilineal kinship. The Nootka and Salish had gone over to the latter, while still preserving traces of the older system.

But the growth of the productive capacity of Pacific Coast society soon led to a more fundamental change: the emergence of classes. Production of a regular *surplus* means that it is possible for part of the community to live in idleness at the expense of the labor of others. Labor is productive enough to maintain both the laborer and his master. *Slavery* was born. Prisoners taken in war, instead of being adopted into the tribe as equals (where all had to work), now became slaves, objects of property. And the chieftains, the men of property, became slave-owners.

Such a development as this was out of the question for the Plains and Eastern Woodlands peoples, with their low level of technique and chronic scarcity of food. (Iroquoian society, with its agriculture and social organization, was evolving towards—but had not yet reached—the level at which class-division becomes possible.)

In the Old World, and in the Maya, Aztec and Inca cultures, agriculture emerged long before class-division appeared. But among the fishing and hunting Pacific Coast peoples, although they had not yet reached the stage of either pottery-making or of agriculture, a class society began to take shape. This happened because of the remarkable productivity of their maritime economy.

Some authorities refer to a three-fold division of this Pacific Coast society into "nobles, commoners and slaves": the use of the first two terms is misleading, since it suggests a feudal structure such as existed in medieval Europe, but not on our West Coast. Others deny that any class division at all was in existence here. They cite as proof the minute gradations of rank as between chiefs and their dependent kinsfolk. Yet they admit that the slaves formed a "distinct section" of society.

The fact of the matter is that the presence of gradations of rank alongside the old, persisting kinship organization was only a symptom of its gradual transformation from a communal society to one founded on private property and wealth. And the fact of division between slave and slave-owner *did* mark the emergence of a class-divided society.

As objects of property, the slaves were wholly without rights; and their enslavement was permanent—and hereditary. "Their lot . . was generally wretched in the extreme. They hunted and fished for their masters, manned . . . canoes, and performed nearly all the drudgery around the village."

With the spread of trade, slaves too became marketable commodities. "Like any other commodity, slaves were bought and sold. The Bella Coola were usually so well provided with salmon that they were able to exchange these fish with the members of other tribes for slaves." When these human chattels were in over-supply, "the value of a slave fell to twenty or thirty salmon." Slaves were also exchanged for adzes and chisels made from the jade found near Yale, on the Fraser. "Even small tools, one or two inches long, were worth from one to three slaves."

Early European navigators reported that among the northern Tlinkit a third of the population were slaves, many of whom had been taken prisoner in wars with the Salish. A similar division was present among the Haida. Alexander Mackenzie in 1793 noted that among the Bella Coola about 30 per cent of the population were enslaved.

These proportions show that while slavery had gained a firm foothold, it was still at an early stage. In fully developed slave-owning societies, the enslaved heavily out-numbered the free: thereby making it imperative for the slave-owners to fashion a machinery of coercion—the *state,* an organization made up of special bodies of armed men, prisons, etc. This stage had not yet been reached on the West Coast.

Though there was as yet no *state,* class cleavage brought from the outset a new kind of antagonism—and a new dimension in brutality. Tlinkit chiefs, at a ceremonial house-raising, caused the living bodies of slaves to be crushed under the heavy cedar house posts. Kwakiutl chiefs, welcoming a fellow slave-owner, used the bodies of slaves as "rollers" to draw the visitor's heavy dugout canoe up on the beach. These are no longer acts of violence of a brute struggle to survive. They express the refined ferocity of men who compete ruthlessly for wealth—at the expense of those who toil.

Spirits, Dreams and Totems

THE WORLD OUTLOOK OF STONE AGE PEOPLES WAS A reflection of their material conditions of existence. Above all, they were at the mercy of the elements, and dependent on the chase for food and clothing. The struggle for subsistence and survival had engendered skills: but about the nature of human consciousness and its relation to the material world there was ignorance and confusion (some of which, in more "refined" forms, persist in our own society).

Hence the prevalence of *animism,* or belief in man-like spirits dwelling in the wind and the thunder, in the moon and sun and stars, in rocks and streams, in plants and trees and living creatures. Thus, among the Crow Indians, the sun-spirit held a place of special honor: while Old Man Coyote was a rascally sort of spirit. These fickle beings and the magic ceremonies employed to placate or cajole them are the raw material of subsequent religion. (As Engels noted: "The first gods arose through the personification of natural forces.") There were creation-myths: the Bella Coola—woodworkers, like the other West Coast tribes—held that their chief spirit had created four spirit-carpenters, who in turn carved the first forebears of man.

In sleep, a person's "spirit" wanders off in dreams; the dream-apparition seems to provide "proof" that there is a soul that can leave the body. As in sleep, so too, it is imagined, in the case of death: the soul is given a send-off, weapons, utensils, ornaments being burned or buried with the corpse. (Some special magic in this respect attached to red ochre, which was placed in the graves of the pre-historic Laurentian people—a custom that was present in Eurasia as well as on this continent.)

As Indian society underwent changes, so did its imagined spirit-world. With the shift from the matrilineal to patrilineal clan organization, the world-creator ceased to be a female spirit and was replaced by a male. (This same change-over from mother-god to father-god occurred in similar conditions in the Old World.) The formation of leagues or confederacies among the Iroquoians and Algonkians brought with it a corresponding change in the organization of their spirit-world.

European missionaries were generally zealous in their search for belief among the Indians in one universal deity. But monotheism, a product of Old World civilization, had as yet no place in Indian mythology. The Jesuit Lalemant complained in 1641 that the Hurons "have no notion of one Deity who created the world or gives heed to its governing."

Communication with the multiplicity of spirits was the job of those who showed an exceptional capacity for having dream-visions: these were the shamans or medicine-men. In their "medicine," magic was mingled with real knowledge of the use of herbs and other remedies.

Out of animism, or spirit-worship, came *totemism*: the belief that each clan or kinship group was descended from some supernatural ancestor—whether animal or plant or natural object. The representation of this ancestral "totem" served as the emblem of the clan.

Among the Mohawk and Oneida there were the clans of the Bear, the Wolf and the Turtle (or Tortoise). In addition to these, the Seneca, Cayuga and Onondaga also had clans of the Deer, the Beaver, the Eel, and the Snipe, Hawk and Heron.

Totemic beliefs attributed a common origin to people and animals, and held that in certain circumstances they were capable of changing into each other: the burial rites of the Kwakiutl implied a belief that the dead could resume the totem-form of the clan ancestor.

The totem-beings of the Algonkian Ojibwa were: the loon, kingfisher, rattlesnake, beaver, porcupine and caribou. On the Pacific Coast there were: frog, raven, eagle (thunderbird), beaver, sea-otter, bear and wolf; killer-whale, salmon, flounder, water-lily, wild rice, wild apple, lichen.

With the change-over from matrilineal to patrilineal family, accompanying the rise of private property, the *clan* totem tended to be transformed into the totem of the *individual family* of the clan chief. The totem-cult became a cult of a male ancestor of the chief. The totem-poles erected in front of the chief's dwelling bore the emblems of his family—once emblems of the clan as a whole.

The introduction of slavery on the West Coast found its reflection in the totemic beliefs and ideology of the peoples there. The animal-totem world itself was now divided into slave-creatures and free. According to the Haida, the Raven—the outstanding totem-figure in West Coast mythology —"had two slaves": and that is why, one legend concludes, the Haida also have slaves. This long-established folklore testifies to the antiquity of slave-ownership in the area. Franz Boas, the American anthropologist, relates a Kwakiutl legend, the obvious moral of which is—once a slave, always a slave, and not even magic can change this. A Tsimshian myth teaches that the Sun has slaves, and slavery has existed ever since the world began.

Thus did primitive mythology reflect—and seek to sanctify—the relationships of the existing social order.*

---

*Modern class society resorts to similar means in order to perpetuate itself. Its ideologists also exert themselves to "prove" that private property and the patriarchal family have "always existed." Even so distinguished an authority as Dr. Marius Barbeau has engaged in such an endeavor. He denies that totemism on the West Coast was really "totemic," or based on belief in the totemic origin of matrilineal kinship groups. The totems, in his view, are merely "family crests," "heraldic emblems." Moreover, he claims, they were borrowed from the Europeans—the thunderbird emblem as an imitation of the Russian eagle, and the beaver emblem being taken from the crest of the Hudson's Bay Company—! This argument apparently is aimed at proving (in a rather roundabout way) that the bourgeois family, like private property, is an "eternal" institution.

Dr. Barbeau's view is set forth in an article: " 'Totemic Atmosphere' on the North-Pacific Coast"—*Journal of American Folklore*, vol. 67 (1954). It is challenged in a study by Julia Averkieva: "On the Question of Totemism Among the Indians of the Northwest Coast of North America"— *Sovietskaya Etnografia* (Soviet Ethnography), 1959.

VII

From Feudal to Capitalist Society. Colonialism and the "New World"

THE STRANGE, WINGED BOATS THAT WERE SIGHTED BY Stone Age hunters off the Labrador coast about the year 1000 must have seemed to come from another world. Indeed, the Norse sea-raiders were people of another epoch: the age of iron. They cleared the Scandinavian forest and built their long, high-prowed ships with a great iron axe. Ruled by military chiefs, they were cattle-raisers and traders; their voyaging ranged from Constantinople to Iceland. They established a settlement in West Greenland about 980: it endured for four centuries, then faded out.*

It was an expedition under Leif Eriksson that sailed from Iceland to the northeast coast of this continent. It led to attempts at settlement, but these were repulsed in bloody collisions with the "Skraelings," as the sagas call the Inuit or Indian inhabitants.

The expeditions of the Norsemen to North America had no immediate sequel. The memory of them mingled with medieval legends of voyages to "islands of the West," supposed to have been made by Irish monks, or by the Welshman Owen Madoc.

The great "Age of Discovery" came when rising capitalism, in the 15th and 16th centuries, shattered the "long winter sleep" of the feudal Middle Ages. The opening up

---

*Our histories generally ignore this fact: as though Greenland were not part of this hemisphere—or, perhaps, because of a general and long-established "blindness" as regards the Arctic?

of America and the birth of colonialism were integrally part of the revolutionary process whereby the capitalist mode of production replaced that of feudalism.

The social system of feudalism was based on the exploitation of serf labor by the holders of great landed estates. The "age of chivalry" rested on the plundering of a peasantry bound to the soil, held in subjection by the military rule of its overlords.* Of the serfs a French troubadour declared: "It is they who keep the rest alive, feed them and give them substance, while they themselves endure the greatest torments."

During the feudal Middle Ages, production (with the iron plow, the loom, the smithy and the water-mill) gradually increased. Growth of exchange, of a money economy, further stimulated it; until in time the productive forces came increasingly into conflict with the cramping property-relations and institutions of feudal society.

The crisis of the feudal system was marked by the growth of the town bourgeoisie ("burghers") and by serf uprisings in the countryside. Goaded beyond endurance, the serfs rose repeatedly in revolt. The 14th century Jacquerie in France and Wat Tyler's rebellion in England were but the best known among hundreds of such outbreaks. Though they were crushed with savage ruthlessness by the armed might of the nobles, these risings gravely weakened the whole structure of feudal rule.

However, those who benefited most directly from the weakening of the power of the nobles were not the oppressed serfs (though these won some concessions) but the

---

*The position of the serf differed from that of the slave. The latter was a chattel, wholly in his owner's power, without any freedom or rights. The serf, while tied to his allotment of land, and obliged to pay feudal tribute in labor or in kind (later, in money) to his overlord—was able in what time was left to him, to work for his own and his family's upkeep: he thus had a small measure of incentive that was lacking to the slave.

rich merchants of the towns. The merchant capitalists were becoming a power, thanks to the deepgoing change that was undermining the feudal economy. New, money relationships based on commodity exchange and a complex division of labor were seeping into the simple, self-sufficient rural economy based on personal ties of vassalage and overlordship. Trade, formerly limited to a few items such as iron and salt, and luxury goods from Asia, now invaded ever wider areas of social life. By the 14th century London merchants were exporting wool and woollen cloth, and importing "grain, cordage, hemp, linen cloth, wax and steel."

Production grew, spurred by the demands of trade. The iron plow came into widespread use, and technical advances were made in spinning and weaving, mining, shipbuilding. Production carried on by wage-laborers working for a capitalist began to supplant the small-scale independent production of village handicraftsmen. In place of feudal tribute and dependence a new form of exploitation was emerging: that based on wage labor, producing profit for the owner of capital.

It is recorded that the workers in the early Flemish cloth industry were treated "rather like horses than men. Early up and late in bed and all day hard work and harder fare (a few herrings and mouldy cheese), and all to enrich the churls their masters, without any profit unto themselves." The nature of wages—a minimum payment for the workers' keep—is seen in the 16th century example of the tin works at Tintern, England: wages were 2/6d a week; the minimum diet for a person was reckoned at two shillings.

The workers' resistance to exploitation took the form of strikes and sometimes uprisings. The Flemish weavers at Douai struck in 1245 (they called it a "takeham"); a general rising of craftsmen in the early 1300's was put down by the Flemish burghers only with the help of the French nobles. The wool-carders of Florence, Italy, took over the town in 1378, and set up a popular-plebeian government that lasted for three years. In France, the stonemasons, carpenters and glaziers who built the great cathedrals organized secret societies to defend their economic interests, often in the form of semi-religious "brotherhoods." A long-drawn strike of the printers in Lyon (broken at last with the help of troops) was being waged at the time of Cartier's third voyage to Canada in 1541.

The growth of trade, the beginnings of industry, were reflected in the rise of the *towns*. The town had its centre in the market place. The market, as trade expanded, became the focal centre not only of a district or region but of the *nation*. This was a new kind of community, made up of people occupying a common territory, speaking a common language, knit together by the relationships of commodity exchange and production; a community that developed its own distinct culture and "national temperament." The formation of the modern nations accompanied the growth of capitalism. The rise of national *states* was its political expression.

The form of these states was the *centralized monarchy*: the product of complex class struggles involving the feudal nobility, still the dominant class; the oppressed but rebellious peasantry; and the bourgeoisie, growing in strength but not yet able to make a direct bid for power in their own right. (Such was the 15th-16th century Tudor monarchy in England, and that of the Valois in France.)

The bourgeoisie, as it grew stronger as a class, came into collision not only with the economic and political institutions of feudalism, but with the feudal ideology and world outlook. Hence, the Protestant Reformation: a struggle of the rising capitalist order against the spiritual authority of the feudal order embodied in the Roman Catholic Church. As against the rigid, obscurantist dogmas of the medieval Church, reformers demanded freedom of opinion and inquiry; in place of the authoritarian hierarchy of the Papacy, they called for a democratic, even a republican, church. Itself the richest feudal landowner in Europe, the Church met the challenge of these new, subversive heresies with ferocious measures of repression.

The ideological struggle of the Reformation merged with the political struggle of the bourgeoisie. In Germany, Luther's defiance of the Pope (1517) opened a round of class battles of which the Peasants' War (1525) was the climax. Left in the lurch by the bourgeoisie, the peasant rising was put down in blood. In France Calvin's teaching (1536) won adherents among the town burghers, particularly those of the Atlantic ports, and among the urban and rural poor. The Wars of Religion (1562-98) did not break the power of the Church, but ended with a compromise that accorded to the Protestant Huguenots a measure of freedom.

The first successful bourgeois revolution was that of the Netherlands (1564-1608): it took the form of a war of the Dutch Protestants for national independence from the rule of Catholic Spain. In England the 16th century Reformation struggles were the prelude to the victorious bourgeois revolution of the mid-17th century, when at the side of the Dutch Republic there emerged the English Republic.

The Reformation was one aspect of the revolutionary ferment in men's minds that accompanied the birth of capitalism. Another was that known as the "rebirth of learning": the Renaissance. With the invention of printing, the bourgeoisie set about breaking the Church's monopoly of learning and of the instruments of propaganda.

Liberating the natural sciences, philosophy and the arts from the grip of medieval theology, the men of the Renaissance proclaimed a new humanism. In place of mysticism and fixation on the supernatural, they strove for knowledge of the real world, and the pursuit therein of the happiness of man.

Just as the introduction of firearms and artillery helped the burghers to breach the walls of the feudal fortresses, so the discoveries of the new science opened the doors to such achievements as the circumnavigation of the globe (Magellan, 1519-22) and the creation of a world market. Copernicus and Galileo, Leonardo da Vinci and Francis Bacon concerned themselves not only with astronomy, art, philosophy: they worked also at such immediate practical problems as those of engineering and fortification, installation of mine pumps, glass and paper-making—and navigation.

Particularly important in this new age of discovery were the changes effected in the range and capability of the main means of long-range transportation—the sailing ship. Fore and aft rigging (learned, like the use of gunpowder, from the Arabs), the replacing of the side steering oar with the stern rudder, widespread use of the magnetic compass and astrolabe (forerunner of the sextant), a two- or three-fold increase in average tonnage (to around 600 tons)—all combined to improve navigation and enable smaller crews to handle bigger ships on voyages lasting weeks or even months. The fast-sailing Portuguese caravel was a model of this new type of ship.

The growth of trade induced a thirst, not only for knowledge but for gold. The search for new sources of precious metals and for new sea-routes to the Indies coincided with the rise in power of the merchants of the Atlantic ports. The centre of gravity now shifted from the

Italian city-republics—the birthplace of capitalism—to Western Europe: a shift that was hastened (but not caused) by the Turks' capture of Constantinople (1453) and of the terminals in Asia Minor of the eastern caravan routes.

The search that ensued for Atlantic pathways to East Asia—either southward around the "bulge" of Africa or westward, across the open ocean—signalled the opening of the age of great geographical discoveries.

The Portuguese, who had taken possession of the Azores in 1440, plundered the coast of Africa in pursuit of gold and ivory and Negro slaves. In 1487 they reached the Cape of Good Hope. In 1498 Vasco da Gama, following the same course, sailed all the way to India. The cargo he brought back to Lisbon netted his backers a profit of six thousand per cent.

The Spaniards and the English, meanwhile, headed out into the uncharted Atlantic. The Genoese Christopher Columbus, sailing for Spain, reached the Bahamas and the West Indies (1492-3). A fellow-Genoese, John Cabot, in the service of England, reached Newfoundland and Cape Breton in 1497; Columbus made his first landfall on the continental mainland only the year following.

Seeking Asia, they had found instead a new continent. An Italian geographer in 1493 spoke of the discovery of "a new world."

Of the effects of this achievement Marx and Engels wrote in the *Communist Manifesto*: "The discovery of America, the rounding of the Cape, opened up fresh ground for the rising bourgeoisie. The East-Indian and Chinese markets, the colonization of America, trade with the colonies, the increase in the means of exchange and in commodities generally, gave to commerce, to navigation, to industry, an impulse never before known, and thereby, to the revolutionary element in the tottering feudal society, a rapid development."

Above all, there was a speeding-up of the accumulation of money-capital in the hands of European capitalists. This "primitive" or primary accumulation of capital was the prelude to the industrial revolution of the 18th century. Marx wrote, in *Capital*: "The discovery of gold and silver in America, the extirpation, enslavement and entombment in mines of the aboriginal population, the beginning of the conquest and looting of the East Indies, the turning of Africa into a warren for the commercial hunting of black-skins, signalized the rosy dawn of the era of capitalist production. These idyllic proceedings are the chief momenta of primitive accumulation."

The other side of the process was the creation, alongside masses of money-capital, of masses of propertyless working people—as a result of the ruin of the peasantry and small producers.

In England, (and later in Scotland and Ireland) masses of small peasants were forcibly dispossessed by the "enclosures," which turned their farms into sheepwalks. Great landowners found the wool-trade a more profitable source of revenue than tenants' rent: so they drove the peasants out. Between 1455 and 1637 half a million acres were enclosed, rendering thirty to forty thousand English peasants homeless. Dissolution of the monasteries added another fifty thousand to the ranks of the dispossessed.

Thomas More in his great work *Utopia* described the brutal process: "Noblemen and gentlemen: yea and certain Abbots, holy men no doubt . . . leave no ground for tillers, they enclose all into pastures. . . . The husbandmen be thrust out of their own, or else either by covin and fraud, or by violent oppression . . . by one means or by other . . . they must needs depart away, poor silly, wretched souls, men, women, husbands, wives, fatherless children, widows, woeful mothers with their young babes, and their household small in substance and much in number.

. . . And when they had wandered abroad till that be spent, what can they else do but steal and then justly . . . be hanged, or else go about a-begging."

A statute of 1572, declaring England to be "with rogues, vagabonds and sturdy beggars exceeding pestered," decreed flogging, branding, and as a last resort death as a felon—for unlicensed begging. The author of a tract written in 1609 speaks of "our land abounding with swarms of idle persons, having no means of labor to relieve their misery. . . . If we seek not some ways for their foreign employment, we must provide shortly more prisons and corrections for their bad conditions."

From the brutalities and degradation that feudal and early capitalist society imposed on the laboring poor there arose the dream of a world founded on principles of justice and brotherhood, with abundance for all instead of for the few. The preacher John Ball, spokesman with Wat Tyler of the English peasants, had declared that "things cannot go well in England, nor ever will, until everything shall be in common."

In Thomas More's imaginary Utopia "there is abundance of all things;" and each, sharing in the work of all, "is sure never to lack."

News of the discovery of a "new world" beyond the seas stirred agonizing hopes. It is not an accident that More wove his story around a conversation with a traveller just back from a voyage with Amerigo Vespucci (for whom "America" was named)—and that he situated his Utopia somewhere in the western Atlantic . . .

VIII

Reconnoitering the Approaches

THE FIRST PEOPLE, AFTER THE EARLY NORSEMEN, TO reach North America from Europe were in all likelihood not the celebrated explorers but unknown whalers or cod fishermen. Working out of Basque, Breton or Portuguese fishing ports, they knew the waters off Iceland and Greenland. They may well have known the Grand Banks also.

What gave the discoveries of Columbus and Cabot their sensational impact was the fact that they took place at the moment when the search for gold and "the Indies" was at fever pitch; and when technical and economic advances in Western Europe made possible the exploration and exploitation of the newly-discovered lands. Spain, the dominant power, secured the Pope's blessing to a division of the world between itself and Portugal, whose navigators had just rounded the southern tip of Africa. The Treaty of Tordesillas (1494) "gave" the Americas to Spain (except for Brazil and, as Portugal later claimed, Newfoundland-Labrador) while Africa and lands eastward were reserved to Portugal.

Just as the merchants of northwest Europe had envied and eventually challenged the monopoly position of the Italian city-republics, so now they eyed covetously the new treasure-house of Spain. "Would that Englishmen had been the first," lamented one poet-adventurer . . . "The land of the Indians whence all the gold cometh had been ours."

From 1480 onward the merchants of Bristol, long active in trading wool and cloth for fish in Iceland, had backed a number of expeditions westward. The first to succeed was that led, in 1497, by the Genoese John Cabot: "a man of the people," as he was described at the time, "of kindly wit and a most expert mariner."

On May 2, 1497, Cabot and eighteen seamen put out from Bristol harbor in a tiny bark, the *Matthew*. For over seven weeks they plied the vast, forbidding reaches of the North Atlantic. Their hope was to reach Japan, "an island . . . rich and replenished with great commodities," the source of "all the spices of the world, and also precious stones." On June 23 they sighted land, and next day came ashore. They had indeed found an island—but not Japan. Their landfall may have been at Bonavista, Newfoundland, or perhaps on Cape Breton Island. Claiming the "new land" for England, Cabot and his men sailed homeward, convinced that they had reached the shores of Asia.

On a second voyage the following year, accompanied by his son Sebastian, Cabot led two ships on a reconnaissance of the Acadian and New England coasts. Once again, in place of Japan's exotic "great commodities" they found only immense quantities of cod. An acquaintance of Cabot's passed on his report to the Duke of Milan:

"The sea is covered with fish which are caught not merely with nets but with baskets, a stone being attached to make the basket sink in the water. . . . And (the) Englishmen, his companions, say that they will fetch so many fish that this kingdom will have no more need of Iceland, from which country there comes a very great store of fish."

Henceforth, the fishery of the Grand Banks was a matter of public knowledge. If earlier it had been known to only a few fishermen, it now drew the fishing fleets of half a dozen nations.

Close in the wake of Cabot came the Portuguese. Joao Fernandez, a one-time farmer or *llavrador* in the Azores,

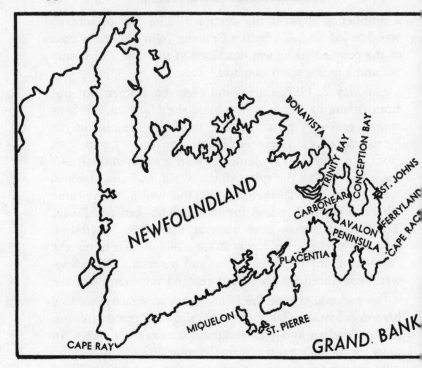

explored the West Greenland coast in 1499, and Labrador was named for him. In 1500-1 Gaspar Corte-Real entered Davis Strait, sailed down the Labrador coast, past both Hamilton Inlet and the entrance to Belle Isle Strait, to Avalon Peninsula. Here he and his men seized 50 or 60 Beothuk Indians and shipped them to Lisbon in one of his ships, to be sold as slaves. He and the crew of his own ship were lost shortly thereafter; and a like fate befell his brother's ship that came in search of him.

The Portuguese were the first to guess that Labrador and Acadia were part of one continent (an eastward projection of Asia, perhaps?). They named the area Baccalaos or "codfish land"; other place-names that recall their pres-

ence are Bonavista, Cape Race (from Razo, "flat"), Conception, and Capes Freels and Spear (from the words for
"cold" and "hope").

Next after the Portuguese came the French. Denys of
Honfleur is said to have entered and been the first to chart
the Gulf of St. Lawrence, in 1506.* Two years later
Thomas Aubert of Dieppe explored the Newfoundland
coast north of Cape Bonavista and took back seven Beothuk men and women as captives to Rouen.

In 1509 Sebastian Cabot sailed in search of "a passage
. . . to Cathay by the north seas": the beginning of four
centuries of search for a "northwest passage" around the
new continent to Asia. He claimed to have reached 67°
North, and reported that there were "great icebergs float-
ing in the sea and almost continuous daylight." At that
point a threat of mutiny forced him to turn back. Had he
entered Hudson's Strait? There is no means of knowing.
(The fact that he later tried to steal from his father the
credit for leading the expedition of 1497 hardly enhances
his credibility.)

In these reconnoitering voyages such lesser powers
as England, Portugal and France were beginning to challenge the dominance of Spain. The empire of the Spanish
Hapsburgs embraced the mid-section of the Americas, and
reaped a harvest of gold and silver through the plunder
and enslavement of the Indians of Peru and Mexico. The
awesome naval might of Spain compelled her rivals to
steer clear of the "Spanish Main" and stake their claims in
the northerly portions of the continent. As the English
geographer Roger Barlow put it, "So there resteth this
way of the north only for to discover. . . ." But he urged

---

*It is referred to as "the Square Gulf" in a work of 1511.

that "no man should think upon the cost in comparison to the great profit that may thereby follow."

"The great profit" was the motive: it worked like a leaven in the mercantile centres of Bristol and London, Lisbon, Rouen and Dieppe. The merchants' profit-hunger fused with that of the royal courts, eager for tribute to swell their treasuries. This mingling of feudal and early capitalist greed is written into the patent that Henry VII granted to a group of English and Portuguese merchants in 1501. Operating out of Bristol, the Company of Adventurers to the New Found Lands were empowered to "search out whatsoever island, countries, regions or provinces of heathen and infidels, in whatever part of the world they may lie, which before this time were and at present are unknown to all Christians, and to set up our banners and ensigns in any town, city, castle, island or mainland by them thus newly found, and to enter and seize these . . . to occupy, possess and subdue (them) . . . as our vassals."

Thus did Christian Europe assert its God-given right to establish the colonial system.

Attempts at establishing permanent outposts of settlement in the areas to the north of Spanish America date from 1518, when the French nobleman De Lery sought, unsuccessfully, to plant a colony on storm-swept Sable Island, off Nova Scotia; and an equally unsuccessful Portuguese effort in 1520 under Joao Fagundez to set up a fishing base in the Bay of Fundy. Shortly thereafter the French monarchy and merchants of the French Atlantic ports launched more extensive operations: the voyages of Verrazzano (1524) and Cartier (1534-42). The chief backers of these expeditions were the rich merchants of Rouen and men like Jean Ango, the leading ship-owner of Dieppe, who had connections with the banking houses of northern Italy (the birthplace of investment banking, as it was of capitalism).

These ventures were part of the intense and many-sided activities that accompanied the national unification of France and that marked the high point of the French Renaissance. The struggle under Francis I for a unified French state brought armed collisions with the Austro-Spanish Hapsburgs, whose domains encroached on most of France's land-frontiers—in Flanders, Lorraine, Piedmont and on the Pyrenees. The thrusts against Spain's overseas empire grew out of the military and political conflict in Europe. (France was at war with the Hapsburg Emperor Charles V in 1521-5, 1527-9, 1536-8, 1542-4.) Within France, meanwhile, the growth of a single national market made headway against medieval barriers and disunity. Reflecting this process was the replacement of Latin by French as the official language (in 1539); and the creative upsurge in literature with the work of such poets as Ronsard and of the great satirist Rabelais.

The gifted Florentine navigator, scientist and man of letters, Giovanni da Verrazzano, was himself a "man of the Renaissance." His "Relation of the Voyage of the *Dauphine*" (the ship in which he cruised along the coast from the Carolinas to Gaspé) contains the first detailed description that we possess of Canada's east coast, and of its early inhabitants. Like Columbus and Cabot, he had hoped to reach "Cathay and the eastern extremity of Asia." Unlike them, he realized that what he had encountered was a whole new continent; and came closer than any before him to guessing (however inaccurately) at its actual shape.*

*A number of maps of the 16th century show New France and Baccalaos (Newfoundland) jutting out from northeastern Siberia; the rest of the Americas projecting southward, separated from China and the Spice Islands (Indonesia) by the "South Sea"— the southern Pacific. (The fact that North America is not joined to Asia was estab-

"A land unknown to the ancients" he wrote, "has been discovered in our day. Another world, distinct from the one they knew, has become apparent . . . This land or New World . . . comprises a single whole. It is joined neither to Asia nor Africa (of this we are sure). Perhaps it joins Europe through Norway or Russia. . . . This continent appears enclosed between the eastern and the western seas, marking the limits of them both."

Of the native peoples he encountered on the coasts of New England and Acadia, Verrazzano noted that some lived in great houses sheltering over 30 persons; and that "in place of iron" they used tools of "flint, jasper . . . or other cutting stone"—"making boats out of a single tree-trunk, hollowed out with admirable skill." Those living to the south raised corn; the northerly hunting people "have no vegetables, and of cultivation we saw not a trace." He noted the absence of any state machinery, and that they "live in complete liberty."*

Some, seemingly, had already had encounters with Europeans: they greeted the intruders, Verrazzano reports, with contemptuous hostility, "jeering and showing their behinds."

Verrazzano's expedition reconnoitered the coast-line between Spanish Florida and Cabot's landfall in Cape Breton. To New England he gave the name "Francesca,"

---

*The Italian geographer Peter Martyr's contemporary account of the early American discoveries bore the title: *De Orbe Novo*—About a New World. Regarding its inhabitants, he wrote: "Among them the land belongs to everyone, like sun or water. They know no difference between *meum* and *tuum* ('mine and thine'), the source of all evils . . . No hedges or walls close in their dwelling places; no laws or judges govern their lives."

---

lished only in 1648, when the Yakut navigator Simeon Dezhnev sailed around the northeast tip of Siberia; the American northwest coast was first charted a century later, by Russian, Spanish and then English mariners.) Verrazzano's big mistake lay in believing that the "South Sea" (or Pacific) was separated from the Atlantic only by a narrow neck of land at Cape Hatteras, North Carolina.

in honor of Francis I; the country to the north of it he called "New France"—a name that was to endure.

Among Verrazzano's crew there may have been a mariner from the Breton port of St. Malo: Jacques Cartier. It was he that the king and the Normandy merchants placed in command of the next search for the "Indies." He sailed with two small ships in April 1534, and made the crossing in three weeks. Rounding the northern tip of Newfoundland, they sailed down through the Strait of Belle Isle into the Gulf. Cartier's reaction to the forbidding, rockbound North Shore struck a note which was later echoed in various ways, none of them encouraging to would-be immigrants. "I am rather inclined," said he, "to believe that this is the land God gave to Cain."

After crossing the Gulf, they came upon an island that Cartier named St. Jean (now Prince Edward Island), and facing it, the shore of what is now New Brunswick. This offered a fairer prospect: "The land along the south side," Cartier wrote, "is as fine and as good land, as arable and as full of beautiful fields and meadows, as any we have ever seen."

At the head of the bay they named Chaleur, Cartier and his men encountered a band of some three hundred Indians. The latter offered them furs, in exchange for "a handful of trinkets." Clearly, these Indians had already been in contact with Europeans; but this was the first case actually recorded of trading in furs. The record testifies to the nature of the "trade" relationship. The Indians were first subjected to a salvo of "fire lances"— murderous projectiles packed with "sulphur, cannon powder, powdered lead, broken glass and mercury." Then, having been brought, presumably, to a due measure of respect, "they bartered all they had [and] all went back naked without anything on them."

Concerning the inhabitants of the New World, Cartier

wrote: "This people can be called savage, for they must be the poorest people on earth; for all together they have not the value of five sous among them, aside from their boats and nets." And in another passage: "These people live as it were in community of goods."

After claiming the Gaspé for France, Cartier and his ships returned as they had come. The next year, 1535, a second expedition under Cartier's leadership made its way past the islands of the Gulf. With the help (be it noted) of Indian guides, the French found "the way to the mouth of the great river of Hochelaga, and the route towards Canada."* At Stadacona, in the shadow of the great rock of Quebec, they halted, and were made welcome by the Indians. Thence, in the smallest of his three ships, Cartier pushed on, through Lake St. Pierre to the island on which stood the village of Hochelaga. Of the welcome accorded them there Cartier writes: "They brought us quantities of fish, and of their bread which is made of Indian corn, throwing so much of it into our long-boats that it seemed to rain bread." In the village there were some fifty long-houses, in each of which a number of families "live together in common." (Evidently these were an Iroquoian people.)

From the summit of Mount Royal, Cartier could survey the sweep of land from the Laurentians in the north to the Adirondacks in the south, and coursing between them the river "with the most violent rapid it is possible to see" —Lachine.

The expedition wintered at Stadacona, and suffered heavy losses through scurvy, until saved by the Indians' showing them a remedy obtained from the sap of an evergreen. When spring came the French sailed for home, treacherously abducting the chief Donnacona and some of his lieutenants, as exhibits for the royal court. In addition

*See Note, p. 66.

to his captives, Cartier brought back tales of a fabulously rich "kingdom of Saguenay," reputed to lie far inland in the continent.

On his way homeward Cartier re-entered the Atlantic via Cabot Strait (instead of Belle-Isle), thus demonstrating for the first time that Newfoundland was an island.

As soon as there was a breathing space in the wars with the Hapsburgs, preparations were set on foot for a new and more ambitious venture. Roberval, a nobleman, with Cartier as his lieutenant, received command of a flotilla of ten ships (the largest, of 110 tons). They were to sail to "the lands of Canada and Hochelaga, which form the extremity of Asia"; as Roberval's pilot explained, "these lands are attached to Tartary" (Verrazzano's contrary view was evidently disregarded). Moreover, they were to plant a colony. Of the 800 persons who embarked, half were sailors, 300 soldiers; the rest included "60 masons and carpenters, and 20 workmen." There were some women, but the number is uncertain. To complete his ship's roster Roberval was empowered to take "criminals and malefactors" from the prisons.

Three of the ships, under Cartier, made the crossing in May 1541, and spent the following winter at Cap Rouge (upstream from Stadacona). In the spring, Roberval not having arrived, they set out for home—only to meet his convoy of ships in the harbor of St. John's, Newfoundland. Ordered to turn back, Cartier gave Roberval the slip and continued homeward. Left to themselves, lacking experience or adequate supplies, Roberval's party passed a bitter winter at Cap Rouge. A third of the settlers died of scurvy. The threat of mutiny was chronic: in one day Roberval had six men hanged. The attempt at settlement was given up in the summer of 1543.

The Austro-Spanish emperor Charles V had watched with suspicion the preparations being made for the

Roberval-Cartier expedition. His spies in French West Coast ports were on the alert to learn its date of departure. When Cartier sailed, swift caravels were sent to intercept him, but failed to do so. However, the emperor's anxieties about the threat to his monopoly of the Americas proved to have been excessive. France's involvement in further wars with the Hapsburgs, and then the outbreak of the Wars of Religion (1562-98), prevented any further effort in New France for close to half a century.

"CANADA," "NEW FRANCE"

The name "Canada" probably came from the Huron-Iroquois *kanata,* meaning a village or settled community. Cartier uses it in his Narrative, 1534-35—"Hochelaga and Canada, also called New France." (For recurrence of the name "Canada" in 1588 and 1627, see pp. 81, 85, below.) During the French regime the two names Canada and New France were roughly interchangeable. In a stricter sense, however, "New France" designated the French possessions in North America in their entirety, (including Louisiana) while "Canada' referred to the colony on the St. Lawrence, from which "Acadia" was distinct. (On uses of the term "Canadians," see Note, p. 198.)

IX

A Northwest Passage?

BY THE MID-16TH CENTURY EUROPEAN NAVIGATORS HAD charted a well-nigh continuous coast line from Argentina to Labrador. There still were hopes of finding a waterway through the "New Lands." But it was becoming increasingly clear that a vast continental barrier lay athwart the westward route to Asia.

For a time, intensive efforts were made to find a possible North East Passage, around Scandinavia and Russia. Sebastian Cabot had a part in the ventures of the Muscovy Company. But Novaya Zemlya and the Kara Sea were as far as they got. Attention turned next to the possibility of finding a North West Passage around America. Magellan had done the like, around the southern tip of South America: but Spain's galleons guarded the seas in that quarter. What of the North?

As long as Labrador was thought to be an extension eastward of Asia, the northern route held little promise. But Verrazzano's belief that America was an island was gaining ground. The Elizabethan seafarer, Sir Humphrey Gilbert, described America as "an island environed round about with Sea, having . . . on the North side the sea that severeth it from Greenland, through which Northern Seas the Passage lyeth." Therefore he had no doubt concerning "our Northwest passage and navigation to India." The search for a North West Passage was to extend over three and a half centuries. First, an entrance had to be found (this was what occupied the Elizabethans); then it was a matter of threading a way through a veritable maze of islands embedded most of the year in ice (this was the phase of the 19th-century endeavors).

It was English seamen who tackled the problem of the Passage. France's early efforts in the St. Lawrence area were cut short by the long-drawn "Wars of Religion." In England, however, there was taking place an upsurge of trade, of the merchant bourgeoisie, and of national consciousness: it was the great Elizabethan Age of the English Renaissance.

Along with a sharpening conflict with imperial Spain there went the wide-ranging pirate-cruises of Sir Francis Drake, and efforts to locate the Passage, "where-through our merchants may have course . . . with their merchandise, from these our northernmost parts of Europe to those Oriental coasts of Asia . . . to their no little commodity and profit."

The starting-point for the search was in the storm- and fog-laden sea between Greenland and Labrador. Gilbert wrote of having seen a chart of Sebastian Cabot's showing a strait or passage "on the north side of Terra de Labrador." The veteran mariner Martin Frobisher sailed in search of it in 1576. In the 25-ton bark *Gabriel* he and his men weathered a storm off Greenland; an accompanying pinnace foundered and the third small vessel in the expedition headed for home. "Although his mast was sprung, and his topmast blown overboard with extreme foul weather," they held to their westward course, "knowing that the sea at length must needs have an ending."

They sighted land: "A great gut, bay or passage" lay before them, dividing "as it were the two main lands or continents asunder." They sailed far up this passage, finding no ending to it, then turned back; they named it "Frobisher's Strait." (Not until 1860 was it established that it was no strait but a deep inlet: Frobisher Bay, at the foot of Baffin Island.)

On the coast they encountered men "in small boats of leather": Eskimo kayaks. "They exchanged coats of seal, and bears' skins and such like with our men," wrote Frobisher; "and received bells, looking glasses, and other toys in recompense thereof."

Returning to England, the voyagers brought with them samples of rock containing a deceptive promise of gold. Two further expeditions (1577 and '78) were diverted to a futile collecting of useless ore in the same area. On the last of these, a flotilla of 15 ships was sent, with a view to establishing a permanent outpost; but furious storms cost them part of their supplies and compelled abandonment of the attempt. At one point they had made their way through pack-ice, gale and fog to the entrance to another sea-lane: Frobisher named it the "Mistaken Straits." Strange irony! His own "Frobisher's Strait" was the "mistaken" one, while this was in fact a real gateway to the north. It was later to be known as Hudson's Strait.

In three successive expeditions (1585-87) the geographer-mariner John Davis of Devon followed up the work that Frobisher had begun. A friend of Walter Raleigh and Humphrey Gilbert, Davis was "a man very well grounded in the principles of the art of navigation." In his later works on seamanship and oceanography he combined vast theoretical knowledge with a wide practical experience.

On his first voyage in search of "the North West Passage to China" he went up the west coast of Greenland ("the land of Desolation," he called it), then sailed northwest across the strait that now bears his name. Land was reached at Exeter Bay (Baffin I.) on the Arctic Circle: the first recorded landfall by Europeans in what is now the Canadian Arctic. From here he followed the coast southward and, passing the "Cape of God's Mercy," entered a passage that Davis took to be a strait: it was Cumberland Sound. A later, deeper penetration of it caused him to

John Davis explored the waters between Greenland and Baffin Island.

doubt that this was the Passage; he leaned to the opinion, however, that "the Northern parts of America are all islands."

On this, as on his other voyages, Davis made detailed scientific observations. He was the first to chart exactly a large area of our northern waters. He also studied the culture and conditions of the Eskimo inhabitants of Greenland and Baffin Island. He compiled a vocabulary of their language; and noted the character of their summer dwellings, "tents . . . made with seal skins set up upon timber"; their carving of "images"; and their method of making fire with a drill, dipped in fish oil, and dry turf.

On the third expedition Davis sailed in a tiny pinnace more than 700 miles up the west coast of Greenland (half the overall length of it)—to 72° 12′ N. the northernmost point reached by him. Here there was "no ice towards the north, but a great sea, free, large, very salt and blue, and of an unsearchable depth." Beyond it, surely, lay Cathay! But contrary winds forced them to turn south. After again visiting Cumberland Sound, and passing Frobisher Bay, the ship's log records that they "fell into a mighty race, where an island of ice was carried by the force of the current as fast as our bark could sail. We saw the sea falling down into the gulf with a mighty overfall, and roaring, with divers circular motions like whirlpools, in such sort as forcible streams pass through the arches of bridges." This "furious overfall" was the entrance to Hudson's Strait. The rush of waters came from the ice-hemmed tides draining out of Hudson Bay.

Thus did John Davis "light Hudson into his strait." In 1610 Henry Hudson led an expedition into the Bay, and explored its eastern shore; there he perished when set adrift by mutineers. Thomas Button in 1613 wintered on the west shore of the Bay, at Port Nelson.

In 1615-16 William Baffin extended the reconnaissance

of the "north water" reached earlier by Davis. He found three openings: Smith Sound (between Greenland and Ellesmere Island), Jones Sound (between Ellesmere and Devon Is.) and Lancaster Sound (between Devon and Baffin Is.); but wrongly concluded that all were merely bays, and that "there is no passage or hope of passage to the north of Davis Straits." The error was not put right for another two centuries.

As doubts grew regarding the existence of a North West Passage, the London merchants became more insistent that their investment show some return. They had diverted Frobisher into a fruitless search for gold; they turned two of Davis's three ships (on his third voyage) on to a fishing venture. The fishery off Newfoundland had been growing all through the 16th century. It brought surer returns than the baffling search for the Passage.

The fishery became the first focus of European settlement in Northern America; and fishermen, the first settlers.

The Cod.

X

The Great Fishery

OFFSHORE FROM NANTUCKET AND CAPE COD, RUNNING some 1,200 miles northeastward, lie a series of submerged plateaus: the fishing banks. By far the largest is the Grand Bank, south and east of Newfoundland's Avalon Peninsula, with an area of 37,000 square miles. Here the cod swarm and spawn each summer. They feed on herring, squid and capeline (a small subarctic fish); and range in size from a few pounds (in the case of shore fish) up to 150 pounds and over.

It was the teeming cod that John Cabot's men had "caught with baskets"; and the cod fishery expanded mightily in the wake of his voyaging. Each year from 1500 onward, between March and October, large fishing fleets congregated on the Banks: Portuguese, Basques, Bretons, Normans, English. They supplied the markets of West Europe and the Mediterranean as far east as Greece, with dried cod—the "beef of the sea."

In addition to the cod-fishers, the Basque whalers had ranged over the North Atlantic ahead of the celebrated "discoverers." (There is one report of their reaching Labrador nearly 30 years before the voyage of Cabot: but it may have been Greenland.)

By the end of the 16th century some 15,000 fishermen were plying the waters of the Banks. The relationships of fishing-masters and men reflected the emerging of the capitalist wages-system. Among the French, agreements of the early 1500's provided that the "marchans et bourgeois" (merchant-proprietors) were to get two-thirds of the "pesche, huile, gaings et prouffics" (fish, oil, earnings and profits). One third went to the men —"compaignons, pescheurs et mariniers" (journeymen, fishermen, seamen). This system of exploitation was amiably described as "giving each his rightful part of such catch as they may take." The "shares" system also prevailed in the English fishery. Among the Basques and Portuguese, the wages-system was the prevailing one.

Among the French, alongside feudal relations, there were some instances of payment in wages. As early as 1510 there is record of a wage-dispute on a Breton ship. And around the same time, a record of the taking of a tithe by abbey monks on the catch of Breton fishermen of Isle Bréhat.

N. Denys, a Frenchman living in Acadia at the beginning of the 1600's, thus describes the hardships of the work: "Although the fish constitutes a kind of inexhaustible manna, I cannot refrain from astonishment of the fact that it sells for so little, having regard to the risks that are run both going and returning. The fishermen upon the bank have nearly six months when the ice freezes upon their lines, whilst they draw them up. This causes them great fatigue. I do not know how men are found for this fishery in which they obtain so little profit. When a fisherman makes on his voyage thirty to thirty-five or forty *ecus*,* that is not bad. And these voyages are of five, six, and seven months, including the time of loading and unloading the vessel, during which time they make nothing."

There were two methods employed in the fishery. In the "green" or "wet" fishery, the catch was salted directly on board ship; in the "dry" or "shore" fishery, the catch was taken ashore and dried on specially built stagings or

---

*Between $67 and $90 in our present currency.

"flakes." The first method required an abundance of salt, and was practised by the French and others well supplied in that respect. The English developed the "dry" method, which the French also resorted to later on.

There was a high degree of division of labor aboard ship and on shore. The fisherman, wearing a long leather apron (sheepskin, with the wool inside and tarred on the outside), used two forty-fathom lines at a time, letting one down as he drew in a catch on the other. He placed the fish he caught in a barrel that stood before him on an out-board staging rigged along the ship's side. The tongues of the cod were cut out and kept as a tally of the amount of each man's catch. Boys carried the fish to the long splitting-tables, where "one man cut off the head and threw it into the sea, a second cut open the bellies and disembowelled them, and a third cut out the backbone. The fish were put in a salting tub for twenty hours and packed away."

In the dry fishery this part of the work was done ashore, where the splitting-tables, washing-troughs and "flakes" were set up, as shown in the accompanying 18th century wood-cut.

There were generally between a dozen and thirty men to a crew. Lescarbot, who explored Acadia with Champlain, tells of one fishing-master who "paid wages to 16 men and his vessel was of 80 tons and would carry 100,000 dry fishes." Each voyage would take three months or so; sometimes several voyages were made in one season, between February and October.

Just as the fishermen were the first to venture into the Western Atlantic, so too they were the first Europeans to establish settlements on the territory that is now Canada. Coming ashore in the coves along the eastern and southern coasts of Newfoundland, they landed to obtain fresh water, or wood, or make repairs to their ships' gear; and

A View of a Stage & also of y manner of Fishing for, Curing & Drying Cod at NEW FOUND
A The Habit of y Fishermen B The Line C The manner of Fishing D. The Dressers of y Fish. E The Trou
which they throw y Cod when Dressed F Salt Boxes G The manner of Carrying y Cod H The Cleansing y Cod. I
to extract y Oyl from y Cods Livers K Casks to receive y Water & Blood that comes from y Livers L Another Cask e
the Oyl M The manner of Drying y Cod

"Fishing for, Curing and Drying Cod."
An early 18th-century engraving.

later, crews stayed on for the winter to erect the "flakes,"
or stagings, build cook-rooms, wharves and boats. By 1552
there were forty or fifty houses in Newfoundland.

The English established their fishing posts in the eastern part of Avalon Peninsula, from Conception Bay to
Cape Race. The French, when they began to go in for the
dry fishery, set up their posts along the southern and western shores of Newfoundland, then at Canso, Gaspé and
the north shore of the St. Lawrence. (Cartier on his first

journey encountered there a fishing ship from La Rochelle.)

The fishermen created the first outposts of settlement; but the fishery did not itself lead to any large-scale colonizing effort. Interest in the "planting" of colonies came somewhat later: with the drive of the West European monarchs and merchants for trade routes to Asia, for markets, for strategic bases overseas.* Also, colonies offered a means of "dumping" the dispossessed and surplus poor. Colonization, wrote the poet John Donne, "shall conduce to great uses . . . It shall sweep your streets and wash your doors from idle persons . . .and employ them." And Humphrey Gilbert in his *Discourse of a Discovery for a New Passage to Cathay* expressed the view: "Also we might inhabit some part of those countries, and settle there such needy people of our country, which now trouble the common wealth."

The words "to inhabit" appear in the charter for Gilbert's colonizing expedition of 1583, which on its way to the mainland got only as far as St. John's, Newfoundland. Gilbert's prospective settlers included "masons, carpenters and blacksmiths;" and, with an eye to hoped-for finds of mineral wealth, "an ore-refiner named Daniel," from Saxony. Mutiny ashore and storms at sea wrecked the venture. Among those lost were Gilbert and the learned geographer Stephen Parmenius, of Hungary.

Newfoundland and the Banks were the meeting-place of ships of many nations, and no one power had any firm claim to territorial possession. But the clash of rival interests was of frequent occurrence. During the struggle between France and Spain, they had raided and burned each other's ships at St. John's; in 1585, with England chal-

---

*"In England this was the period when the capitalist era began, and the first advocates of colonial expansion appeared." (G. O. Rothney, *Newfoundland*, p. 4).

lenging the power of Spain (the Armada met its defeat in 1588), English ships made a devastating assault on the Spanish fishing fleet. When the war with Spain ended, England's position of strength in the fishery was assured. Yet it was not one of decisive dominance. France remained strong, and the new sea-power of the Netherlands was being forged in the successful revolutionary war with Spain.

The fishery now began to be prized as a "nursery for seamen." The ships of the fishing fleets provided, it was held, a training-school for the national navies that were taking shape. "If these should be lost," declared Sir Walter Raleigh, "it would be the greatest blow ever given to England." In the century following, the number of English ships in the Newfoundland fishery grew to 300, with three thousand seamen; and it was estimated that the jobs of some 20,000 in England depended on activities (shipbuilding, supplies, etc.) linked with the fishery.

In 1610 there was founded a "Company of Adventurers and Planters of the City of London and Bristol, for the Colony and Plantation of Newfoundland." Among its shareholders was the celebrated Francis Bacon, one of the fathers of modern science (Marx calls him the founder "of English materialism and generally of the experimental sciences of modern times"). Bacon wrote in support of the projected settlement, pointing to "the gold mines of the Newfoundland fishery, of which there is none so rich."

The venture was led by John Guy, a merchant of Bristol, who brought out "peasants and artisans" (including sawyers) to establish a permanent settlement. At Cupid's Cove, Conception Bay, they constructed a fort, farm buildings, a warehouse, wharves, a grist mill and a saw mill. The Company's instructions ordered them to engage in fishing, obtain cod oil, make "masts, spars and deal boards," and look into the possibility of carrying on sheep raising. The instructions contained the warning: "If any persons employed in this service shall be found to be seditious, mutinous or in any manner unfit," they were to be sent back to England "by the next return of any ship . . . to be discharged, giving advertisement of their behaviour."

To the fishermen already established in the area, the "planting" of the colony loomed as a threat to their livelihood. They petitioned the king, James I, citing numerous grievances: that the settlers "have put sundry of the Petitioners from the chiefest places of fishing there . . . That they have taken away great quantities of salt, casks, boats, stages and other provisions . . ." Also, that the Company arrogated to itself rights of government: to which the fishermen declare that "they are altogether unwilling to be ordered by the Planters." Unable to get redress of their grievances, the fishermen at one point attempted to destroy the Company's mills.

Thus began a conflict that was to dominate the history of eastern Newfoundland for close to two centuries. Behind the clash of colony and fishery—in which settlers and fishermen were the immediate contestants and sufferers—stood the rival merchant-capitalist interests of the company shareholders in London and Bristol on the one hand, and the West Country fishing-masters and merchants in Cornwall, Devon, Somerset and Dorset, on the other.

XI

The Fur Trade of New France

THE CARTIER-ROBERVAL ATTEMPT TO FOUND A COLONY of settlement on the St. Lawrence in 1541-43 ended in failure and no new attempt was made in the half-century that followed. Yet at home the forces making for colonial expansion continued to grow. The founding of France's first bank in 1544 (at Lyons, the silk-weaving centre) was a landmark in the country's merchant-capitalist development. With the rise of a national market came a unified currency; by the mid-century France had "developed a more modern financial system than had Spain, the Netherlands or England" (Marx).

In the "Wars of Religion" (1562-98) the centralized monarchy experienced a profound crisis. This long-drawn civil war was a confused tangle of interwoven conflicts: resistance on the part of the most reactionary feudal elements (backed from abroad by the Hapsburgs) to the central power (supported by some of the lesser nobles and the bourgeoisie); clashes of rival groups of the landed nobility; and in the latter stages, a tidal wave of mass peasant uprisings against oppression by their overlords. Driven beyond endurance by the hunger and devastation that accompanied the war, the peasants fought pitched battles: 12,000 insurgents made a stand in Normandy, 40,000 in Périgord. In Britanny they fought, as one chronicler records it, "to abolish the nobility . . . for only thus could be established the equality that ought to reign on earth."

To meet this threat, the strife-torn ruling classes halted their hostilities. The peasant risings were crushed, the wars ended in a compromise. It was embodied in the Edict of Nantes, proclaimed in 1598 by the new king, Henry IV —the one-time Huguenot leader, turned Catholic. The national monarchy was preserved and strengthened, but the Church was made secure in its vast holdings. At the same time the Huguenots secured certain concessions, being allowed to practice the "reformed religion" in restricted areas and to hold official posts.

The sea-port towns were strongholds of the Huguenot merchants. Even during the civil war they had attempted one colonial settlement in Florida, which was promptly wiped out by rival Spaniards, and another in Brazil, likewise short-lived. Toward the war's end, the merchants revived the schemes of colonial enterprise. In this they were joined by some of the nobles; and the royal court (its coffers much in need of replenishing) began granting them charters of monopoly. At once there were vociferous complaints from those not included in the monopoly arrangements. The burgesses of St. Malo in 1588 protested against "the interdiction of trade with Canada," declaring that a trading monopoly was "a thing prejudicial to the generality of this community." When all the estates of Britanny joined in the protest—nobles, clergy and commoners—the king yielded; he conceded "that from all time commerce and trade has been free to our subjects . . . with the savages and others . . . as well in peltries and fish as in other commodities."

But the wealthier nobles and merchant capitalists, seeking the protected profit that monopoly promised, kept up their pressure and soon secured new charters. These included a requirement that the merchant adventurers should establish colonies of settlement as well as fur-trading posts: strategic state interests (particularly the struggle with Spain) called for steps toward outright occupation of the "new lands," even though settlement might come into conflict with the needs of the "trade in peltries."

This trade had grown up gradually out of the early contacts of the fishermen with the Indians. By the close of the 16th century progress in the technique of felting, in the making of beaver hats, combined with the demand for furs on the part of rich merchants and court aristocracy to provide a growing market for beaver pelts. (It is characteristic of the peculiar pattern of early French capitalist development that fur, a luxury product, should become the staple of its North American colony.)

The Marquis de la Roche, who earlier had obtained colonizing rights and the title of Viceroy of Newfoundland, in 1598 sought to "plant" a colony on storm-swept Sable Island, east of the Nova Scotia coast. He shipped out sixty "beggars and vagabonds"— dispossessed peasants and urban poor—taken from the jails; and left them on the desolate island. They mutinied, and four-fifths of them had perished before the starving survivors were brought back to France, five years later. Around this time another unsuccessful attempt at establishing an outpost of settlement was made at Tadoussac, this time by the Huguenot merchant Pierre Chauvin.

In 1603 a company of Dieppe and Rouen merchants sent an expedition up the St. Lawrence. Led by the mariner Pontgravé and with Samuel de Champlain as geographer, the reconnaissance covered roughly the same ground as Cartier had done. The following year they attempted a colonizing venture in Acadia. A party of threescore workmen under the command of the Huguenot De Monts wintered at the mouth of the St. Croix River. From here Champlain charted the coastline southward as far as Cape Cod; and visited the future site of St. John in the Bay of Fundy. After a grim winter—more than half the men died of scurvy—they moved to a more sheltered haven in the Annapolis Valley. Here, at Port Royal, they built a "habitation," mill and workshops: the first actual French settlement in North America. (Two years later the English founded their first permanent settlement at Jamestown, Virginia.)

Accompanied by a miner from Slovenia, one Master Jacques, Champlain examined Minas Basin at the head of the Bay of Fundy in the hope of finding copper or other mineral deposits—but without success. This miner— in Champlain's words "a native of Sclavonia, a man well versed in the search for minerals"— was in all likelihood the first Slav to come to Canada.

Although Port Royal enjoyed a milder climate than the "disagreeable country" (as de Monts described it) north of the St. Lawrence, Champlain concluded that in Acadia "there is not so much profit and gain in the trade in furs." So it was agreed to turn once more to the "river of Canada." In 1608 Champlain directed the founding of an outpost of settlement at the foot of the great rock of Quebec. In the years that followed he laid the ground-work for the French fur-empire: exploring the trade routes, conducting military operations, initiating agricul-tural settlement as a base of operations for the trade.

Samuel de Champlain came of a seafaring family in Brouage, a port to the north of Bordeaux. He served in the Wars of Religion under Henry IV; later he sailed under Spanish command, acquiring a notable mastery of the arts of map-making and navigation. (To this period belongs an expedition to the Caribbean, the account of which is of doubtful authenticity.*) Thereafter, he return-ed to the service of France; and his work of exploration

---

*See Reference note.

in what now is Canada bears witness to his consuming passion: discovery, the widening of man's knowledge of the world.

Because of the epoch in which he lived—that of the dawn of capitalism and colonialism—his gifts and energies were bound to the service of the trading companies and the monarchy. Yet he was able to see beyond his masters' immediate narrow aims, and grew to love this vast land, its forests, rivers, lakes. "The farther we go," he noted in his log-book, "the more beautiful is the country. . . . New France is not a kingdom but a new world, fair to perfection."

The vision of the potential that this "new world" contained was sound. But the pathway to its fulfilment was devious and grim, its initial starting-point being the ruthless subjugation and plundering of the native peoples: an operation in which Champlain played a significant part.

Here, as elsewhere, the "rosy dawn" of capitalist accumulation was no idyllic story.

From the outset, the ruling powers in the colony were the feudal-mercantile companies and the Catholic Church. Very soon the settlers were in conflict with them both.

As regards the position of the Church, a two-fold conflict developed. First, there was the struggle of Calvinists against Catholics. Protestant merchants played a predominant part in organizing the trading companies, and many of their employees were of the same faith.

A second conflict arose from the efforts of the Jesuit Order to oust the Franciscan Recollets and secure a monopoly of religious authority in the colony. When the first contingent of Jesuits reached Quebec in 1625, they faced universal hostility: "All refused unanimously to receive them"— until the Recollets agreed to give them shelter. (A charitable gesture that was followed later by the Recollets' own expulsion, thanks to Jesuit intrigue at court.) The coming of the Jesuits was protested in a pamphlet that circulated among the garrison and the settlers at Quebec. It was "notoriously libellous," according to a contemporary Jesuit chronicler, who also noted that at Tadoussac the Calvinists, "loudly and with rough voices," "made the whole place ring with foolish and impious ditties."

In 1628 the king's troops laid siege to La Rochelle, the Huguenot stronghold on the French Atlantic coast. That same year Protestants were barred from settling in New France.

As for the trading companies, their interest lay in fur profits, not colonization; and they systematically sabotaged the requirement of their monopoly grant that they bring out settlers. A contemporary observed: "The country is still sparsely populated and deserted, and this through the negligence and lack of interest of the merchants who have been content to gather in furs and profits, without engaging in any expense for the cultivation, settlement or progress of the country."

In 1621—there were then only eleven settlers—they (including Champlain) held a "general meeting of all Frenchmen inhabiting this country of New France," drew up a statement of grievances and sent it to the court in Paris. This earliest protest against monopoly was but the first of many.

In 1627 a new monopoly was set up: that of the "Hundred Associates" or Company of New France. In it were combined both feudal and merchant capital interests. Its charter granted "in perpetuity . . . in full property, jurisdiction and seigneurie, the fort and habitation at Quebec, with all the said country of New France, called Canada." Itself a vassal of the king, the company was in turn empowered to grant feudal holdings of land or seigneuries.

By this time there were 76 settlers around the trading post at Quebec. They were cultivating some 18 or 20 arpents of land.* Carpenters, brought out from France, had started to build a water-mill. But in the summer of 1628 English ships appeared in the St. Lawrence, and their commander Kirke demanded surrender of the post.

English colonization was spreading on the Atlantic seaboard (Plymouth was founded in 1620) and in Europe merchant-imperial rivalry with France had erupted in open war.

After holding out for the winter, Champlain's small force surrendered Quebec in 1629. But at the time of its surrender, hostilities in Europe had already ended. Three years later, in exchange for an arrangement to pay the dowry of Charles I's French queen, France recovered Canada.

Traders and missionaries now extended the area of French occupation toward the interior. In 1634 fur merchants established a post at Three Rivers. The Jesuits built up their mission in Huronia, the area between Georgian Bay and Lake Simcoe. A group of wealthy Church supporters undertook to finance the founding of a missionary, trading and military outpost on the Island of Montreal: led by the soldier Paul de Chomedey, sieur de Maisonneuve, a group of settlers in 1642 founded Ville-Marie (Montreal).

At the time of the founding of Montreal, there were only some 300 settlers in New France. To the south, New Holland on the Hudson had a population of 10,000; while Massachusetts had two and a half times that number.

The main labor force for the trade in furs was made up of thousands of Indians who hunted and trapped, prepared the pelts, and carried them hundreds of miles to the trading posts.

---

*Arpent: about 5/6 of an acre.

To people who knew only stone tools and implements of wood or bone, the trade-goods of the merchants: iron, knives, awls, hatchet heads and kettles—were things of wonder, of well-nigh magical power . . . things, in the words of one French traveller, that could render the Indians "powerful aid in ameliorating their wretched condition." According to the Jesuit *Relation* of 1611, "the savages, who have neither copper, iron, hemp, wool, vegetables, nor manufactured articles of any kind, resort to the French for them, giving them in return the only thing of value they have, namely, furs."

To the traders, the "wretched condition" of the native people was an invitation to shameless plundering. As one trader himself described it: "One gets a beaver robe for a portion of tobacco, sometimes for six knives, sometimes for a fathom of small blue beads, etc." Another says that in exchange for furs they gave the Indians "paint, porcelain and other rubbish."

The French 18th-century materialist Raynal in his history of merchant companies denounced the plundering of the Indians in Canada; he asserted that "ruse and perfidy have been the basis of our commerce with them"; and contrasted the "implacable greed of the most civilized peoples of Europe" with the attitudes and relationships of native, primitive society: "Inequality of condition, which we hold so necessary for the maintenance of society, is to the savage the height of lunacy."

The Jesuit *Relation* of 1626 reported that the merchants "deal principally in Beavers, in which they find their greatest profit. I was told that during one year they carried back as many as 22,000. The usual number for one year is 15,000 or 12,000, at one pistole each, which is not doing badly."*

---

*Pistole: about $10 in our currency.

The extension of the trade required the establishment of outposts on the main canoe routes. Working out of Quebec, Champlain and his men set up trading posts at Three Rivers and the island of Montreal; they followed the Richelieu to the lake now called Champlain; they journeyed nothwestward up the Ottawa, across Lake Nipissing, down the French River to Georgian Bay, eastward to Lake Simcoe and thence to the Bay of Quinte. The routes they followed were already well-established, since the Indians had built up earlier a trading network of their own. What to the Europeans was "discovery" was, in some respects, at least, rather in the nature of a conducted tour: everywhere Indians guided them, paddled them, taught them woodcraft. In time, on the basis of this indispensable assistance, the French built up a corps of their own canoemen, or voyageurs—but the basic workforce remained the Indian hunting peoples.

The European traders not only took full advantage of the Indians' poverty; in order to reduce those with whom they traded to even greater dependency, they fomented fratricidal wars among the tribes. H. A. Innis, the outstanding authority on the fur trade, observes: "Alliances were formed and wars were favored to increase the supply of fur. The net result was continuous and destructive warfare." Thus Champlain at Tadoussac in 1603 pledged French military assistance to the Algonquin-Montagnais who were then at war with the Iroquois; six years later he joined a war-party of theirs in an invasion of the Iroquois-Mohawk territory up the Richelieu.

In Champlain's later negotiations with the tribes, promises of arms and aid in war recur repeatedly, as inducements to continue trading with the French. Inter-tribal wars were not new: the Algonquin-Montagnais had long since driven out the Iroquois people whom Cartier had encountered at Stadacona and Hochelaga, and the conflict in which Champlain intervened may have been a continuation of this earlier struggle. But the European intervention transformed what had once been sporadic, local contests waged with bows and arrows into murderous wars of mutual extermination waged with firearms and extending over vast territories. The arrival of the English in Virginia and of the Dutch on the Hudson (1609), challenging the French in Acadia and on the St. Lawrence, signalled the onset of the long struggle of the European powers for colonial territory and trade in northeastern North America. The chief victims of this struggle were the Indian peoples.

XII

The Iroquois Resistance

THE FRENCH FUR-LORDS BUILT THEIR POWER IN NORTH America on the backs of the native peoples. Those who declined to become dependent, exploited "allies" had to wage war in order to survive. Such were the tribes of the Iroquois Confederacy. Their lands lay athwart the path of the French penetration, which was striking ever deeper into the interior of the continent.

Emissaries of Champlain, Etienne Brûlé was on the Ohio in 1615, and by 1634 Nicolet was in Wisconsin. Champlain, appealing to Richelieu to send him troops, argued that this military aid would enable the French colonizers to become "absolute masters of these peoples, establishing the order that is needed, which will augment the practice of religion and an incredible amount of trade." Because the Iroquois stood in the way of French expansion, he urged that they be destroyed.

Like the Algonquin and Huron "allies" of the French, the Iroquois came to depend increasingly on European trade goods. They obtained them from the Dutch at Albany, in exchange for furs. But by the early 1630's the supply of beaver in the Iroquois country south of the lower Great Lakes was dwindling rapidly. It became an urgent necessity for the Iroquois to get furs from the Hurons living to the northwest. As the French traveller La Hontan later commented: "The Iroquois, being unprovided with beaver skins to be given in exchange for Guns, Powder, Ball and Nets, would be starved to death" or obliged to leave the country. During the 1620's and

30's the Iroquois tried repeatedly to come to an agreement with the Hurons. Such an arrangement, as the Jesuit *Relation* noted, would have greatly benefited the Dutch . . . "to the very notable detriment of the Gentlemen Associates of the Company of New France." Father Gabriel Sagard, a Recollet, who innocently hoped that it might be possible "to promote a peace between the Hurons and the Iroquois" was promptly put straight: "Some members of the Company advised me that it was not expedient, since if the Hurons were at peace with the Iroquois" the latter would induce them "to trade with the Dutch and divert them from Quebec which is more distant."

Thus Company policy and profit required the perpetuating of a murderous inter-tribal war. Efforts to establish peace were calculatingly disrupted.* This cynical policy in due course resulted in the destruction of Huronia, the wiping out of the Jesuit missions there and mortal jeopardy to the entire French colony.

By 1640 there were no more beaver to be caught in the country of the Iroquois, who for some years had been raiding the Huron fur fleets on the waterways to Quebec. As the Iroquois position became desperate, scattered and intermittent small-scale clashes gave way to outright war. When Montreal was founded under religious auspices in 1642, it was not so much a mission settlement as an advance military outpost in a highly exposed position. "The Iroquois . . . have blocked up all the passages and avenues of the River," reported the Jesuit *Relation* of 1644;

---

*"The Iroquois were eager for peace and the Hurons also were willing; but the possibility was frustrated by the intriguing French who, with the priests as envoys, put a stop to any negotiations that might divert the trade." (G. T. Hunt, *Wars of the Iroquois*.)

A century later a priest, Father Aubery, was urging that the Abenaki of the Maritimes be urged to keep up hostilities with the English: "This war is very necessary if we are not to risk losing the whole South Shore of the St. Lawrence and . . . all of Canada."

"We are now as it were invested and besieged on every hand." A colleague added: "Our habitations are no longer aught else but prisons." The Recollet Sagard commented on "the boldness of the savages in having dared, without fear of swords or muskets, to press through so many distant forests to attack the French in the territory of the habitation."

The war that raged from the middle 1630's to the 1660's was not such as Europeans were familiar with. It was a guerilla war of the forest and river. As Champlain remarked: "the mode of warfare which they practise is altogether by surprises." The French had to learn woodcraft, the use of snowshoes and how to handle the canoe, before their superiority in firearms could become in any way decisive.

The Iroquois strategy was to strike first at the dependent Huron allies of the French. In this they were aided greatly by the fact that Huronia was fatally weakened from within. In the first place even the limited successes of the missionaries in securing converts had led to deep divisions within the Huron ranks. What this meant in practice is revealed in a priestly comment about the experiences of one war party, that "Our people"— the converts —"always wanted to camp separately so as to avoid all contact with the sinful ones."

More serious by far, however, in opening the way for a crushing Huron defeat, were the successive waves of smallpox and other diseases that ravaged the tribes who were in contact with French trading posts and missions. Contagion swept through the crowded Huron lodges and out to the Algonquin hunting camps in three frightful epidemics in the years 1635 to 1640. "The terror and fright of war" says the *Relation* of 1642, "followed upon mortal sickness which in previous years spread mourning and desolation on all sides." Contemporary accounts report that the

Huron population was cut down in the space of a few years from 30,000 to 12,000.

In 1643 the Iroquois expelled the Neutral Nation, who were suppliers of foodstuffs to the Huron traders, from the Niagara Peninsula. Next year the Ottawa and St. Lawrence were under blockade as far as Quebec. If no help should come, the Jesuits warned, it would mean "ruin for the Faith and for the trade."

In 1645 Governor Montmagny sued for peace. During negotiations at Three Rivers the Iroquois sachem Kiot-saton pointedly reminded the Hurons of his people's earlier offers of peace, and of their rejection of them. The treaty finally agreed on contained a secret clause whereby the French abandoned their Algonquin allies (except a handful of Christian converts), leaving them to face the Iroquois as best they might. The Hurons, for their part, apparently promised the Iroquois to supply them with furs. However, they proceeded the following year to carry huge shipments of furs to the French, while by-passing the Iroquois: a course that led promptly to a disastrous renewal of the war.

In 1649-50 the Iroquois struck a blow that shattered Huronia. Its villages were destroyed, its population dispersed. Bréboeuf and his fellow Jesuit missionaries perished at the stake: victims of a policy of which they had been the co-authors. By 1653, when the Iroquois defeated the Eries,* the whole French trading system in southern Ontario had been wrecked. The fur trade was brought to a standstill. It was not revived until the French traders, some years later, enlisted a new labor force from the tribe of the Ottawas, living to the north and west of Lake Huron.

Having destroyed the Huron allies of the French, the

---

*Eries: Iroquoian tribe living south of the lake of that name.

Iroquois now turned upon the colony itself. Their on-slaughts ranged from outposts on Lake Michigan to the Isle of Orleans below Quebec.

The whole country was terror-stricken. "Nothing in the world is more cruel than an Iroquois war," wrote the 18th century chronicler La Potherie: "Then the habitant trembles as he eats, no one who leaves his house may count on returning: his sowings and reapings are abandoned."

In 1650 the desperate Quebec authorities sent an envoy to New England, with the aim of negotiating an alliance ". . . no matter what rupture might take place between the Crowns of England and France." This first venture in what might be called an independent Canadian foreign policy was not much of a success: the envoy, a Jesuit, was welcomed by his Puritan hosts, but the negotiations, involving representatives of four English colonies, finally bogged down.

By 1657 the Iroquois offensive penetrated in a great arc to the north and east of Quebec, driving the Montagnais out of the country of the upper Saguenay. Two years later it reached as far as Tadoussac. Montreal lay under siege, and the settlers feared for Quebec itself. Rumors of a further impending attack spread panic in the spring of 1660. Early in May, as Iroquois parties were gathering on the Ottawa and the Richelieu, a group of sixteen young Montrealers led by Dollard des Ormeaux "conceived the plan of risking themselves to set an ambush for the Iroquois," as one contemporary described the venture. The encounter took place upstream from Montreal, at the Long Sault on the Ottawa. Although heavily out-numbered by some seven hundred Iroquois the Montrealers, with four Hurons and forty Algonquins stood their ground. The fighting raged for a week. None of the French survived; only a few of their allies managed to escape. However, for that year at least, the threat to the French settlements was stayed.*

It was no more than a breathing-spell. The following year Tadoussac was burned, its hundred inhabitants fleeing to Quebec. Far to the north the Iroquois reached Necouba, the meeting-place near the height of land between James Bay and the St. Lawrence. "We are at war more than ever," wrote the governor, D'Argenson, "and still more in the throes of famine."

The only hope for New France lay in speedy help from home. What Champlain and Montmagny had sought in vain was obtained at last when establishment of direct royal rule over the colony in 1663 was followed, within three years, by the sending out of troops for its defense. The Carignan-Salières regiment (which had at one time been employed against the Turks in Hungary) was transferred from the West Indies to Quebec. Its mission: to break the power of the Iroquois, "to carry the war to their doors, to exterminate them utterly."

In the operations that ensued, signs of friction appeared between the "Canadian" forest fighters under Le Moyne and the French regulars led by de Tracy. The latter "wanted to apply the methods of defense used in Europe, which were most unsuitable for this country, to whose experience in the art of war they attached too little attention." The differences between Frenchmen from

---

*A lively debate has raged recently about the significance of the episode. A nationalist "mystique" having exalted the band of Frenchmen to the point of sanctification, rude reminders have been brought forward, of their relation to the plundering operations of the fur trade. What is wrong, asks Abbé Groulx, if "the hope of some booty" (in furs) *was* "mingled with their selfless deed?" (*Le Devoir*, May 9, 1960). The fur trade, after all, was the basis of the colony's existence! In any event, one immediate result of the stand made at Long Sault was that a record convoy of furs from the northwest got through— Radisson and 300 Ottawa tribesmen bringing 60 canoe-loads to Montreal, worth 200,000 livres.

France and the colonists, already growing conscious of their common identity, were just beginning to make themselves felt.

The French troops, seconded by Le Moyne's detachment from Montreal, invaded the Mohawk country southwest of Lake Champlain. They left the native villages in ashes, their cornfields laid waste. For a number of years there were no further Iroquois attacks on the settlements of New France.

What had happened, meanwhile, to the Algonquin and Montagnais "allies" of the French? They were well-nigh wiped out—not so much by the successive Iroquois offensives as by the epidemics carried among them by their French masters. Of all those living north of the St. Lawrence between the Ottawa and Labrador, no more than a pitiful handful survived the calamity.

XIII

"Workers and Plowmen"

Settlement in New France for a long time made little headway. Neither the fishing nor the fur-trading interests required it on any sizeable scale. Only slowly and with difficulty did the posts at Port Royal and Quebec gain any sort of foothold as centres of colonization.

At Port Royal the apothecary Louis Hébert had planted vines and sown wheat; in 1617 he brought his family to Quebec and started a farm. "Along with the experience he has of his art," observed one fellow-colonist, "he takes pleasure in tilling the land." The grant ceded to Hébert at Quebec in 1623 stated that "he has by his painful labors and industry cleared lands, fenced them, and erected buildings for himself, his family and his cattle . . . to encourage those who may hereafter desire to inhabit and develop the country of Canada."

After making a clearing in the forest the early settlers broke ground with spade and pick and mattock. The first to use a plow was Hébert's son-in-law, Guillaume Couillard, in April, 1628. But the ox-drawn plow did not come into general use until the latter half of that century—due to the scarcity of draft animals, and the specialized work required to make the plowshare and other parts.

The type that finally became common was the heavy wheeled plow, drawn by a pair of oxen (or, later, horses). It took two persons, one at the handles guiding the plow, the other driving the team. Next to the plow in importance was the triangular harrow, with wooden teeth; it was generally horse-drawn.

Farming in 17th - 18th-century France.
(From Diderot's Encyclopédie.)

These, with such hand-implements as the hoe, rake, spade, pick-axe, scythe, sickle and flail, were the means of labor of the rural settler. Neither the implements nor the methods of cultivation underwent any great change during the French regime. Crop rotation was practised in a rudimentary way: one year grain, the next year hay. Little use was made of manure, and the soil suffered in consequence. With the exception of fall wheat (the development of which aroused some interest on the part of the French authorities), the practice of farming in New France differed little from that in the Old World. An 18th-century observer described as follows the labor of the Canadian habitants:

"They till the land with plows, as in Flanders; they plow once in autumn, and as soon as the snow melts around the end of April to the beginning of May they plow and scatter the seed and then harrow to cover it; only half of their land is sown each year; they know only wheat and oats, some sow peas, Indian corn, beans and tobacco, depending on the soil; harvest-time is at the end of August . . ."

Some of the French settlers (including the Héberts) had remained during the English occupation. Now efforts to bring out more settlers were resumed. Robert Giffard, a surgeon who was the holder of a seigneurie, recruited emigrants from west-central France with offers of land-grants. His efforts led some 50 families, over the years, to leave the west-central province of Perche for Quebec.

But it was not only the agricultural settlers with grants of land who laid the foundations of New France. At Port Royal and again at Quebec, workmen made up the bulk of the new arrivals. The list of those sailing for the "habitation" at Quebec in 1619 included not only army officers, traders, priests—but "ouvriers et laboureurs," workers and plowmen. Of the habitation itself, Champlain wrote: "I employed the workers to build in stone and wood, and everything was so well managed that in a short time we were able to support a lodge for the few workers, part of whom began to build a fort. . . ."

Du Creux, the earliest historian of Canada, noted in 1664 that those who had left France for the colony were for the most part "Workmen and soldiers . . . nearly all the inhabitants were either one or the other."

The workers who were shipped out to serve at the trading posts and missions were recruited by merchants and shipowners in the seaport towns. In Dieppe and La Rochelle, Bordeaux and Rouen, merchant capitalist interests controlled not only the fur trade of Canada, but slave-trading operations in the Caribbean. Wage-labor and a "free" labor market were only beginning to emerge in France; the prevailing form of hiring workers was to take them on as indentured bond-servants (*engagés*). By the terms of hire, the indentured servant was bound to work for his master (a seigneur, a well-to-do colonist, a religious order or a trading company) for anywhere from three to five years.

One of the earliest of such contracts, signed at La Rochelle, records that "Charles de Menore, on the 3rd of February 1634, engages Daniel Benesteau, carpenter from Puy-Belliard in Poitou" (western France). No time-limit is specified, nor wage-rate. Generally these worker-bond-servants received wages: in the early years those working for the fur companies were paid in kind: "Pelts are the form of money most highly prized," says the *Relation* of 1636; "Laborers would rather get their pay in this money than any other." Sometimes they obtained a portion of the land they cleared. Many of those who worked for the religious orders received nothing but board and lodging. Thus the "declaration of servitude" of Jean Guérin states that he is to be "a domestic servant during his lifetime," with his priestly employers "promising to maintain him according to his condition with food and clothing, without other wages or claims on his part . . ."

What was needed, wrote the Jesuit LeJeune, was "good lads or married men who are robust, able to handle the axe, hoe, spade and plow."

Between 1638 and 1644 several groups of workers were shipped from La Rochelle to Cape Breton, where a trading post was in operation at Fort St. Pierre. Among those sent out were Hélié Grimard, worker in heavy timber; Jean Vanuel, tailor; Jean Bonnard, a master nailsmith, "to fashion nails and work at the forge" at a wage of 120 livres a year.* Bonnard's wife accompanied him, an arrangement which in the early years was the exception rather than the rule.

For the years 1638 to 1660 there are records in La Rochelle of the sending to New France of 25 workers in heavy timber, seven long-saw men, 48 plowmen and 11 day laborers. With work getting under way at Quebec and then Montreal, on fortifications, churches, and dwellings for officials and wealthy merchants, there was a demand for stonemasons and workers in related trades. Thus the fort at Quebec was at first "a rampart rather than a citadel, being composed of logs, which Champlain's workmen had loosely joined together, filling the chinks with mud." Then Champlain's successor Montmagny had a more finished structure put up, "skilfully fashioned of oak and cedar by the carpenters."

The sponsors of the founding of Montreal drew up a plan in 1640, providing for an advance party of 40 workmen to clear the forest, then the sponsors were "to increase, year by year, the number of workers, as far as possible, then send oxen and plowmen . . ." "Providence gave M. de Maisonneuve very good workmen " (de forts bons ouvriers) — remarked Dollier de Casson, the brawny soldier-priest who was the chronicler of Montreal's beginnings. Among these builders of the new settlement were: Nicolas Godé and his two sons, all three carpenters; L. Loisel, a locksmith; G. Boissier, Jean Mattemasse, U. Tessier and Gilbert Barbier, workers in timber.

Gilbert Barbier's nickname was "Minime" (which may be translated familiarly as "pee-wee" or "shrimp")—but despite his being the smallest, he was "by no means the least either in fighting or in his trade." He was, says De Casson, "a very clever carpenter," remarkable for "his courage . . . and the services he has rendered on this

---

*Livre: roughly equivalent to our present dollar.

island, whose buildings have nearly all been made by his hands or by those whom he has taught."

Many of the workmen fell victims in the fighting with the Iroquois.

At the mission in Huronia in 1648 there were six Jesuits, eight soldiers, nine workmen and three young boys. Jean Guiet, carpenter and interpreter, worked on the squared timbers of the mission buildings; Pierre Tourmente was the stonemason, Louis Gaubert the blacksmith, and Charles Boivin the master-builder. (Two of his brothers also were carpenters in New France.)

It is of interest to note that the carpenters at Quebec in 1657 established a *confrérie,* or religious-fraternal organization of the type that had arisen among workers of many trades during the Middle Ages in Europe. This *confrérie* was under the patronage of St. Anne. Its founder was Jean Levasseur, a master-carpenter (joiner) who like others then in Quebec had belonged previously to a similar organization in Paris. In addition to religious observances, the *confrérie* provided a means of mutual help to its members in times of sickness, accident or poverty. Its officers included an Intendant, elected annually, as were a secretary, treasurer, an almoner and two "Mothers of the Poor," and a perpetual spiritual director—the curé. The members (who included others as well as carpenters) were organized in groups under neighborhood or group leaders. In 1658-9 there was an exchange of letters of greeting between the Quebec and Paris *Confrérie de Ste. Anne.**

Although by no means a trade union in the modern sense, the *Confrérie* of carpenters of Quebec required of

---

*A second confrérie was that organized by Montreal armorers and metalworkers in 1676. Led by Pierre Gadbois, Jean Rousquet and others, they "formed a society" and observed the feast-day of their patron saint, St. Eloi, on December 1 of each year.

French carpenters at work.
(From L'Encyclopédie.*)*

its members "zeal for the public welfare" and opposition
to "manifest injustices and shameful dishonesties"— the
latter responsibility being the special concern of the group
leaders.

The conditions and treatment of the workers shipped
out to the colony doubtless provided plenty of instances
of "manifest injustice." The hiring and transporting of
indentured servants grew into a lucrative business. "The
indentured servants," according to one account, "have become the object of a special commerce, a speculation."
With widespread unemployment and impoverishment
driving the craftsmen and dispossessed peasants into the
seaport towns in search of work, the shipowners took full
advantage of them. Wages, which in the 1630s were often

150-200 livres a year (and sometimes over 300 livres)—fell to 70 livres as a general rate, but often to 45 or 50.

"It was the poor who were the most numerous in offering themselves" we are told; the principal reason for leaving France was "misery, first of all, or at least poverty." The bond-servants faced an uncertain future: for most there was no sure promise of obtaining land; to the other uncertainties of emigration were added the hazards of a month's long crossing of the Atlantic. Of a large group of indentured servants brought out by the colonizer Pierre Boucher in 1662, no less than a third perished during the crossing in the scurvy-ridden ships.

XIV

Feudal New France

THE MILITARY RESCUE-OPERATION THAT CAME WITH the establishment of direct royal rule accorded the colony a breathing-space. The period of 20 years following Tracy's invasion of the Mohawk country (1665) witnessed the consolidation of the economy and social-political structure of New France.

This society was an extension overseas of the system prevailing in 17th-century France. Feudal tenure of land, merchant-capitalist commerce, a feudal-absolutist monarchy: these were the institutions transplanted to North America. Here they were modified by the colonial character of the new community, the dominant role of trading interests in colonial enterprise, its relation to the native peoples, and the geographical environment.

The pattern of feudal relationships was based on the holding of land. Under the seigneurial system, the colony was granted by the king to a vassal (a trading company), who in turn granted it to a number of seigneurs, each of whom assigned plots of land to feudal tenants or *censitaires*. Under French feudal law, these holdings were not granted in outright ownership:* the true owner was the king, and estates were held in trust, as it were, conditional on the fulfilment of certain obligations.

One peculiarity of the feudal tenure in New France was the requirement that holders of seigneuries should sub-

---

*Later, under British rule, when capitalist property relationships supplanted those of feudalism, the seigneurs claimed and secured outright ownership of the estates they held—thereby fraudulently enriching themselves. Cf. *French Canada*, ch. V.

grant land to settlers: an obligation that was often evaded, especially by the fur companies. (The charter of the Company of New France in 1627 required that it bring out 4,000 colonists within 15 years, but even by 1663 there were only 2,500 settlers.)

Another distinguishing feature was that while the censitaire was legally bound to till the allotment he had been granted, the presence of the adjoining forest, the domain of the fur-trade, made escape from bondage far easier than it was for the feudal peasant in France. Several thousands became *coureurs-de-bois,* free-lance "runners of the woods" illicitly engaging in the trade, or in smuggling, as well as hunting and fishing, often in the company of a band of Indian trappers. It is estimated that during the French régime as many as 15,000 took to the woods in this manner.

Despite these and other special features, the system of landed property relationships in New France was nonetheless definitely a feudal one.

The first land grants—those secured in 1623-26 by Louis Hébert, by the trader de Caen, and by the Jesuit Order— were all conceded in the form of seigneuries. From 1627 to 1663 the Company of New France (the Hundred Associates) held the entire colony as its feudal domain; and during its period of tenure it sub-granted some sixty seigneuries—to officials, merchants, army officers, religious orders.

These last—Jesuits, Sulpicians and others—occupied a particularly strong position in the colony, obtaining huge estates in the vicinity of Quebec and Montreal. During the French régime the Church acquired over two million acres—about a quarter of all the land that was granted.

A pioneer in land-grabbing on a grandiose scale was the manager (or intendant) of the Company of New France, Jean de Lauzon. In his own name, in that of his infant son, and those of cronies acting as "fronts" for him, he laid hands on estates embracing the entire south shore of the St. Lawrence, westward from the Chaudière valley (across from Quebec) to Montreal. Thirty years later, there were still no more than thirteen settlers in the whole of the Chaudière valley: an example of the way such land-grabbing operations as Lauzon's impeded the development of the colony.

Following the expedition of the Carignan-Salières regiment against the Iroquois, 25 of its officers were awarded seigneuries along the Richelieu and the St. Lawrence. About 400 men of the regiment were settled as their censitaires. This scheme of feudal-military colonization, designed to provide a strategic rampart against the Iroquois resistance, was at the origin of such centres of settlement as Sorel, Chambly, Contrecoeur, Soulanges.

The seigneurial system, in the colony as in France, was a system of feudal exploitation. Its cornerstone was the right of the seigneur to appropriate unpaid labor of the censitaire. Its most common forms were the surrender by the censitaire of a set proportion of his crop or other produce and a specified number of days of labor—as an unpaid tribute to the seigneur. Whether rendered in money or in kind or in the form of labor-rent, this forced tribute was inherent in the relationship. The system presupposed a level of productivity that enabled the producer to pay to the overlord this tribute (surplus-labor) as well as to maintain himself and family. Upon the relationship of feudal exploitation there was built up the rest of the social structure—including the corresponding form of state rule. "The specific economic form in which unpaid surplus-labor is pumped out of direct producers, determines the relationship of rulers and ruled . . ." (Marx)

The seigneur extracted surplus-labor from his censitaires in numerous ways. First there was the payment of feudal dues or *cens et rentes.* The *cens* was a small payment made in recognition of the seigneur's overlordship; it was generally from one to eight French *sols* or sous. The *rentes* or annual rent was more substantial, varying from one to five *livres* according to the size of the plot. It was "a lucrative source of finance to the seigneur." Payment—which was made each year at the seigneur's manor on the feast of St. Martin—was made either in money or in produce, according to the seigneur's choice. (At Montreal the Sulpicians demanded payment in capons in lieu of cash.)

The *lods et ventes,* a charge originally fixed at one-twelfth of the value of the holding, were exacted on each change of tenancy.

The *corvée* of so many days' compulsory, unpaid labor for the seigneur, was a more burdensome exaction. In the earlier period, up to six days of *corvée* were required of each censitaire during the year; but after 1700 the number increased, in some cases to as many as 30 days annually. Since these days fell in the busy sowing, haying, harvesting and plowing seasons, their value to the seigneur was greater than their number alone suggests. Early in the 18th century protests against the *corvée* were so widespread that the home government ordered its suspension in the colony; but this edict was never promulgated there, so the seigneurs continued to impose the *corvée* and later even increased its amount.

Another exaction was that of *banalité,* or milling rights, whereby the censitaire had to grind his grain in the seigneur's mill (paying him a share—generally one-fourteenth—of the flour).

The *banalité* was a source of widespread grievance. "Complaints were common," reports one authority. The wife of the seigneur de Ramezay complained that "certain *habitants* of her seigneurie at Sorel evaded and refused sending their grain to her mill, although they are so

obliged by their contracts and by virtue of the regulations . . ." So the Intendant issued an order: "We forbid
the said *habitants* to take their wheat to be ground elsewhere than the mill in question, on pain of a fine of ten
livres. . . ."

But there was also another grievance connected with the
banalité: in some cases the seigneur, living at Quebec, did
not bother to have a mill erected on his estate. The Intendant in 1707 reported that this was "a privation from
which the habitants suffer a great deal, being in no position, due to their meagre means, to build one themselves . . ."

Additional forms of feudal tribute included: charging
rent for the use of pasture land; "the reservation of the
right (of the seigneurs) to take from all land granted all
the wood they might want; the preference of buying what
the farmer might have for sale; the reservation of all pine
and oak trees; the eleventh part of the fish caught by
farmers in front of their houses gratis. . . ."

In the innumerable disputes that arose between seigneur and tenant it was of no small advantage to the former that he was by feudal right and custom empowered to
sit in judgment. With the establishment of royal courts
in the colony, cases of "high" and "middle" justice (those
involving criminal charges) were taken over by the courts;
but it is to be noted that the seigneurs insisted on retaining their powers of "low" justice, "in order to keep their
position of being able to force the habitants to pay their
'*cens et rentes*'."

What the revenues derived by the seigneurs from feudal
exactions amounted to is a question that cries out for research. The weight of "official" historiography has hitherto been heavily on the side of efforts to smother the facts
of exploitation; and to present instead an idyllic picture
of an alleged "rural equality" as between seigneurs and

tenants. Thus even a historian such as M. Guy Frégault in his thorough and well documented study, *La Civilisation de la Nouvelle France* (1944), makes the assertion that "The seigneurial régime was not established in order to enable a privileged class to live by the labor of a lower class, but with a view to endowing the country with the socio-economic organization which suited it."

At the opening of the 18th century, censitaires and engagés (indentured servants) numbering with their families some 18,000, were maintaining by their labor ninety or so seigneurs, lay and ecclesiastical (apart, that is, from what these gentry pocketed from the trade in furs). About half the entire population were concentrated on the ecclesiastical seigneuries. These were the most efficiently run, and also the least loquacious about the size of their revenues. Seven hundred censitaires and farm-hands worked for the Quebec Seminary, 2,000 for the Jesuits, 3,000 for the Sulpician seigneurs of Montreal.

It is recorded that the seigneur of Terrebonne, La Corne, extracted an annual tribute of 12,000 livres from his feudal tenantry. Whether this was more than the average or less, it seems clear that the seigneurial system was "the socio-economic organization which suited"— the interests of the seigneurs.

XV

Seedlings of Capitalism in Canada

THE RULING CLASS IN NEW FRANCE WAS AN AMALGAM: feudal, clerical and mercantile. As in 17th century France, the feudal structure was interwoven with merchant-capitalist elements: in the colony these were proportionately stronger than in the mother country. But in North America as in France the state power—the absolute monarchy—upheld the rule of the seigneurs. Even the policy of Louis XIV's minister Colbert, of encouraging trade and manufactures, was aimed at fostering sources of royal revenue outside the domain of the pampered aristocracy. The bourgeoisie were taxed heavily, and firm bounds were set to their ambitions. Yet despite its being designed to buttress feudal rule, Colbert's policy did in fact help promote a growth of capitalist commerce and manufacture, both in France and the colony.

Inauguration of direct royal rule (1663) led not only to military but also economic intervention on behalf of New France. A more vigorous effort was made to send out settlers. The French population of Canada grew from 3,215 in 1665 to 24,951 in 1721. It was they—censitaires and indentured servants—whose labor wrested fruitful farmland from the dense Laurentian forest. It took one man a year of uninterrupted toil with axe and saw to clear an acre and a quarter of bush.

In 1666 they had cleared about 9,300 acres. By 1706, close to 40,000. Wheat, the main crop, totalled just over 100,000 bushels in 1685, and 212,000 in 1706.

At Montreal in 1648 Maisonneuve ordered the building of a windmill not far from the fort. By 1660 flour mills were also in operation at Three Rivers, as well as at Quebec. The census of 1666 listed nine millers in the colony; in 1685 there were 41 flour mills in operation. As has been pointed out, under the seigneurial regime owner- ship of a mill was the monopoly of the big landowners; and many were the grievances and complaints in relation thereto. In 1671—a year of crop failure—there were pro- tests against millers' profiteering and adulterating the flour. The year following, the censitaires of Montreal were involved in a struggle over malpractices of the miller of the Seminary of St. Sulpice (the seigneurs of the Island); he was accused of taking bribes and discriminating against the poorer settlers. The clerical seigneurs jealously upheld their monopoly, preventing all others (including even the religious order of the Frères Charron) from building mills; thus as late as 1703 "the inhabitants of Montreal suffered from the lack of flour mills, some of them having to cover a distance of six leagues to get their wheat ground."

Under the feudal regulations governing trade and in- dustry, the number of bakers was limited. In 1677 at Que- bec there were complaints that the price of loaves was too high, and the quality inferior. Some time later, public protests led to all nine bakers at Montreal being brought to court and ordered to lower their prices. One of them at least countered by lowering the quality of his wares; his biscuits, according to the authorities, were such as "cannot be eaten by humans"; so they were confiscated— and sent to feed the poor at the hospital!

To begin with, it was an almost wholly self-sufficient pioneer economy that prevailed in the countryside. What- ever had been the trade of the settler in the old land, here on the farm of necessity he learned to combine with fron- tier agriculture the work of a carpenter, stonemason and wheelwright. Much of the burden of domestic industry was borne by the woman: "She baked bread, wove cloth, and, with her daughter, made clothing for the entire household. In wintertime she looked after the processing and preparation of flax and hemp and candle-making; in spring, the tapping and boiling down of maple sap . . . in autumn, the preparation of the local spruce beer."

By degrees, as population increased, villages grew up, and craftsmen established themselves: carpenters and cabinetmakers, stonemasons, tailors, cobblers, blacksmiths and gunsmiths, etc. The appearance of these village artisans marked the separation of specialized, small-scale production from the all-embracing "natural economy" of the pioneer farm.

Division of labor within the community—*social* division of labor—led to a growth of production, and of exchange of commodities (goods produced for the market). As wealthier elements accumulated capital from trade, and technique developed, investment in larger enterprises became possible—and therewith, wage-labor on a growing scale. At first, however, it was a matter of employing only one or two "helpers"; then, by degrees, the exploiting of wage-labor took on larger dimensions—in lumber camps, sawmills, tanneries and shipyards. Thus did the evolution of the colony reproduce, in a different setting and on a tiny scale, the path traversed in France: industrial beginnings within a feudal framework.

Colbert's mercantilist* policy sought to increase the royal revenues by securing a favorable balance of trade. In order that the colony should benefit the treasury and not be a

---

*Mercantilism: an economic theory and policy typical of the period of "primary accumulation" (15th to 18th centuries), prior to the Industrial Revolution. Inspired by the drive for merchants' profit, it held that the national interest required the accumulation within the country

drag on it, he sought to make it self-sufficient. The executor of this policy was the able administrator Jean Talon, Intendant of New France from 1665 to 1672. Colbert instructed him: "The rule and object of your conduct is to enable the colony to suffice unto itself." Talon was told that "one of the greatest needs of Canada is to establish manufactures and attract craftsmen thither . . . for up till now it has been necessary to transport to that country cloth with which to clothe the inhabitants, and even shoes for their feet. . . ."

The Intendant applied himself to promoting the infant industries of Canada. Under his direction and aided by a royal subsidy, Bissot, a censitaire of the Lauzon seigneurie, set up a tannery employing a dozen laborers. The enterprise throve, and he and his son-in-law Charest became two of the wealthiest citizens of the colony.

Since the early days of the colony the Recollets and then the Jesuits had operated breweries. Talon started a larger one in 1670. In addition to the brewery and tannery, he promoted the establishment of cloth shops, millineries, shoe-making; tar, potash and cordage works; and actively promoted saw-milling, ship-building, prospecting and an iron works.

Talon also took steps to initiate the growing of flax; soon thread and cloth were being made in small shops as well as on the farms. By 1671 he was able to report to Colbert that in a couple of years "the inhabitants, through their own cultivation and manufacture, would have the major part and perhaps all of the cloth needed for their use." Woollen cloth of coarse varieties was being made (there were a few sheep in the colony). Moreover, wrote

---

of the greatest possible amount of gold or silver; or, for the same purpose, restrictive trade measures to ensure a surplus of exports over imports ("For then," wrote Francis Bacon, "the balance of trade must of necessity be returned in coin or bullion"). In pursuit of this, mercantilism not only favored merchant monopolies, but to some extent promoted home manufactures.

Talon: "Close to a third of the shoes are being made from the leather of the country, and I have at present where-with to clothe me from head to foot; nothing in that re-spect now seems impossible, and I hope that in a short time, if it is well administered, the country, will want nothing from old France except a few necessities."

That year the Intendant reported: "I established work-shops which kept close to 350 men occupied during the whole summer." A present-day economic historian com-ments on Talon's report: "The capitalist system put in its appearance on the banks of the St. Lawrence." It was not yet, assuredly, modern capitalist machine industry; but the "manufactory," or large workshop employing hand-labor, was indeed a capitalist enterprise, based on the exploita-tion of wage-workers.

In the forest industry and ship-building, large scale operations were started. As early as 1630 Nicholas Denys had organized the cutting of the stand of oak in Acadia. He shipped square beams and barrel staves to France in exchange for provisions and supplies. Lumber was ex-ported from the Quebec area in the 1650's. The Jesuits were then the possessors of a profitable sawmill at Que-bec, and later of another at Cap de la Madeleine. The first sawmill in the Montreal district was that built in 1670 for the Sulpicians.

Colbert looked to New France as a potential supplier of materials for the navy. For this purpose he had Talon make a survey of forest resources; the Intendant described these as "a treasure to be carefully conserved."

In addition to ordering masts and planking for the naval dockyards in France, Colbert had a start made on shipbuilding in the colony. In 1667 workers built a vessel of 120 tons burden at the mouth of the St. Charles River at Quebec. Listed as long-saw men who made planking for the decks were Pierre Beaucousin and Jacques Grumault.

These early Canadian shipbuilders received a shilling a day for their labors. The record of Talon's administration contains references to disputes over wages, and to something resembling a "slow-down" strike at the Quebec dockyard.

In 1670 Talon brought out six carpenters and three smiths, and recruited a score of young lads to work under their direction and learn the carpenter's trade. In a memorandum to Louis XIV he wrote: "I have sent into the workshop soldiers and habitants who could not handle an axe, and who are learning the trade in a way that leads me to hope that in a few years such workers will be trained here as are skilled enough to work wherever His Majesty may assign them." That year, in November, all the carpenters available were sent to the bush to "cut down, saw and square" timber for a 400-ton ship that was planned at Quebec. The ship, which was not finished till five years later, was designed to carry 46 guns.

In 1687 two merchants of La Rochelle in partnership with a "marchand bourgeois" of Quebec set up a couple of large double sawmills at La Malbaie. Thirty men worked at these mills, which achieved an annual output of some 30,000 planks, 800 beams and a hundred or so masts.

However, despite the stimulus of French naval needs, problems of labor shortage and lack of capital and equipment limited the growth of the logging industry.

In 1664 the Compagnie des Indes Occidentales had been granted the right to forge weapons, make bullets and manufacture cannon in the colony. Colbert nursed hopes of building up a Canadian iron industry to serve the needs of the French naval arsenals and shipyards. He urged "the seeking out of iron mines which the country possesses and which would consume a prodigious quantity of wood." Talon had exploration carried on north of

Three Rivers, and deposits were located on a stream called Rivière Noire, a tributary of the St. Maurice. But for
for the time being little came of the effort.

Hoping that mining would become "an essential in the
king's business and in the establishment of Canada,"
Talon sent a search party to the Lake Superior region.
They found traces of copper, but no large deposits.

In Acadia the presence of coal had been noted earlier;
in 1671 Talon had a shipload of it brought from Cape
Breton. Attempts at this time and later to organize shipment of coal from Acadia to France did not materialize;
but some was exported to the French West Indies for use
in the sugar refineries there.

As part of his policy of building a self-sufficient mercantile empire, Colbert strove to promote a three-way trading
system embracing New France (and the French Newfoundland fishery), the French West Indies and the
metropolis. Under Talon's leadership merchants at Quebec built several 50-ton vessels, loaded them "with fish,
wood, vegetable oil and beer, all products of Canada, and
shipped them to Cayenne and La Tortue, in the Islands."
Later they had a 120-ton brigantine built to take lumber
and fish to La Rochelle and bring back wine, brandy and
other merchandise.

These beginnings were followed up sporadically; but
the trading system Colbert had visualized never really
materialized. The economy of New France, though growing, could not be counted on as a regular source of exports. New England, far more favorably situated geogra-
phically (as well as economically), became the main supplier of the French West Indies.

Administered by Colbert and Talon, France's colony on
the St. Lawrence for the first time struck root and began
to grow with some expectation of success. Agriculture,

small local industries for domestic needs, and lumber and shipbuilding all made some headway. These advances laid the initial groundwork for eventual industrial growth in Canada.

The feudal-absolutist monarchy during this period fostered economic enterprise in order to enhance its revenues and strengthen its military-strategic positions in the struggle with the naval powers, Holland and England in particular. The régime of Louis XIV saw in a growing trade and industry "the necessary condition of national greatness and its own magnificence." (Marx). Taking over the administration of New France, Louis pointed to trade as "the source and principle of abundance," and to colonies as "the chief and most important part of trade."

True, the framework of feudal relationships and institutions limited and confined economic growth in Canada as in France; but at least in the early part of his reign (till the 1680's and the wars at the turn of the century) Louis XIV favored policies of trade and manufacturing expansion. Historically, Colbert's protectionist system served as "an artificial means . . . of forcibly shortening the transition from the old mode of production to the new" (Marx). As yet, the new capitalist element was not strong enough to pose any real threat to feudal-absolutist rule. So for the time being the monarchy protected it (and taxed it!) for its own purposes of enrichment and aggrandizement.

The Rulers and the Ruled

T HE CANADIAN GOVERNMENT," SAYS PARKMAN, "WAS essentially military." The armed forces of the absolute monarchy were the instrument of power in the colony. Their mission: to cope with the Iroquois resistance, ward off encroachment by the rival forces of Dutch or English colonizers—and keep the settlers in order and imbued with a proper respect for feudal and merchant-capitalist property.

Here, as elsewhere the *state* as the organ of class rule took the form of "bodies of armed men and prisons" (Engels). Establishment of royal rule brought a further elaboration of the state machinery. The military Governor was joined by a civil administrator: the Intendant, having charge of police, the administration of feudal justice, finance and economic affairs. Sharing executive authority with these temporal officials was the head of the Church: the Bishop of Quebec. (Until the appointment of the first bishop, Laval, in 1659, the superior of the Jesuits represented the clerical power.) Union of church and state was a vital feature of feudal rule: its vestiges, in present-day Quebec, are with us yet.

While governor, bishop and intendant represented the combined general interests of feudal absolutism, clericalism and merchants' capital, the particular interests of groups of traders found expression in the governor's appointive council.

A common interest in the profits of exploitation in the fur trade united the various sections of the ruling class.

Thus, the governor Denonville wrote regarding the clergy: "The Indian tribes can be kept quiet thanks only to these missionaries; the Fathers alone are able to win them for our interests and restrain them from rebellion, which otherwise would break out from one day to the next."

On the other hand, sectional interests within the ruling class caused chronic and sometimes acute friction. The military and the priests were often at loggerheads; so were priests and traders; also, local traders and those of France.

Complaints of clerical domination and intervention in every aspect of life were many and frequent. Colbert had to instruct Talon to uphold the civil power against the pretensions of Laval and the Jesuits, too little inclined "to confine themselves to matters spiritual." Louis XIV himself noted that the clergy "assumed an authority that exceeds the bounds of their true profession." Lamothe Cadillac, fur-trader and supporter of Frontenac in the governor's quarrel with Laval, spoke of "odious and insupportable ecclesiastical domination." The traveller, Baron de La Hontan, observed that "In *Canada,* the Politick, Ecclesiastical and Military government, are all in a manner one thing"— and he complained bitterly of clerical prying and censorship.

Numerous testimonials bear witness to the severity of the system of "thought control" imposed by the secular and clerical authorities. Public meetings were severely limited. No printing-press was allowed in the colony during the whole of the French régime. "It is of very great consequence" wrote one intendant, "that the people should not be left at liberty to speak their minds." In 1661 two men, Daniel Voil and Laviolette, were executed —for blasphemy. A decade later a certain Paul Dupuy was thrown in irons and branded on the face with a *fleur-de-lis* for having spoken with approval of the English revolution and the beheading of Charles I.

"There is not a heretic here," reported Governor Denonville with satisfaction. Each arriving ship was visited and its passengers "screened" by the Jesuits to ensure that none should slip into the colony.

The monopoly of Catholicism was far more complete in Canada than in France, where the liberties accorded to Huguenots under the Edict of Nantes (1598) remained in effect for close to a century. In Canada, they were suppressed, at the insistence of the Jesuits, from 1628 onwards.

This offensive of militant clericalism was part of the Catholic Counter-reformation. Fighting to beat back the bourgeois-protestant Reformation, the Papacy in 1534 had set on foot a special clerical-political organization: the Jesuit Order. Working everywhere in the service of feudal reaction, it concentrated its efforts on winning influence over key figures in the courts and ruling groups of various European powers. The fact that Cardinals Richelieu and Mazarin directed French affairs from 1624 to 1661 reflected the strength of political clericalism. The French king's confessors were generally Jesuits; by using this office, "they often gave direction to the colonial policy of the Court."

The presence of Dutch and English Protestant colonies in North America, adjoining New France, lent strength to the Jesuits' insistence that heretics should be barred from the colony. The existence of a "pagan" native population served to justify large-scale missionary efforts; and these in turn (despite their sparse results in terms of converts) the Jesuits sought to develop as a base for theocratic rule. (In Paraguay in 1610 the Jesuits succeeded in setting up a clerical state based on exploitation of the Indian population; it lasted until 1768.)

Within the Church itself, the domineering attitude of the Jesuits evoked strong resentment. The Sulpicians at

Montreal quarreled with them; the Recollets, ousted through Jesuit intrigue over a third of a century before, were brought back to the colony in 1669 by Talon to serve as a counterweight to Jesuit influence.

Friction between church and state, and within each of them, was not the only inner conflict in New France. More significant in terms of forces making for fundamental change were the rise of a local Canadian class of merchants, challenging the mercantile monopolists of France; and the sporadic outbursts of popular opposition to feudal-absolutist rule.

Even in Champlain's time there had been signs of local traders asserting their collective interest as against that of the chartered companies. But the formation in 1645 of the Compagnie des Habitants signalled quite definitely the emergence of a Canadian mercantile bourgeoisie.

It is worth noting that the appearance of this social grouping was accompanied by the first embryonic beginnings of a national spirit and of elective institutions. As early as 1651 the settlers were using the term "Canadois" to refer to themselves, as distinct from old-country Frenchmen. And two years after the Compagnie des Habitants was formed, the authorities conceded to the inhabitants of Quebec, Three Rivers and Montreal the right to elect spokesmen or "syndics."

The syndics, elected annually, were allowed to attend the governing council, make representations on matters affecting their constituents, but not to debate or vote. The first syndics to be elected from Quebec and Three Rivers respectively, were the engineer and "bourgeois" Jean Bourdon and the trader and explorer Jacques Hertel, who had been one of Champlain's "young men" in the Indian country. In 1663 a carpenter, Jean Le Mire, was elected to the post at Quebec, and again in 1667. In 1648 the practice was introduced of having the appointive members of the council elect, in consultation with the syndics, two representatives of the inhabitants as council members with full rights.*

One reason for granting these concessions may well have been the pressure of the small traders and settlers, who in no uncertain terms voiced their resentment at the activities of the "leading families." A group of these wealthier merchant-seigneurs, headed by the La Potheries and de Repentignys, had got control of the Compagnie des Habitants, and barred the rest of the settlers from taking part in the fur trade. (The receipts of the company in its first year, close to 200,000 francs, brought it a profit of between 30 and 50 per cent.) Late in 1645 a near-mutiny broke out, the leaders being one Maheu (a settler), Marsolet (an interpreter) and Robineau (a young army officer). It took the intervention of the governor, Montmagny, to put down the protest movement.

In 1657, the governing council was radically reorganized: four of its six members were made elective (two from Quebec, one each from Montreal and Three Rivers). This was a remarkable development for a colony of absolutist France. Its significance was tempered, however, by the fact that the power of the governor remained supreme; and that involved in this "popular representation" was not a recognition of political rights but a matter of administrative function within the trading company: electors and elected alike were limited to members of the Compagnie des Habitants.

---

*M. Gustave Lanctôt says this decision "marked a new stage in the political evolution of the colony, since it placed an essential part of its administration in the hands of the people in the person of their two representatives on the Council." (*Histoire du Canada,* (1959) t.i. p. 247). Considering that these two representatives, permanently a minority, were co-opted by the non-elective majority, M. Lanctôt's characterization seems more than a little exaggerated.

A present-day French Canadian historian, M. Roger Bilodeau, has described the merchant-seigneurs of New France as "the first Canadian oligarchy": "At the summit of Canadian society reigned a big bourgeoisie..." This "Canadian ruling class" sought to "dominate the large-scale commerce of the day—that of furs—and have the colonial government, in which they [were] represented, serve the needs of the trade."

It is perhaps an overstatement to speak of a "big bourgeoisie" in 17th century New France. And to say that its "effort to raise and keep itself at the head of trade and the administration, drawing after it, consciously or otherwise, the [rest of the] collectivity," represented "the continuing conquest of political and economic liberty"; or that in 1645-65 "The Canadians . . . possessed a government that was almost the equivalent of independence, a 'self-government' within the framework of the French empire" —all this assuredly overstates the reality.

Yet in essence, that was certainly the *direction* of the trend: formation of a Canadian mercantile bourgeoisie, pressure on its part for a voice in government. It is very likely that these growing pretensions of the colonial bourgeoisie were a factor in the decision of the monarchy in 1663 to assume direct control and provide New France with the state institutions corresponding to those of a French province. (The elective element in the governing council was eliminated with the introduction of the new set-up; although the right of electing syndics was preserved.)

Moreover, within a year the king restored the trade monopoly to a chartered company—the West India Company. This move Bilodeau characterizes as "a threat of ruin for the Canadian bourgeoisie."

The latter fought back; and soon gained a strong ally in the Intendant, Jean Talon, who was enthused with the possibilities of the colony's development, providing the colonists were accorded some leeway to promote it. If the king, he wrote, envisaged Canada as nothing better than a mere trading-post, then the Company's monopoly made sense; but if he "saw this country as a fair expanse in which can be founded a great kingdom . . . or at least a very considerable State"— then freedom of trade should be permitted, for it was the trade alone which attracted "the most considerable among the inhabitants."

Colbert replied sharply: the king could by no means agree with Talon's talk of "making Canada into a large and powerful State." Such a plan would call for large-scale emigration, which would carry with it the danger of depopulating France; Talon should concentrate on "causing Justice to reign, establishing a good police," and more in the same vein. The danger of colonial movements toward independence was, clearly, not left out of account. Talon himself in one despatch had referred to the need, in view of the great distance of the colony from France, of special measures designed to guard against "changes or revolutions" leading to the setting up of some independent power.

Of this, there was as yet no real danger. But the local merchants were strong enough to uphold their interests, and the West India Company ended by withdrawing from the scene.

If the growth of a local colonial merchant bourgeoisie was one source of conflict and difficulty for the ruling power, another, far more deep-going, was the chronic unrest among the mass of the censitaires and indentured servants: the working people of New France.

The outstanding authority on the seigneurial system, W. B. Munro, claims that this institution "gave to the monarchy a most effective means of ensuring the docility of its colonial population . . ." Contemporary evidence suggests that this "docility" was largely a myth. One intendant described the inhabitants of New France as being "naturally indocile"; another observer speaks of them as "the most indocile and independent of peoples."

The spirit of unruly independence asserted itself particularly—but by no means exclusively—at the fringes of the feudal colony. The Acadians, remote from the centre of authority at Quebec and trading regularly with the neighboring New Englanders, showed a robust disregard for their lawful rulers. "They lived," it was said, "like true republicans, not acknowledging royal or judicial authority."

A far wider field of heady freedom from seigneurial restraints was the "pays d'en haut," the upper country of river, lake and forest northwest of the St. Lawrence settlements. Here the coureurs-de-bois, freebooters of the fur trade, found adventure and profit; they organized into gangs, carried on illicit trade with the Dutch and English, returned from time to time to Montreal, where their roistering was a frequent cause for scandal. Talon's successor Duchesneau noted in 1679 that there were five or six hundred of these lawless adventurers in the woods, led by the trader Du Lhut. Their offense lay above all in "claiming to be independent" of authority. And this contagion of independence was rampant in the settlements as well.

Frontenac complained of his inability to arrest the outlaws, among other reasons "because of the contact they have with the inhabitants who warn them . . ." Another governor, De la Barre, found the people of the Montreal-Richelieu area "indifferently inclined to obedience." In 1680 there was a "sedition" in Montreal: the riots which occurred were connected on the surface with a conflict among thieving officials, but underlying the outburst was mass indignation at despotic, arbitrary rule.

The censitaires resisted the imposition of church tithes; they compelled a reduction in the tithe-rate from 1/13 to 1/26 of the harvested grain.

The most widespread and continuous expression of popular unrest was the colonists' stubborn refusal to pay taxes which in France were mandatory. In the face of this opposition even the colonial officials advised against attempts to impose such taxes: citing on one occasion, the poverty of the inhabitants, on another the impossibility of getting taxes out of them, especially for military purposes. When Louis XIV "in 1704 proposed to levy a *taille* or land-tax in New France to help pay for the costs of administration, the Governor and the Intendant repeated again and again that it was not practical because the people of the colony were profoundly opposed to such a tax; it was never levied."

Resistance to tax-payments was a marked feature of the peasant-plebeian struggles that were under way in France also in this period. There, in addition to the heavy feudal tribute, a crushing load of taxation ground down the rural poor. (The nobles and clergy alike were exempt from taxes.) In the first half of the 17th century the tax burden in France increased from 17 million to 44 million livres annually. Throughout the century there were repeated risings of peasants and urban poor. In 1624 in the South there were outbreaks in town and countryside. In 1639 there took place in Normandy a general rising of the peasants ("Va-nu-pieds"—the Barefoot Ones) in the course of which the insurgents were at one moment masters of Rouen. An earlier official report on conditions in that province had said: "Picture to yourself the poor villagers of Normandy, bareheaded, thin, in rags, weak with hunger, without a shirt to their back or shoes to their feet, resembling rather ones dragged from the grave than living men." In 1646-7 there was mass resistance to the tax-

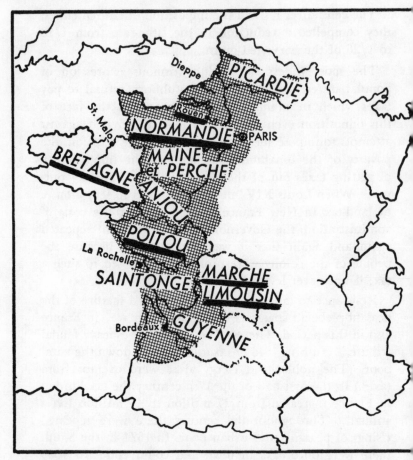

Western France in the 17th century. Shaded: the main areas of emigration to Canada. Underlined: areas of peasant-plebeian revolts in the same period.

collectors in west-central France, and in 1664-5 risings there against the hated salt-tax.* In Britanny there was a widespread peasant revolt in 1675.

---

*Among released prisoners shipped out to Quebec, not a few were peasants who had resisted or evaded payment of this tax.

These struggles were put down with ferocity by the armed forces of the feudal-absolutist state. But they left a heritage of hatred of oppression and a tradition of revolutionary-popular struggle that triumphed later in the crisis of the Old Régime.

It is interesting to note that some of the main areas where peasant uprisings took place were also those from which most of the settlers in New France were drawn. Despite the rigorous "screening" by the authorities, there can be little doubt that among the peasants and indentured servants who went to Canada not a few carried strong memories of resistance to oppression; and that the tradition of militant struggle in Old France played its part in the New, in the resistance to taxes, "indocility" and "spirit of independence" that were so often noted by the ruling officialdom.

XVII

The English Revolution. Contest for Empire

I HAVE THE HONOR TO INFORM YOU," TALON WROTE TO Colbert in 1665, "that Canada is of very vast extent, that to the North I do not know its limits, so distant are they from us, and that to the South there is nothing to prevent our bearing the name and arms of His Majesty to Florida, New Sweden, New Holland and New England, and through the first of these countries, penetrating as far as Mexico."

Such was the scheme of empire that was taking shape in the minds of the French colonizers. In 1671 Talon's lieutenant De Lusson was at Sault Sainte Marie; here in the name of Louis XIV he proclaimed French sovereignty over the continent "in all its length and breadth," bounded "on one side by the Northern and Western Seas, and on the other by the South Sea." One line of trading expansion led northwestward, over Lake Superior (Radisson pursued it, and later La Vérendrye). Another ran southwest, from Frontenac's fort at the St. Lawrence opening (1673), through the post at Niagara (1676), on to the Ohio and Illinois country, down the Mississippi, explored by Marquette, Jolliet, La Salle (1673-82).

The urge to embrace the continent, far from following any unified plan, was beset with contradictory impulses. The fact that the beaver areas were receding, and eagerness to establish profitable advance outposts, drew the traders ever deeper into the mid-continent. Royal policy, as voiced by Colbert, was concerned to establish a firm economic base in the Quebec-Montreal area and was fearful of a hazardous over-extension of communication lines in the interior. At the same time Louis XIV, moving toward the pinnacle of European power, was resolved to suffer no challenge from his rivals in America.

New France, meanwhile, generated its own expansionist forces, and its own internal conflicts. The Canadian merchant bourgeoisie, headed by such families as the Le Moynes, Le Bers and La Chesnayes, dominated the northwestern trade that was based on the labor of the Ottawas. Newcomers, the governor Frontenac and his protégé La Salle, challenged their dominant position. The Jesuits, who earlier had staked out claims for a theocratic western empire of their own, bitterly opposed the Frontenac-La Salle group.

The squabble over fur-profits and political dominion was argued on a moral plane: the iniquity of selling Indians brandy so as to rob them of their furs. The traders, wrote the Ursuline nun, Marie de l'Incarnation, in 1669, "go into the woods and carry drinks to the savages in order to get their furs for nothing when they are drunk. Immorality, theft and murder ensue . . ." This practice had been forbidden by the authorities in 1633, 1642, 1657; but it continued unabated. The drive for trading profit readily overrode both "moral" arguments and clerical concern about demoralization and loss of prospective converts. The brandy traffic flourished: as the clergy intervened with threats of excommunication, the civil power countered, asserting its jurisdiction by authorizing the sale of brandy. The ones to suffer were the Indian peoples. Not only were they cheated and plundered the more effectively, but their resistance to European diseases was undermined, hastening in many areas their near-extermination.

The French penetration of the interior, across the lower Great Lakes to the Mississippi watershed, soon led to new fratricidal wars among the Indian peoples and a renewal of the Iroquois resistance. But on a wider arena it meant collision with the other merchant-imperial powers who had undertaken to partition the Americas. Among the powers of Western Europe a deep-going shift in relationships was under way. Some idea of its nature is needed in order to grasp what followed in the ensuing century in North America.

During the first half of the 17th century Spain, linked with the empire of the Austrian Hapsburgs, was dominant in Europe and held an immensely rich domain in Mid-America. In the Thirty Years War (1618-48) a league of Protestant states born of the bourgeois Reformation challenged the feudal Catholic Hapsburgs. France under Richelieu, the Catholic cardinal, sided intermittently with the Protestant powers; utilizing the alliance, however vacillating and unstable, in order to strengthen the hold of the centralized monarchy on borderlands threatened by Hapsburg encirclement. (France's war with Spain continued till 1659.) Spain emerged weakened from the long war. Moreover, its rigid feudal structure stifled capitalist development; hence its economy was unable to digest the silver stream of booty from Peru and Mexico, and stagnation and decline were the result.

Meanwhile Holland, which a half century before had won its independence from Spain and established a bourgeois republic, as a result had forged ahead and was the foremost trading and maritime power in Europe. Colbert estimated that of the 20,000 ships in the seaborne trade of Europe, some 16,000 belonged to the Dutch merchants. (England had 3-4,000, France only 600.) Thus tiny Holland, thanks to its capitalist development, had become a power—with colonial outposts in India and Indonesia, and a fur-trading colony astride the Hudson with four times as large a population as New France.

But a mightier rival than the Dutch was in the making. Across the Channel, the English bourgeois revolution of 1642-49 released an aggressive upsurge of economic and political energies. The monarchy, which under the Tudors had been an ally of the rising bourgeoisie, by the 17th century had become a bulwark of feudal-aristocratic reaction. The Stuarts leaned strongly toward a military tie-up with Spain, neglected the fleet, fettered the power of the merchants and manufacturers. The sharpening contest between king and parliament over control of the public purse reflected the fundamental conflict between feudal-aristocratic state and property relations on the one hand and the fast-growing power of the bourgeoisie on the other.

Unlike the Dutch, whose strength resided primarily in a vast accumulation of commercial capital, the English bourgeoisie were manufacturers as well as merchants. To the wool and cloth industries of the 15th-16th centuries were added brass foundries, paper works, tin mines—and above all coal: its output increased 14-fold between 1560 and 1680, and thousands of workers were employed mining it and shipping it from the Tyneside.

It took seven years of civil war and the execution of the king to establish bourgeois rule in England. The "supremacy of Parliament" meant the rule of the great merchants and allied gentry who controlled it. When radical spokesmen of the urban and rural poor—of those who had fought the battles and made the greatest sacrifices in the cause of Parliament—advanced proposals for the complete abolition of all vestiges of privilege, they were ruthlessly suppressed. The Republic and the Protectorate (1649-60) rested on an alliance between the bourgeoisie and a large section of the landed interest. The Restoration of the monarchy (1660) amended the terms of that alliance, but did not alter its substance.

The re-established monarchy existed, not by "divine right" but by decision of the landlord-mercantile interests that controlled Parliament. The Church regained its estates. The landed aristocrats—in a move that in fact carried the bourgeois revolution a step forward—secured, in place of feudal tenure, outright ownership of their domains. Thereby, Marx notes, they "vindicated for themselves the rights of modern private property in estates to which they had only a feudal title."*

The triumph of the capitalist order brought with it an aggressive colonialism. The sporadic piracy of the Elizabethans, the lackadaisical indifference of the early Stuarts, gave way to a new, vigorous colonial policy.

Up till now, colonies had grown up in America either as settlements of dissident, opposition elements (Puritans in New England at one stage, Catholics in Maryland at another) or else as feudal estates granted to such titled landowners as Sir William Alexander (the grant of Nova Scotia in 1621) or Lord Baltimore (part of Newfoundland, 1622). Merchant capitalist groups had made the most of whatever opportunities the royal charters granted; but they got less than vigorous backing from the Stuart monarchs of the pre-revolutionary period.

In 1650 the Committee on Trade of the English Republic was instructed to concern itself with the colonies in America and elsewhere, and advise how they and their productions might best be organized to the benefit and advantage of the Republic.

In 1651 the first of a series of Navigation Acts proclaimed the resolve of the English bourgeoisie to build up its

---

*A similar operation was put through by the seigneurs in Canada in 1854. See footnote to p. 105, above.

own sea-borne trade. By requiring that goods imported by England be carried in English ships, it struck hard at the huge Dutch carrying trade. By barring foreign ships from bringing goods to England from Asia, Africa or America it struck not only at its Dutch competitors but at the trading rights of English colonies. Certain colonial products enumerated in a further Navigation Act (1660), including sugar, tobacco, cotton—could be shipped only to England or her possessions: a measure that for the first time made explicit the proposition that "the interests of the Mother country" were "the end for which the Colonies had a being." The Navigation Acts (which endured for two centuries) became fetters on the colonial economies, and an issue in their later fight for independence.

In 1654 the Protectorate initiated a series of measures that directed the authorities to "apprehend lewd and dangerous persons, rogues, vagrants, and those who have no way of livelihood," and to "treat with merchants and others for transporting them to the English plantations."

Aggressive colonialism needed military—and above all naval—force in order to succeed in the face of rivals such as Holland, France and Spain. In 1649 the English fleet could muster a mere 39 ships. In 1660 it numbered 229. The result of a prodigious effort, this was "much the largest and most powerful sea-force (England) had ever possessed." Cromwell, acting for the new ruling class of merchants and manufacturers, created not only the New Model Army, but the modern Navy.

It was not long idle.

Bourgeois rule in England led quickly to an armed collision with Holland, her chief rival and competitor in trade. In the words of General Monck, Cromwell's lieutenant, "The Dutch have too much trade, and the English are resolved to take it from them." The Anglo-Dutch war of 1652-4 was but the first of three, in which the English step by step asserted their predominance. The greater development of English manufactures, and Holland's concentration on commerce, decided the eventual outcome of the contest. In the words of Marx: "The history of the decline of Holland as the ruling trading nation is the history of the subordination of merchants' capital to industrial capital."

In 1655, a naval expedition to the West Indies captured Jamaica: a blow challenging Spain, and England's first successful and enduring acquisition by force of colonial territory from a rival imperial power.

The Cromwellian Protectorate thus inaugurated the systematic regulation of colonial trade (monopolizing their raw materials as a means to building up manufactures and capital at home); and launched the drive for colonial expansion that led to the build-up and aggrandizement of the modern British Empire.

In 1664, just on the eve of the second Dutch war, the English seized New Holland, ousting their rivals from a strategic area of North America. The acquisition of the Dutch fur-trading colony on the Hudson, which for 40 years had lain as a wedge separating New England from the other possessions to the south, created a continuous string of English colonies along the coast between Spanish Florida and New France. In 1654 a force of 500 men, led by Robert Sedgwick, a Cromwellian officer, had captured Port Royal and two other forts in Acadia; the English held them until 1667, when Charles II gave them back to France.

The consolidation and rapid growth of the English colonies on the Atlantic seaboard contrasted sharply with the painfully slow efforts of the French colonizers on the St. Lawrence. Concentration on the fur trade, the lack of ice-free ports—these were factors in the lagging of New

France. But the very failure to surmount them (by developing Acadia, for instance, and linking it with Quebec) reflected more deep-going causes. The social-economic structure of feudal-absolutist France was an obstacle to the kind of growth that the English colonies experienced. The forces that impelled New England forward were those that brought on and carried through the English bourgeois revolution. The roadblocks in the way of New France were such as the Cromwellian revolution cleared away.

The advance in trade and early forms of manufacture was reflected in the growth of a colonial bourgeoisie, which increasingly asserted its own interest as against that of the imperial metropolis. The bourgeois-parliamentary struggle in England had its extension and counterpart across the Atlantic: here, assemblies of colonial burgesses contested and sometimes successfully defied the power and prerogatives of royal governors. As early as 1643 the four New England colonies on their own had established a confederation in their common interest; thirty years later we find the Lords of Trade and Plantations complaining that the Massachusetts merchants "do not conform themselves to the laws, but take a liberty of trading where they think fit."

The colonial striving for freedom of trade and full self-government was curbed in some measure by external conflict. In New England, the Indians' resistance to being robbed of their lands reached a climax with the short-lived rising of 1675-6 of three allied tribes led by Metacom ("King Philip," the colonists called him). In addition to the continuing conflict with the native peoples, the English colonists came into collision, increasingly, with neighboring New France. Colonial friction, in the fur trade and the fishery, merged with the larger imperial conflict between France and England.

XVIII

Anglo-French Conflict: First Round of Wars

THE FUR TRADE BUILT UP BY THE DUTCH AT ALBANY was taken over by the English in 1664, as well as the trade-alliance with the Iroquois. Soon after, to this challenge to New France from the south, was added a new threat from the north. Two independent traders, Radisson and Groseillers, embittered against the French authorities, had led the English to the beaver country flanking Hudson Bay. An expedition that brought back £19,000 worth of furs, in exchange for £650 of trade goods, was enough to whet the appetite of investors. So in 1670 Charles II granted a charter to a group of wealthy noblemen and merchants, conveying to them trading rights and sovereignty over the entire Hudson Bay drainage basin. The charter ignored the claims of France in the area (to say nothing of the rights of the native peoples dwelling there). It required that the "Governor and Company of Adventurers Trading into Hudson's Bay" conduct a search for a passage from the Bay to the "South Sea" (the Pacific). But what had drawn them to the enterprise was fur profits through plunder of the Indians—exploration could wait (and did). The Company limited its exertions to building fortified posts on the shores of the Bay, drawing thither the Cree and Chipewyan trappers by means of offers of better and cheaper trade goods than the French could command.

Soon the French began to feel the effect of the pincer movement on their far-flung trading network: Indians beyond Sault Ste. Marie were carrying their peltries north, instead of east; and at the same time a contraband trade carried on by coureurs de bois at Albany was on the increase (the English there paid three times the price offered by the French).

The Montreal fur merchants headed by the Le Moynes were concerned about the threat in the northwest, where their own operations were centred. The Frontenac-La Salle combination, on the other hand, were interested in the Ohio-Illinois country. The only reaction of the governor to the intrusion from the Bay was to send a lone Jesuit to reconnoitre, bearing a message of salutation to the English commanding officer. For their part, the Canadian merchants in 1682 organized their own "Compagnie du Nord" to counter the northern fur enterprise of the English. But to challenge the latter's well-entrenched position military means were needed; and not until 1686, under another governor, did the Montreal merchants manage to get a military expedition launched against the Hudson's Bay Company posts.

Frontenac's commercial and imperial ventures in the direction of the Mississippi, meanwhile, led to a new round of Indian wars. The trading system in the midwest depended for success on the exploitation of the Illinois people. Neighboring Lake Michigan tribes urged them to resist the French traders' blandishments: "Our families and yours," they warned, "will henceforth be reduced to servitude by the French . . . they will be strong enough to make slaves of us all, unless we prevent their undertaking."

But the Illinois yielded to French pressure. Thereupon, the Iroquois, who three decades earlier had struck first at the Hurons, then the base of the French trading system, now warred upon the Illinois. Achieving a measure of success, they turned next to challenge the French.

Soon the threat of a general Iroquois onslaught loomed over the scattered settlements of New France. An inveterately complacent Frontenac ignored the warning sent by a Jesuit in the Iroquois' country, that the Five Nations were planning to "fall upon Canada and crush it in a single campaign." Recalled to France, he left the colony ill-prepared for defense.

An expedition under Governor Denonville in 1686 drove as far west as Niagara and laid waste the villages of the Seneca. Far from being deterred by this show of force, the Iroquois laid siege to Fort Frontenac (compelling its abandonment soon after) and attacked Fort Chambly on the Richelieu. Then, in the summer of 1689, they raided La Chine on the outskirts of Montreal, killing over a score of the inhabitants and taking twice that many prisoner. For months thereafter the whole district lived in terror.

At this moment, new forces were thrown into the balance. War with England was added to war with the Iroquois, and soon overshadowed it. With the overthrow of James II and the coming to power, by Parliament's decision, of William of Orange—the Revolution of 1688—England broke the Stuarts' ties with the French court and joined the coalition of France's enemies. With the War of the League of Augsburg ("King William's War": 1689-97) the contest between England and France began in earnest. For the first time, their colonies were caught up in a major military struggle.

To the New England and Albany merchants England's declaration of war offered an opportunity to take the offensive against their colonial competitors to the north. In New France the outbreak of war provided a sanction for the Montreal merchants' military forays against the English posts on Hudson Bay.

Frontenac, who returned as governor at the outbreak of war, organized a series of ferocious border raids on Schenectady, Salmon Arm and other settlements in New York State and New England. These operations were in lieu of a land and sea offensive against the town of New York, which Paris was unready to support and which New France alone was not strong enough to undertake.

The English colonies, however, showed themselves quite able in 1690 to mount an expedition against Quebec. First, the New England merchants sent a force to seize and pillage Port Royal. Then a naval expedition of 30-odd ships under William Phips set sail for Quebec. It arrived only in October, with an early winter closing in. A planned simultaneous land invasion from New York up the line of the Hudson-Richelieu did not get beyond Lake George.

A summons by Phips to surrender brought Frontenac's rejoinder, that he would "answer with the mouths of his cannon and his musketry." Some 1300 troops were landed on the Beauport shore, below Quebec, with the aim of crossing the St. Charles to attack the town from the rear in conjunction with a bombardment and landing from the river-front. Co-ordination failed, supplies ran short, and the Canadian militia (the French regular troops were not engaged) put up a brisk defense. The landing force was withdrawn, and shortly thereafter a storm dispersed the invading fleet.

The other focus of conflict in North America was Hudson Bay. In 1686 an overland expedition under de Troyes had captured the English posts on the shore of James Bay; in 1694 Pierre Le Moyne d'Iberville led a naval detachment that captured the key English position of Fort York, at the mouth of the Hayes River. Two years later the English retook it. In 1697 the French sent a squadron to the Bay. During the engagements that ensued, Iberville performed the spectacular feat, with one ship of 50 guns, of defeating three English ships of a combined strength of 114 guns. Fort York once more was in the hands of the French.

Together with the fur trade, the fishery was a major object of contention. By the 1660's the English fishing fleet off Newfoundland numbered 300, with 15,000 men employed; the French had 400 ships, 18,000 men. During the war in the 1690's the French, based at Placentia, carried out a series of devastating raids on the English settlements along the east coast and captured St. John's. It was retaken soon after, but nearly all the small fishing ports (except for Carbonear and Bonavista) had been ravaged.

As the war ended with the Peace of Ryswick in 1697, the French had somewhat strengthened their North American positions (Acadia was returned to them). But in the decisive European theatre the outcome was a draw, and the peace was no more than a short breathing-space.

Before turning to consider the next round of warfare and its consequences, two aspects of the North American struggle call for consideration.

The outbreak of war in 1689 had the effect of subordinating the Iroquois resistance to the English military effort. At first, the war situation encouraged the Iroquois to go on the offensive; but as the English colonies demonstrated their ability to threaten Quebec, and showed signs of expansionist land-grabbing policies (of which Governor Dongan of New York was an aggressive exponent)—the Iroquois policy began to undergo a change.

What the Five Nations had been fighting for in the past half century was not merely their middleman's position in the trade with the English, but independence—and survival. As one of their chiefs declared, during negotiations with the French: "The English and the French, without any right, have usurped the grounds they now are possessed of; and of which they have dislodged several Nations, in order to make way for their building of Cities, Villages and Forts."

To fight on as auxiliaries of the English would not advance but undermine such freedom of action as still was left to them. So the Iroquois in 1701 made peace with the French, and during the ensuing twelve years of war they adhered to a policy of neutrality. Iroquois statesmanship was fully equal to the demands of history; as contemporaries noted more than once, its subtlety and sagacity were thoroughly a match for the diplomatic wiles of Europeans. The new policy was described by the 18th-century historian Charlevoix as being "to hold the scale evenly balanced between the two nations, whose mutual jealousy made the Iroquois sought by both and ensured their safety." . . . "To preserve a balance between us and the French," wrote Peter Wraxall, a New York official, "is the great ruling principle of the modern Indian politics."

The Revolution of 1688 that overthrew the Stuarts had widespread reverberations in the American colonies. "The impact of that event" writes Herbert Aptheker in *The Colonial Era* "was tremendous throughout the colonial world and led to revolutionary attempts . . . notably in New England, New York, Maryland and North Carolina. . . . The assertion of the supremacy of Parliament in the affairs of England bulwarked the claims of colonial legislatures for their supremacy in terms of colonial government."

There was a rising in Boston, another in Maryland. In New York, which since its seizure from Holland had been ruled despotically by its merchant-landowners, a rebellion led by Jacob Leisler secured the granting of a representative assembly. Solidarity between the governments born of popular struggle fostered the growing sense of an American community.

Thus, revolutionary-democratic currents were strongly to the fore at the time of "King William's War." And to militant Protestants, the French Catholic régime on the St. Lawrence stood as a bulwark of reaction. Yet the thesis of Professor S. D. Clark (in his valuable and stimulating *Movements of Political Protest in Canada: 1640-1840*) surely makes too large a claim. He describes the conflict as "the first American War of Independence"; and says: "With revolution in England and political chaos in New York, the movement of 1689-90 assumed something of the character of a general uprising of the American peoples."

The national-democratic element was present, assuredly—but it was a subordinate one. The major, and decisive framework was the imperial struggle for trade and colonies. Phips' expedition did not negate these overriding aims: it served them. Professor Clark appears rather to skirt around this fact when he writes: "Confused though it may have been by the conflicts of empire, the war carried on by the Iroquois and the English colonies in the years 1649-90 had as its very clear purpose the destruction of a system of economic and political control imposed upon the settled communities of America from the outside." Moreover: "A combined uprising of French and English colonists would bring to an end old-world rule in America . . ."

The catch is in the "would." Though there were rebellious elements in French Canada as well as in the English colonies, and though those in the latter were far more advanced (thanks to the English bourgeois revolution)—not only did they *not* combine forces against the imperial powers, they remained politically subject to them and, objectively at least, served their military purposes. Subjective aspirations are not a substitute for actual transformation in class structure or colonial rule. The American Revolution, like the French, lay far in the future: which is not to deny by any means that the seeds of both were already planted and germinating.

The renewal of hostilities in "Queen Anne's War" or the War of the Spanish Succession (1702-13) stemmed from a dynastic quarrel over Bourbon and Hapsburg claims to the Spanish throne; but basically what was involved, along with dominance in Europe, was England's resolve to prevent Louis XIV from acquiring the colonial empire of Spain and the profitable monopoly of the trade in slaves.

The main theatre of operations was in Europe, where Marlborough's armies and the English fleet struck telling blows at the power of the French. In North America there was only sporadic fighting: fierce raids in Newfoundland and Acadia, chiefly. In 1705 the idea of colonial disengagement and neutrality was mooted at Quebec; and the French Colonial Minister Pontchartrain actually authorized negotiations by the colonists to that end. The English authorities, however, cut short the parleys.

French efforts to extend their colonial empire in America had been continuing meanwhile. Iberville, after conducting raids on the English outposts in Newfoundland, had established a fort upstream from the mouth of the Mississippi; and another, Fort Louis, was built on Mobile Bay. It was in the course of a naval campaign against the English in the West Indies that the indefatigable and audacious Canadian commander, Pierre d'Iberville, died in Havana. Born in Montreal of the wealthy fur-trading Le Moyne family, he had become the outstanding military figure in New France.

As the war drew to a close, the British attempted a major blow against Quebec. But the invasion fleet met disaster, being shipwrecked on the north shore of the St. Lawrence with a loss of over 700 men.

The war in Europe and at sea seriously weakened the position of feudal-absolutist France. It no longer possessed unchallenged hegemony on the Continent; and the rising power of England, based on capitalist manufacture, compelled a re-division of bases and colonial possessions. Together with Gibraltar, England obtained the coveted *asiento*—the exclusive right to transport and sell African slaves in the Spanish Indies. In North America France surrendered Acadia, its share of Newfoundland, and all of Hudson Bay.

The first round of Anglo-French wars had ended; the crisis of French absolutism had begun.

Progress and Crisis: 1713-1745

BETWEEN THE FIRST AND SECOND ROUND OF ANGLO-French wars (1689-1713; 1745-63) came an interval of peace that witnessed both the high point in New France's growth and the onset of its severest crisis.

The Treaty of Utrecht (1713) sounded a first note of crisis-warning. The surrender to the British of Acadia (except for Cape Breton) and of the Hudson Bay posts that Iberville had taken was a step towards the dismemberment of New France. The acceptance of a British "protectorate" over the Iroquois and their territory, far inland from the English settlements, threatened to sever Louisiana from Canada.

The rulers of New France reacted to the decisions taken at Utrecht by setting out to nullify as far as possible their negative effects. To the southwest, on the Ohio and the Illinois, the French constructed a chain of forts; they strengthened their position on the lower Mississippi with the founding of New Orleans (1718); and at the other end of a great arc of empire, on Cape Breton (Ile Royale) they started the building of a massive fortress: Louisbourg.

To the loss of Hudson Bay the fur traders on the St. Lawrence responded by an intensified drive to win the West. By securing positions on the Saskatchewan they might intercept the movement of Cree and Assiniboine trappers down the main river routes to the Bay. At the same time they penetrated to new territories rich in beaver. These were the objectives pursued in the 1730's and 40's by the La Vérendryes, who established trading posts almost as far westward as the foothills of the Rockies.

Thus the French answered Utrecht and its threat of ultimate dismemberment by seeking to sever the arteries of their rivals' Hudson Bay trade, and to outflank and encircle the Atlantic seaboard colonies.

This expansionist policy, linked with the building of a transcontinental fur empire, called for fantastically extended lines of communication; and these of necessity were military as well as commercial. The strain of constructing and maintaining them—in the face of Indian resistance and Anglo-colonial competition—required a strong and growing base of operations on the St. Lawrence. Moreover, the steadily growing population and resources of the Thirteen Colonies served notice on Paris and Quebec: it was necessary that New France be strengthened drastically before another trial by arms should come.

The colony could—and did—make headway in the interval that peace afforded. But it was beset by inner difficulties. One of these was the ever-simmering conflict between the Canadian and the French merchant-capitalists. The former had organized the Compagnie du Nord, in competition with the Hudson's Bay Company. After a time, a French mercantile group secured the dominant interest in the firm, elbowing the Canadians aside. In 1700 the latter organized a new venture, the Compagnie de la Colonie. It foundered as a result of wartime difficulties and a glut on the French fur market.

Then, in 1717, the French Compagnie de l'Occident secured for itself a monopoly of the Canadian trade. Vehement protests by the Montreal and Quebec merchants succeeded only in getting the monopoly privileges of their rivals suspended for short intervals. An important section of the Canadian traders—especially the Montrealers—

carried on a roaring contraband trade at Albany; the Intendant Bégon (whom they accused of trying to corner the whole trade for himself) lamented that 50,000 livres worth of furs was being smuggled annually to the English: an amount equal to a quarter of the entire Canadian fur trade.

Another deep-going inner contradiction was the oft-cited conflict between "the fur trade and settlement." What lay at the root of this conflict? A contradiction between the requirements of two distinct stages of capitalist development: primary accumulation, represented by merchants' capital and the fur trade; and the beginnings of capitalist production, of manufacture, whose new relationships were emerging within the old framework of feudal-rural society. These two processes, though related, were by no means identical. The merchants who achieved the "primitive accumulation" of capital, through extracting fabulous profits from "trade" with the Indians, had little interest in the small (and as yet relatively less profitable) hemp-works or tanneries or other forms of early capitalist production, such as Talon had tried to foster.

Certainly, here as elsewhere, the growth of *trade* itself acted as a dissolvent, eating away at the old fabric of feudal seigneurial relationships. The fur trade in Canada did this, by turning censitaires into voyageurs and coureurs-de-bois, and by implanting a mercantile, money economy on the St. Lawrence.

But the advance towards the new capitalist mode of production came from within the growing rural-handicraft economy—as a result, initially, of intervention by the state and the pressure of military needs. Talon's organizing of enterprises and measures to stimulate the economy had been an example of such governmental intervention. The process went forward on a bigger scale, both in France and in the colony, from about 1730 on.

For one thing, the construction and operation of the great Louisbourg fortress not only employed hundreds of workmen: it provided a market for surplus wheat from the farms on the St. Lawrence. Between 1720 and 1740 the crop increased from a quarter of a million to 635,000 bushels (one year—1734—it reached 738,000). In the same period the censitaires and farm laborers extended the cleared land to over 70,000 arpents: more than four times what it had been in Talon's day. Cattle increased from 18,000 to 39,000 head.

This advance in agriculture brought with it a limited, partial change-over from the "natural economy" of the self-sufficient pioneer farm to production for the market: commodity production. Reporting on the state of agriculture in 1737, the Intendant Gilles Hocquart described both these features: "The country people are all skilful with the axe; they themselves make most of their tools and farm implements; build their houses and barns; quite a few are weavers, making rough cloth and a fabric they called *droguet* (a kind of serge), which they use to clothe themselves and their families." Then, turning to the cultivation of wheat, the main farm product: "The country not only provides it for the subsistence of its inhabitants, but also for the trade at Ile Royale (Cape Breton) and in the Islands" (the West Indies). It should be noted that France, whose agriculture was similar, not complementary to that of the colony, did not provide a market; and attempts to get around this by a three-way trade with the West Indies were never much of a success.

These beginnings in commercial farming meant some growth in the *home market*: an indispensable condition for any development of industry. They also led to sharper differentiation in the countryside, with richer farmers employing more *engagés*, and poorer ones being taken on as *métayers* or share-croppers. (Neither in the colony nor in

France did full-blown capitalist farming based on wage labor become widespread—much less, predominant—as it did in England. There, the mass expropriation of the small producers, the wiping out of the yeomanry, created a mass of "free" laborers; in France, this process was much more gradual, and very much less sweeping.)

If progress in agriculture was one feature of the economic advance in this period, another was the renewed growth of a number of fields of industrial enterprise—in lumber, ship-building and iron-working. Here—on however modest a scale—were the real beginnings of capitalist production in Canada.

As in France, the first large industrial enterprises were started with direct financial aid from the state, or on the basis of military orders. "You would infinitely benefit this colony," wrote an official at Quebec, "if you would obtain your masts and planking from this country." The French naval dockyards needed timber, masts and spars; their orders spurred the infant lumber industry in New France.

One Intendant, Dupuy, in the 1720's projected the idea of a planned conservation and development program for the forest industries of New France, and made this prophetic observation: "Wood should be considered as the fruit of Canada which will replace fur, which is everywhere diminishing. Wheat and wood will comprise the bulk of its trade . . . [we should] use, and not abuse them."

Early in the 18th century a number of seigneurs (both laymen and ecclesiastics) became lumber magnates. One was the Sieur de Ramezay who went into the business on a grand scale: he had workmen making masts at mills on Baie St. Paul, at Sorel and outside Montreal. Le Moyne, Baron of Longueil, was another. The Abbé Le Page had a sawmill among his other enterprises in the seigneurie of

Terrebonne; and the sawmills belonging to the Seminary at Quebec brought in "large revenues." There were mills operating on Cape Breton, on the Badeck River, and at least one in Labrador.

By 1739 New France had 70 sawmills in operation. Those of M. de Ramezay were putting out annually 8,000 feet of planking and 4,000 beams.

One record of the period describes a new wonder: "mills with a hydraulic saw . . . a single mechanical wheel turns out as much as do twelve hand-powered saws, each of which requires three men . . ." Already in those infant days of capitalist production, the revolutionizing effect of machinery begins to make itself felt: one power-driven saw doing the work of thirty-six men . . .

Simon Sicard is recorded as the builder of one of the earliest of these water-driven sawmills in New France; a Sulpician chronicler who visited it declared himself "delighted to observe the mechanism working, so regularly and with such precision" ("avec tant de régularité et d'accord").

Ships were the means of trade (and of trade wars); so in Canada, as in a number of other countries taking the path towards capitalist development, the shipyard was one of the earliest centres of wage-labor.

Champlain had seen the possibility of developing naval construction on the St. Lawrence; workmen at Quebec had built a barque in 1628. Carpenters who came out with Maisonneuve built two small vessels. Flat boats for troop transport were built on Lake Ontario in 1673. When La Salle commanded at Cataraqui (Fort Frontenac) he had ships' carpenters construct barques for defense and for transporting furs; he had the great "Griffon" built on Lake Erie, for service on the Upper Lakes (it was lost in a heavy storm soon after it was launched).

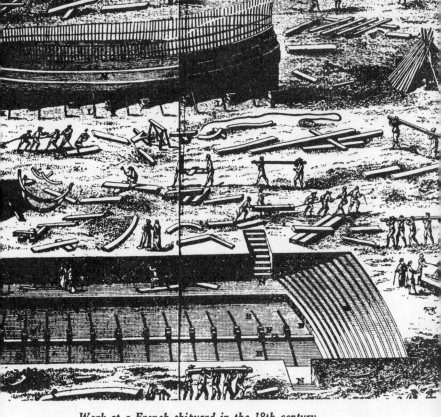

Work at a French shipyard in the 18th century.
(From L'Encyclopédie.*)*

In the first quarter of the 18th century shipyard work-ers at Quebec produced a number of warships—including one carrying 36 guns.

In 1739 a war vessel of 500 tons—the "Canada"—was on the stocks. The men building her, it is recorded, toiled "from before sunrise till long after sunset." That same year Canadian shipyard workers put out ten merchant vessels. Rouen and Bordeaux shipping interests had a hand in financing merchant marine construction in the colony. The Quebec and Montreal forest areas provided oak and pine in vast quantity, and of excellent material (though the French shipbuilders and government seem never to have evaluated properly the treasure-store of

Canadian timber). The iron-mines and forges on the St. Maurice, near Three Rivers, provided the nails and iron-work for ship construction at Quebec.

The Intendant Hocquart, writing about the early Canadian shipyard workers, observed "The carpenters of the country display an extraordinary facility in learning and perfecting their skill"; but he complained that they were used to a rough style of work. Six carpenters had built a ship of 130 tons in six months, at Quebec; they received about 400 francs each for their work.

In October 1741, workers in the Quebec shipyard went on strike. Thereupon the employers fired a number of the Canadian workers, replacing them with French ships' carpenters, who had been sent out from Rochefort. These too struck, supporting the demand for reinstatement of the Canadians. The Intendant Hocquart had the strikers imprisoned, declaring his determination "to put down from the outset and once and for all by means of prison and irons their mutiny which had gone to the length of resisting orders." The government succeeded in breaking the strike: the long, bitter process of learning by experience and struggle was beginning for workers in Canada, even in those earliest days of capitalist production.

At the opening of the century the Intendant Raudot urged Paris to authorize a large-scale program of naval construction in New France. He pointed to the example of New England which was busily building ships both for its own commerce and for sale in Europe. He put his finger on the main obstacle in the way of a serious growth of shipbuilding in Canada: "So long as the colony depended on the merchants in France, and did not itself organize its own commerce, it would continue to languish." Some ships, as we have seen, were built for the French navy. But the ministry preferred that the colonials should limit themselves in the main to supplying lumber and masts—to be used in the dockyards of France. They might also provide cordage: Talon had encouraged the growing of hemp for that purpose, and in 1732 the authorities sent to Canada three master cordage-workers and seven journeymen.

In 1740 the monarchy stopped the practice of subsidizing private shipbuilding; a few years later the Canadian authorities were informed that it was "the intention of the King to undertake no further construction of vessels in Canada."

The difficulties that beset the infant iron industry in New France were more acute than those that retarded shipbuilding.

Jean Talon had given some impetus to opening up the iron mines on the St. Maurice River. But the enterprise had not got under way when the war years came. In 1717 a proposal was made for getting the St. Maurice works started in production. Iron was badly needed for machinery in the sawmills and also for shipbuilding. A royal memorandum turned down the proposal, on the ground that there were enough iron mines in France as it was. The Intendant Bégon, though he suggested that conditions in Canada might justify making an exception, hastened to state his agreement with the precept that "the motive for establishing colonies is to benefit the manufactures from the kingdom." If a colonial iron industry would compete with that in France, then let it perish at birth. Let the Canadians grow hemp!—such was the retort from Paris to urgings in favor of the enterprise. "His Majesty does not wish them opened" stated one official communication regarding the mines.

Not until the 1730's—and then only on grounds of military necessity, and with considerable reservations—did the French government give permission for an iron works in

The St. Maurice Forges.

Canada. François Poulin, Montreal merchant and seigneur of St. Maurice, obtained the concession for the workings. Later other merchants and officials were associated with the enterprise.

In 1736 the home authorities were still deep in doubt as to the wisdom of it: wrote the Minister of Marine (and Colonies): "Despite all the advantages which the enterprise offers the colony of Canada, I have deemed it proper, before proposing its adoption to the king, to examine whether it might not be inconvenient to authorize it, having in mind the present state of the iron trade in France and the existing forges established in different provinces of the kingdom."

However, the project slowly got under way. The employers brought out two iron-workers from France; and sent a Canadian named Labrèche —"a skillful and clever workman of the country"— to study the method of making bar iron then in use in New England.

After the construction of a forge and workers' barracks was completed, and bellows and other equipment were brought from France, the St. Maurice Forges at last were in operation. But after they had produced their first ton of iron, technical difficulties and the proprietor's death caused the works to close. Shortly thereafter a reorganized company brought more iron-workers from France; and an enlarged works with two furnaces went into production under the direction of a French forge-master, Olivier de Vézin. Financial difficulties, however, continued to accumulate and in 1741 the company went into bankruptcy. From then on it was operated by the state.

By 1742 the works was turning out 5,000 pounds of iron daily.* Its products ranged from cast-iron pots, stoves and plowshares to bullets and mortar shells. In time a number of cannon and mortars were produced; at one point, by way of experiment, 27 lbs. of steel was smelted. For a period the forges supplied the French naval dockyards at Rochefort and Brest with bar iron. But the plan for a large arsenal in the colony itself never materialized.

Peter Kalm, the Finno-Swedish naturalist who visited Canada in 1749, had this to say about the St. Maurice forges:

"The iron-work, which is the only one in this country, lies three miles to the west of Trois Rivières.** Here are two great forges, besides two lesser ones to each of the

---

*Annual production only reached the figure of 400,000 lbs. The furnace was closed down in winter-time, the freezing over of the stream interfering with the operation of the water-wheel which worked the bellows. The forges were kept going, though at reduced output.

**The distance was actually nine miles.

Stove-making and hardware: an 18th-century workshop.

great ones, and under the same roof with them. The bellows were made of wood, and everything else as it is in Swedish forges. The ore is got two French miles and a half from the iron works, and is carried thither on sledges. It is a kind of moor ore, which lies in veins, within six inches or a foot from the surface of the ground. ... The iron which is here made was described to me as soft, pliable and tough ... they cast cannon and mortars here of different sizes, iron stoves, which are in use all over Canada, kettles, etc., not to mention the bars which are made here. They have likewise tried to make steel here, but cannot bring it to any great perfection, because they are unacquainted with the best manner of preparing it."

The St. Maurice Forges at this time employed 120 men. Problems of working hours and labor discipline were on one occasion at least the subject of a special decree of the Council at Quebec. A system of payment in provisions and other goods resulted in the workers constantly finding themselves in debt to the company. According to a report of the Intendant: "The workers, dissatisfied with their pay which they receive in the form of merchandise, became disgusted and then they mutinied; insubordination and ill-will reigned." Their protests won them some concessions and the Minister instructed the Intendant that they were to be paid their wages in cash.

Technical difficulties, shortage of skilled labor, corruption on the part of the managing officialdom and huge debts chronically bedevilled the enterprise. Kalm noted that its operations (which had shown a profit in the seven years preceding) showed a deficit. He was told that the labor shortage was to blame for the failure to cover operating costs: "This result is attributed to the insufficient population, the inhabitants of the country having enough to do to cultivate their lands, and only at considerable expense and trouble can workers be obtained from elsewhere."

Undoubtedly this was a factor; but it needs to be seen as part of the larger problem. Feudal-absolutist society in France did not allow the kind of mass emigration that would make available large numbers of "free" laborers, unburdened by property or feudal ties. That same social structure was responsible for the chronic lack of capital that plagued the various merchant companies and inhibited the growth of manufactures. Abbé Le Page, entrepreneur and seigneur of Terrebonne, was but one among many to voice the plaint: "Scarcity of money is the reason why there are such difficulties in the way of succeeding in different enterprises in Canada today."*

The "seedlings of capitalism" planted in Talon's day were stunted in their growth. In the first place the system of colonialism stifled expansion: as one authority notes, "It was government policy to discourage the establishment of industries in the colonies." Furthermore, the colonial pattern of New France, dominated by the fur trade, was particularly inimical to the growth of a stable local market-

---

*See Note, p. 164.

economy and its advance to one based on manufacture and wage labor.

In the second place, the fact that this was the colony of a feudal monarchy vastly aggravated the difficulties of growth. The authors of a recent economic history point out with good reason: "Feudal forms of social organization"— no matter how they were modified by North American conditions —"inevitably inhibited the development of a commercial economy." This retarding influence was not lessened but intensified in the 18th century.

In the mid-17th century the central monarchy was still allying itself with the bourgeoisie in order to curb the power of the great nobles: hence Colbert's policy of encouraging manufactures, even in the colony of New France. But before the century ended, class relationships began to undergo a change: a period of reaction set in, and the monarchy became the rallying point of the feudal aristocracy and the Church against the pressures of the bourgeoisie and the revolutionary threat of growing peasant-plebeian struggles.

The crisis-period of the "Old Régime," of the feudal order in France, was now beginning. The repeal of the Edict of Nantes (1685) put an end to toleration of Huguenots within France, and signalled the onset of the new clerical-reactionary trend. The severe losses in the ensuing quarter-century of war not only weakened the régime externally but led to sharpening conflicts within. At the core of these was the contradiction between the slowly expanding productive forces and the constricting framework of outworn property relationships. The engineer Vauban wrote that six-tenths of the French population were in a state of pauperism, while three out of four "fare very badly." Luxury and extravagance at the court of Versailles, poverty and hunger among great masses of the people—these poles of parasitism and pauperization were the surface-symptoms of the crisis of a social system. 1789 was in the making.

In New France as well the ferment was at work. Here, the effort to move beyond the system of mercantile plundering that the fur trade stood for, and to develop capitalist manufacture, was blocked by the combined deadweight of feudal relationships, absolutist rule (serving feudal interests) and colonial status.

These roadblocks to progress stayed even the slight advance that has been noted in forest industry, shipbuilding, iron-working. One more example might be cited, in consumer goods. After the Treaty of Utrecht, hat manufacture was started at Quebec and Montreal; the small enterprises of local capitalists, Huppe, Chauffour and Cotton, were turning out annually 1,200 partly-felted beaver hats. In 1717 the fur-trading monopoly in France secured the suppression of this colonial industry. They could invoke the recent words of Louis XIV concerning colonies: "They are established solely for the utility of the country that forms them . . ." Or those of his minister, instructing an intendant: he was to "bear in mind that the Colony of Canada is good only insofar as it is useful to the Kingdom." One more attempt by a capitalist in Canada to get permission to establish a hat manufacture (in 1730) met with flat refusal from Versailles: there was to be no colonial competition with the manufactures of the realm!

With the coming of François Bigot as Intendant in 1748 a new privileged group of speculators, financiers, racketeers in provisioning and munitions attached themselves to the colony. The monarchy was already underwriting 70 per cent of the costs of administration. The zealous endeavors of Bigot and his entourage pushed up the state expenditures to dizzy heights. War preparations and then the onset of hostilities offered them wide scope. By 1743 government expenses were somewhat less than a million livres (about three times what they had been early in the century). By 1752 they topped four million—and in 1759, thirty million.

A memorandum written the year before the fall of Quebec stated that "The Canadian . . . is disgusted and discouraged at the immense fortunes he sees being made by private individuals who, sent from France to govern him, are far more eager to despoil him, profiteering in funds allocated to the colony."

In France, repeated waves of peasant revolt and risings of the urban poor were battering the foundations of feudal rule. The action of the masses of the people was in itself a powerful crisis-factor in the obsolete social structure.

In New France, the conditions of frontier life, the scattered pattern of settlement, the constant threat of Indian resistance, and the extent to which the economy rested on exploitation of the native peoples—all this tended to limit and blunt the edge of class struggle. But it did not by any means remove it. The idyllic patriarchal picture of these times that has become traditional, is a piece of flagrant deception.

The "spirit of independence," the "indocility" that officials complained of in the preceding century, far from disappearing, grew more pronounced. The colonial yoke engendered a national resentment that merged with social protest.

Throughout this period between the wars, prices rose steadily in both France and Canada. Consumer goods were dear enough already in the colony; but in the aftermath of war the situation worsened considerably. To meet the shortage of currency, Intendant de Meulles in 1685 had started the practice of issuing "card money": playing cards cut into pieces and stamped. During the war this paper currency served on a large scale to purchase war supplies; but no sooner was the war ended than Paris discounted it at less than half its face value.

The hardship occasioned by soaring prices called forth vigorous protest: as in 1714, when housewives went on a mass delegation to Quebec, to petition the authorities for curbs on high prices of the goods they had to buy for their families.

Unrest was reported in the early 1720's in the towns; but it was not confined to them. Governor Vaudreuil* in 1725 noted the spread of "the same spirit of mutiny and independence among all the inhabitants of the country-side."

As in France, the seigneurs during this period put increasing pressure on their tenantry. Popular protest had forced the enactment of measures penalizing those landlords who failed to fulfil their responsibilities toward their tenants; but while under the Edicts of Marly (1711) a few seigneurs were deprived of their grants, the edge of the legislation was turned against the censitaires. The seigneurs on occasion sought to encroach on the common pastureland; there is a record of the censitaires resisting such an atttempt by their overlords, the Sulpician monks of Montreal.

As in the earlier period, the inhabitants stoutly resisted impositions of taxes. At Montreal the townspeople demonstrated against paying a proposed tax for fortifications. When the Governor appeared in person they defied him and forced him to decamp in un-viceregal haste.

In 1728, protests against the Intendant Bégon's speculations and profiteering in farm produce approached the boiling-point: in the countryside the peasants at one stage actually took up arms. Paris made administrative changes,

---

*Father of the Vaudreuil who was governor at the time of the British conquest.

the Intendant was replaced, and the disturbances subsided.

In 1733 there were further incidents, the inhabitants defying "daily the orders sent them for the King's service." In 1737 the colonial officials asked that more troops be sent from France because the people "are beginning to become numerous" and have been allowed "a little too much freedom." Twelve years later, more troops were requested—according to Governor La Jonquière in order "to hold in check the inhabitants who, I understand, are somewhat mutinous."

Such was the state of affairs in New France when the court at Versailles plunged recklessly into a new round of wars.

FUR PROFITS
AND NEW FRANCE

In a typical year, 1685, metropolitan France extracted 392,250 livres in net profit, 179,514 l. in tax-returns and graft, 84,000 in purchases of provisions, as a result of the trade in furs. Between 1675 and 1760, no less than 72% of the revenues from the trade went to the metropolis, while 14% remained in the hands of Canadian merchants. Comments Jean Hamelin, from whose work the foregoing data are drawn: "The export monopoly, held for most of the time by a metropolitan company or the royal farmers of the revenue, together with the tax of one quarter on the beaver pelts, prevented the accumulation of capital in the colony." (*Economie et Société en Nouvelle France*, Laval 1960.)

XX

Cultural Achievement in New France

CLEARING THE FOREST, STARTING AGRICULTURE, PUTTING
up homes and forts and churches—the working people not
only built New France: they were also the main creators
of her cultural heritage. The appearance of a new culture, at once French and Canadian, dates back to the work
of Quebec and Montreal stone-masons who became architects, carpenters who were also wood-carvers and sculptors; and stems from the growth of the varied forms of
folk art, painting, instrumental music and song.

As an extension overseas of the French culture of the
16th-18th centuries, that of New France continues a development that has its roots in the European Middle Ages
and Renaissance. As modified by North American conditions, this culture takes on an identity of its own. It is the
second culture to grow in what now is Canada—after the
Indian-Eskimo Stone Age culture, which was the first, and
which was itself a formative influence in shaping the ways
of life in New France. (The "style" of the voyageur, the
canoeman, is the most notable instance of this.)

The transplanting of 17th century feudal rule to the
colony in North America set the framework in which education, letters, art and science had to grow—or whither—as
best they might. The transplanting at the same time of the
seeds of capitalism meant that the forces of conflict at work
in the colonial economy and politics were present in the
realm of culture also.

As in medieval society, education and "social services"
were in the hands of the Church: the biggest feudal land-

owner, the agency of ideological rule, fused with the feudal-absolutist state machinery. So schools (and hospitals and poorhouses) were church institutions. At Quebec in 1635 the Jesuits started the first college on the continent north of Mexico. Following a project of Talon's for a school of arts and manufactures, the church and civil authorities established an art school at St. Joachim in 1668, in order to train craftsmen to decorate religious edifices; and later, in response to the needs of war and navigation, the church founded at Quebec and Montreal schools of mathematics and hydrography. No school of medicine existed in the colony and doctors had to be brought from France. Midwives were in some instances elected "by plurality of votes" of the women of a parish.

The dominant concern of the clergy was with missions and with the training of priests.* Schooling of the children of seigneurs and merchants came a poor second. The Intendant Hocquart complained that "All the education received by most children of officers and gentry amounts to very little; they barely know how to read and write . . ." He suggested (apparently without result) the appointment of army school-masters to teach cadets "geometry, fortification and geography."

As for workers and farmers, they were up against very great difficulty in getting any education for their children. While the settlers stoutly resisted the imposition of taxes for military purposes, Governor Vaudreuil noted their "readiness to provide board and lodging to those [teachers] who come to the back concessions, in consideration of the advantage they derive for the instruction of their Children." Moreover, "all the expense and upkeep and subsistence of school-teachers in the parishes [are] charged to

---

*"The heads of the Church are of course concerned above all with the religious instruction of the young and the recruitment of the clergy" (Abbé Groulx).

the inhabitants." Eventually, there were 44 schools in New France, 25 for boys, 19 for girls.

The limited provision for education was characteristic in a society that was in many ways a replica of feudal-mercantile relationships in Europe. But the fact that in the whole period of its existence New France was never permitted a printing-press was a glaring expression of the stifling influence of feudal-colonial reaction. To the Church, Canada was a base for the Counter-Reformation, a preserve of the Jesuits. The exclusion of any means of printing served the interests of the clerical monopoly. The civil power, concerned at the "indocility" and "spirit of independence" of the colonists, concurred in this. Progressive or radical ideas could be spread only orally, or in hand-written form—or through printed works smuggled in from abroad.* (Baron La Hontan in 1690 was enraged to find that during his absence a priest had rifled his small library and torn to shreds volumes considered "licentious.")

Yet New France produced the beginnings of a literature. Printed in France, it comprised largely chronicles and journals: Jacques Cartier's *Short Narrative* (one of the earliest editions of which was printed in Italy), the writings of Champlain, and Lescarbot, the narrations of the Recollets Gabriel Sagard and Chrestien LeClercq, the voluminous *Relations* of the Jesuits (a modern edition of them runs to 70 volumes). Early histories were Du Creux's History of Canada (in Latin, 1664), Dollier de Casson's History of Montreal (1674), Charlevoix's History of New France (1744). La Hontan's *Voyages in North America*, which breathed the spirit of anti-clerical, anti-colonialist radicalism, had to be printed in Holland and smuggled into France.

---

*Such was the situation when an anti-Jesuit leaflet circulated at Quebec in 1626—and hand-written leaflets were still being resorted to in the period of the American Revolution.

HISTORIÆ

Poxo D. 1
Typogxαch

CANADENSIS,

SEV

NOVÆ-FRANCIÆ

LIBRI DECEM,
Ad Annum vsque Christi MDCLVI.

Auctore P. FRANCISCO CREVXIO, è Societate IESV.

PARISIIS,
Apud SEBASTIANVM CRAMOISY, Et SEBAST.
MABRE-CRAMOISY, Typographos Regis,
viâ Iacobæâ, sub Ciconijs.

M. DC. LXIV.
CVM PRIVILEGIO REGIS.

Title-page of François Du Creux: History of Canada or New France.
Paris, 1664.

The theatre, which was flourishing in France during this period, had a lively (though almost wholly amateur) existence in the colony. Inspired by the lawyer-poet Marc Lescarbot, the first party of settlers in Acadia entertained themselves with such dramatic presentations as: "The Theatre of Neptune in New France, played on the fields of Port Royal, November 14, 1606, on the return of the Seigneur de Poutrincourt from the land of the Armouchiquois." On the eve of the Conquest, in 1757, Montcalm's *Journal* records that the garrison at Fort Niagara composed and played a comedy, "Le Vieillard Dupé" (The Old Man Duped).

Between these two landmarks, theatricals were more than once the occasion of conflict, sometimes of disorders. Under Frontenac's governorship, in 1693, plays by Corneille and Racine were performed by officers of the garrison; and preparations were made to play Molière's stinging satire of sanctimonious clerical hypocrisy, *Tartufe*. A violent row ensued, the bishop and the Jesuits blasting the governor and all patrons of theatrical iniquity, whereupon the performance was called off.

Formal music was largely in the hands of the Church. Father Amadour Martin (b. 1648) is the first Canadian composer of whom there is record. The gentry and officials at Quebec were entertained on occasion with chamber music. It is reported that the Intendant Raudot organized for the young people (of the "upper class," presumably) "a concert of combined vocal and instrumental music, which provided a delightful harmony."

The people sang the songs of the provinces of old France, altering them in response to the conditions of life in the New World. They also made up songs of their own, some of them satirical and charged with a spirit of revolt. Early in the 18th century the authorities issued a decree "forbidding all persons, and particularly those of Batiscan,

Champlain and Sainte-Anne, to compose, circulate or sing defamatory songs, on pain of extraordinary prosecution and punishment in accord with the exigencies of the case."

Popular festivities—with music, song and dance, punch-and-judy shows and fireworks—were dear to the hearts of the pioneer settlers. Saints' days—and from 1636 on, particularly the eve of St. John's day, June 24 ("la Saint-Jean Baptiste")*— were the occasion for these community celebrations. In them the gaiety of temperament and sociability of the families of New France found lively expression. Too lively, in the opinion of the Jesuits, who "by no means appreciated (*ne goûtaient point*) the popular aspect of these festivals," finding them "vulgar." In 1743 Bishop Pontchartrain decreed the suppression of seventeen calendar feast-days, ordering that they be moved to Sunday. A particular target of ecclesiastical censure were workers' celebrations on the saint's-day of the patron of their trade: St. Eloi of the iron-workers, the shoemakers' St. Crispin, the charcoal-burners' St. Thibault, and others.

(Toward the end of the 18th century and early in the 19th the clerical authorities again took measures to suppress these popular—and potentially "subversive"— festivities.)

One feature of the French and Canadian culture that was developing in New France was its national homogeneity: restrictions on immigration stood in the way of any large admixture of other national cultures than the French. Yet this feature should not be exaggerated. The mingling with the Indian peoples not only produced the Métis (mixed Franco-Indian) of the western fur country; it strongly influenced the culture of the settlers on the St. Lawrence.

---

*In its origin, a primitive feast of sun-worship, around the time of the summer solstice, the longest day in the year.

Moreover, persons of many European nationalities found their way into the colony. Thus, the Carignan regiment (recruited in Savoy) included a number of Italians who later became settlers. There were Italians among the clergy—such as the 17th century Jesuit missionary Bressani.

There were Hungarians also: five Hungarian Jesuits were at Three Rivers in 1719; one, Nandor Konosak, later published in Budapest a detailed study of the Indians. A Hungarian Protestant, Arom Joos, is reported to have been tried in Montreal by the Jesuits in 1757 for "revolutionary activity"; his fate is unknown. Another anti-Jesuit, Istvan Vass, after a stay in Canada, in 1758 published a scathing indictment of the Order in a pamphlet entitled *Autour des Jésuites*.

German miners were brought to work at the St. Maurice forges, and probably also Czechs from the famed Johannestal mining region of Bohemia.

Jews, like Huguenots, were barred from entering New France. Yet there appear to have been one or two Portuguese Jewish families in Montreal early in the 18th century. In 1738 a Jewish girl, Esther Brandeau, arrived by ship at Quebec disguised as a boy. She was arrested and kept prisoner for a year; attempts to convert her to Catholicism having failed, she was deported to France. It was not until after the British Conquest that Jews were able legally to enter Canada.

A few worker-settlers of British and Dutch origin slipped into New France from Albany. In 1660 there is mention of the presence at Montreal of two Irish workers, a Fleming and a Dutchman.

There were a few Negro slaves in the colony: but the greater number of house-slaves were Indians taken in the Ohio-Illinois country.*

*See Chapter XXVII on Slavery in Canada.

Thus, there were representatives of not a few nationalities within the community of New France: but they were proportionately far less numerous than in the Atlantic colonies. Large-scale immigration of various national groups came only after the Conquest.

The spoken language of New France was the French of the 17th and 18th centuries. The modern French language was then still in the process of crystallizing and was far from having established itself throughout France as a uniform speech of the nation. (French, instead of Latin, was adopted as the language used in French official documents only four years after Cartier sailed up the St. Lawrence.) The regional differences of speech in the score or so of provinces from which the settlers came blended in the common language of the colony. A few Indian words found a place in this Canadian French.

Thus it was neither a "patois" (speech of a village or small rural district) nor the "purest 17th century French." It was a regional French, in the process of living development; it acquired a measure of uniformity in the colony earlier than was the case in France. It was above all a spoken language. The French language in Canada had the salty flavor of the provinces, and bore the imprint of the character of the working people of France.

The decorative arts in New France were first and foremost handmaidens of the Church. Painting, sculpture in wood, gold and silver-smiths' work, embroidery, weaving, all served to make resplendent the interiors of church and monastery, seminary and nunnery. But there was also some portrait painting: most notably by Claude François, the Recollet "Frère Luc," who had studied in France under the great master Poussin and was the first professional painter to work in New France. His portraits of Jean Talon and Bishop Laval are outstanding. Although his stay in the colony was very brief (1670-1), his work exerted lasting influence. One of his religious paintings, of the "Holy Family" ("Sainte Famille à la Huronne") depicts in addition to the traditional figures that of a young Indian girl with a glimpse of the rock of Quebec in the background.

In rare instances the everyday life of working people was portrayed: as in the painting (1740) attributed to the soldier-painter Paul Beaucourt, of a logger trapped beneath a fallen tree while his dog runs off in search of help; and others by the same artist, of seamen shipwrecked in the St. Lawrence, and of men who had lost their way being rescued from the cold and snows of a stark forest. These were "votive" works, offered to the Church in thanksgiving for the subject's life having been saved.

Wood sculpture developed from the mid-17th century onward as an important Canadian art-form. Most of the work was done in white pine. Many of the sculptors were originally carpenters or cabinet-makers who developed their skills to the level of fine art. Jacques Leblond and Denis Mallet taught sculpture at the St. Joachim school around the turn of the century. Four members of the Levasseur family of carpenters and wood sculptors did outstanding work during the 18th century. Flanders-born Gilles Bolvin at Three Rivers was another leading sculptor of the period.

The stonemason Jean Maillou (1668-1753), born in the colony, became Royal Architect of New France. He was one of many French and Canadian craftsmen who built manor houses, homes and churches that came to have a distinctive character: an adaptation of French tradition to North American conditions. Medieval French folk architecture evolved into a new, Canadian style in the low, massive, steep-roofed farm cottage and its enlarged version, the manor house or the city mansion (e.g. the Château de Ramezay in Montreal). The same character emerged in the early Quebec churches, blended with the baroque: severe exteriors and—in dramatic contrast—interiors dazzling and resplendent with ornate decoration. (This baroque style was characteristic of the Catholic Counter-Reformation; the Jesuits are credited with inspiring it.)

The growth of capitalist trade and industry in the 17th and 18th centuries in Europe brought with it a broad advance in several fields of natural science. Newton's law of gravity, Harvey's discovery of circulation of the blood, Buffon's work as a naturalist, Réaumur's discoveries in physics: these are just a few examples of the work then being done to enlarge man's knowledge of the real nature of the world. Together with gains in science there grew up elements of a scientific-materialist world outlook. Pierre Bayle, Fontenelle and other philosophers challenged the still-dominant mystical-spiritualist outlook that was a carry-over from the Middle Ages. With the work of Diderot, D'Alembert and others on the great Encyclopedia (started in 1751) philosophical materialism made fresh headway in its struggle against obscurantism.

New France, despite the firm grip of clerical reaction on its institutions, was not wholly untouched by the progress of science and advanced ideas.

Michel Sarrazin (1659-1735), came to Quebec from Burgundy as an army surgeon in 1691; in addition to strenuous work in combating the numerous epidemics that swept through the colony, he made a thoroughgoing study of the plant and animal life of the St. Lawrence region. His work in classifying large numbers of plants led to one group of them being named after him. In 1699 he was named a corresponding member of the French Academy

ENCYCLOPEDIE,

OU

DICTIONNAIRE RAISONNE
DES SCIENCES,
DES ARTS ET DES MÉTIERS,

PAR UNE SOCIÉTÉ DE GENS DE LETTRES.

Mis en ordre & publié par M. *DIDEROT*, de l'Académie Royale des Sciences & des Belles-Lettres de Prusse ; & quant à la PARTIE MATHÉMATIQUE, par M. *D'ALEMBERT*, de l'Académie Royale des Sciences de Paris, de celle de Prusse, & de la Société Royale de Londres.

Tantùm series juncturaque pollet,
Tantùm de medio sumptis accedit honoris! HORAT.

TOME PREMIER.

A PARIS,

Chez
BRIASSON, *rue Saint Jacques, à la Science.*
DAVID l'aîné, *rue Saint Jacques, à la Plume d'or.*
LE BRETON, *Imprimeur ordinaire du Roy, rue de la Harpe.*
DURAND, *rue Saint Jacques, à Saint Landry, & au Griffon.*

M. DCC. LI.
AVEC APPROBATION ET PRIVILEGE DU ROY.

Title-page of Vol. I of the great Encyclopedia of Diderot and D'Alembert (1751).

of Sciences, founded by Colbert. (Newton was made a member the same year.)

Sarrazin sent the Royal Botanical Gardens in Paris many specimens of plants; of one, he wrote: "There grows here a plant that is thought to be the *ginseng* of Tartary or China, which the Indians have found . . ." and he suggested that his correspondent should obtain "some dried roots to rejuvenate you if you are aged, or to well sustain your youth if you are so lucky as to still be young."

The annals of the Academy for 1704 contained a remarkably detailed and accurate study by Sarrazin of the anatomy and life-habits of the Canadian beaver. Later, he made similar studies of the musk-rat, the North American badger and the porcupine. (He began research on the skunk, but complained that "it stinks execrably, enough to cause the abandonment of an entire county.")

Sarrazin was in regular correspondence with the physicist Réaumur at the Academy and was acquainted with the astronomer and man of letters, Fontenelle. Réaumur esteemed highly the conscientious, painstaking methods of his correspondent at Quebec —"one of those observers who may well grasp things that have been missed by great masters in matters they have dealt with."

Although he carried a heavy load of work at the Quebec hospital, and was for a time a member of the governor's council, he found himself unable to afford the scientific instruments needed for research. In one letter to Paris he refers to the work of looking after 80 patients who had just been disembarked, performing a major operation, dissecting a sea-cow (as part of his research as a naturalist), suffering atrocious headaches the while: "Not to mention the trouble the Jesuits will try to make for me, even though I've looked after them gratis for thirty years. . . . However I breathe not a word of it in this country."

Michel Sarrazin, Canada's first scientist, died in 1735 and was buried in the cemetery of the poor. It has been truly said of him that he took his stand in defense of the tradition of "Galileo, Harvey and Descartes . . . [against] all the pedants and impostors justly satirized by Molière."

The Finnish-Swedish botanist, Peter Kalm, who visited Canada some years later, said of Sarrazin: "He was possessed of great knowledge in the practice of physic, anatomy, and other sciences, and very agreeable in his behavior. He died at Quebec of a malignant fever, which had been brought to that place by a ship, and with which he was infected at a hospital, where he visited the sick."

After Sarrazin, the outstanding scientific worker in New France was Jean-François Gaulthier, physician, lawyer and naturalist, named in 1750 a corresponding member of the French Academy of Sciences. Gaulthier instituted the keeping of precise meteorological records, with particular reference to health conditions. He pursued further the study of maple syrup (which Sarrazin had commenced). On the instructions of the governor, La Galissonière (himself a fervent student of the natural sciences), Gaulthier prepared a detailed questionnaire on plant and animal life and mineral resources, which was sent to all commanders of military posts in Canada. The replies and scientific specimens collected were forwarded to Paris.

"It is certain," wrote Gaulthier to a French colleague, "that Canada contains many rarities and things of interest in the field of natural history. It is a wholly new country from which nothing has been drawn as it were, because we have hardly ever had a governor or intendant who would take an interest in this sort of research. The Marquis de la Galissonière is the first to begin to put things on a sound footing." Buffon, with whom Galissonière was acquainted, drew on materials sent from Canada in preparing his master-work, *L'Histoire Naturelle,* the first edition of which appeared in 1749.

La Galissonière was one of those members of the aristocracy who came under the influence of the new ideas of the 18th century Enlightenment. He urged the introduction of a printing-press in New France; the official reply was negative, however, "the King not judging it appropriate to undertake the expense of such an establishment."

Peter Kalm on his visit to Canada in 1749 got to know both the governor and Gaulthier (with whom he went out collecting plant specimens). He commented on the questionnaire, which was also submitted to "learned men who travelled in the country," and remarked: "I have found among people of distinction here generally more taste for natural history and letters than in the English colonies, where the sole preoccupation of each seems to be to make a quick fortune, while learning is held in universal contempt."

The influence of the materialist thought of Diderot's *Encyclopédie* did not make itself directly felt in Canada until the latter part of the 18th and the early 19th century. But it may be of interest to note that the article *Colonie* in the Encyclopedia, by the political economist Véron de Forbonnais, developed the critical analysis of colonialism which the essayist Montaigne had first initiated and later the political scientist Montesquieu had amplified. "These colonies being established solely for the utility of the metropolis, it follows that . . . the colonies would be of no more use, if they were able to do without the metropolis; thus it is a very law of nature that the arts and cultivation in a colony must be confined to such and such objects, according to the convenience of the country of domination."

The article on *Canada* (in Vol. VI of the *Encyclopédie*) bears the same critical tone. It opens with these words:

"Canada, that immense territory of North America, bounded on one side by the Ocean and the Mississippi River, has no known limits towards the north, where it merges with those cold lands into which European avarice and curiosity have not yet penetrated."

Referring to the Hurons and Iroquois, it says "generally, the ruling passion of all these peoples is love of liberty."

qu'on donne par jour fur les vaiffeaux por-
tugais , à chaque matelot ·ou homme de
l'équipage.

CANADA , ʼ(*Géogr. Hift.*) cette im-
menfe contrée de l'Amérique feptentrio-
nale , terminée d'un côté par l'Océan & le
fleuve Miffiffipi , n'a·point de bornes con-
nues vers le nord , où elle fe confond avec
ces pays froids où l'avarice & la curiofité
européennes n'ont pas encore pénétré. Québec en eft la capitale. Quoique le *Canada* foit
auffi voifin de l'équateur que le pays que
nous habitons , le froid y eft plus piquant,
& l'hiver plus long que dans les régions
tempérées de l'Europe ; les vaftes forêts
dont cette terre nouvelle eft couverte , les
lacs & les fleuves dont elle eft coupée , &
peut-être l'élévation du terrein , font les
caufes de cette différence de climat , fous
le mêmes paralleles ; au refte le fol eft fertile , & on y a tranfporté avec fuccès plu-
fieurs de nos végétaux , tels que le froment,
& quelques légumes , le cedre , l'acacia,
maintenant l'ornement de nos jardins , le
pelu dont découle une réfine qui fournit le
godron. La tige de ces arbres s'éleve à
une hauteur beaucoup plus confidérable
qu'en Europe. Le commerce des pelleteries
étoit l'objet principal de l'établiffement des
François dans ce pays ; les forêts y font

Beginning of the article on CANADA *in the* Encyclopédie.

Of commerce in New France (which Voltaire had
argued was of scant worth): "The trade in furs was the
principal object of the French in establishing themselves
in this country. . . . It cannot be denied (in spite of Voltaire) that the fur trade, costing little in itself, was a
source of wealth. The Indians bore all the expense of the

hunt, and sold the finest furs for crude tools, which to them were treasures more precious than our luxury fabrics and metals, which are but riches of opinion . . ."

The Encyclopedists and Raynal, author of the *Philosophical and Political History of Trading Companies*, developed a vigorous critique of the colonial system. They did so from the standpoint of the radical wing of the French bourgeoisie: opposition to the feudal-mercantilist trading monopolies, advocacy of freedom of trade. The critique had the limitations of its bourgeois exponents: at times it veered to a position of liberalized, "enlightened" colonialism.

Yet the revolutionary edge of the criticism was not wholly blunted. The Encyclopedists proclaimed the equality of man, therefore they were led to denounce racism. They stood for universal peace, and therefore condemned colonial wars. Raynal warned the crowned heads of Europe: "It is the decree of destiny: either you will renounce colonies, or else they will renounce you."

The radical criticism of the Old Régime was contributing to its deepening crisis. In New France, factors of crisis were at work as well.

Conquest of Canada: (I)

THE PEACE SETTLEMENT OF UTRECHT (1713) LASTED
little more than a quarter of a century; then the struggle
for dominance in Europe and empire in America broke
out afresh.

As in the earlier round of wars, the chief prize in the
New World was the vast treasure-house of enfeebled
Spain. At Utrecht the British had wrested from the French
the monopoly of the trade in Negro slaves, transporting
them from Africa for sale in Spanish America. A slave
bought in Africa for £10 worth of trade goods would fetch
six times that amount in the Spanish Indies. Each year,
the slave ships from Liverpool and other English ports
were crammed with 4,800 slaves: cargoes of suffering, and
of profit. The slave trade opened the door to smuggling
operations in other commodities. When the Spanish
authorities took reprisals against smuggling, the English
traders and ship-owners whipped up a patriotic war-fever.
George II, declaring himself "touched with the many
hardships and injuries sustained by my trading subjects
in America," declared war on Spain in 1739. (The jingo-
ist anthem "Rule, Britannia" made its appearance the following year.)

Warring on Spain, the British were challenging France,
their rival in the race for booty in the Americas.

War with France came in 1744, with a quarrel over the
succession to the Hapsburg throne: a dynastic squabble
masking the contest for trade, colonies, and dominance in
Europe.

In the quarter century of peace both France and England had expanded their trade; and the clash over colonies now embraced India as well as North America. But whereas the growth in British commerce was laying the groundwork for her Industrial Revolution and eventual world leadership as a capitalist power, the French economy was hobbled by a feudal-absolutist structure that was already showing signs of a profound crisis. The two successive wars—that of the Austrian succession (1744-8) and the Seven Years' War (1756-63) — further deepened this crisis.

In North America these wars were phases of one longdrawn struggle. The early military operations centered mainly in two areas: Acadia and the Ohio. The latter was a focal zone of conflict because here the westward line of Anglo-colonial expansion cut across the French line of communication with the Mississippi and Louisiana. The English had already threatened this life-line by building their first fortified post on Lake Ontario—at Oswego in 1727. (The French post, Fort Rouillé, built in 1749 on the present site of the exhibition grounds in Toronto, was intended to counter their rivals' Fort Oswego.) Possession of the Ohio country was crucial for control of the fur trade and for dominant influence over the Indian tribes of the interior. Anglo-American merchants proclaimed that their major war aim consisted in "taking possession of the trade in furs, which is of inestimable value." The American colonists hoped to put an end to the ever-present threat that came from being "surrounded with the encroachments of the French." The latter for their part feared that "to admit the English to the centre of their domains [would] make it easy for them to seize next either Louisiana or Canada."

On each side there were signs of divergence and friction as between the interests of the colonists and those of their imperial metropolis. The French Canadian traders pressed for a policy that became known as *"le système canadien"*: it aimed at harassing the English, undermining their positions in the Ohio area, but avoiding a head-on collision. Versailles, however, imposed a policy of moving towards a showdown; and installed at Quebec a new clique of officials to carry the policy through.

On the English side, the Albany merchants looked to the defeat of their rivals as a means of annexing the whole fur territory of the northwest. But London, the seat of empire and of the Hudson's Bay Company, was not planning any such enlargement of the colonials' trading empire. It was more likely (as later events made plain) to try to exclude them from the interior, once it fell into British hands.

On the Atlantic seaboard military operations opened with a bid by the French to recover Acadia, which had been surrendered at Utrecht. They captured Canso, but failed to take Port Royal. The New England merchants thereupon decided to launch a major operation of their own: to attempt the capture of the great French fortress of Louisbourg on Cape Breton. They raised a volunteer expeditionary force and in May 1745, with the backing of a British naval squadron, moved against the French "Gibraltar of the North."

At the time the attack was launched, the Louisbourg garrison was in a state of open mutiny. Led by a soldier named Dupaquai, the men had rebelled on Dec. 27, 1744 and arrested the governor and the commissary (one François Bigot). The grievances that had driven the troops to revolt were reflected in the demands they set forth, which included: provision of firewood for their unheated, vermin-infested barracks; a stop to the practice of officers withholding the men's pay and robbing them through officer-operated canteens; an end to swindling by the commissary.

When the English attacked in May, the mutiny had still not been quelled; however, the men agreed to fight in defense of the fortress. For the defenders an unfortunate detail was that the cannon-balls sent from France were of the wrong calibre for the fort's guns. The well-informed New Englanders brought along with them a supply of the size required; and after capturing a key French battery across the bay, bombarded Louisbourg into submission.

The fall of the fortress carried with it a double postscript: Bigot, a very smooth operator, made money for himself out of the capitulation by selling to the victors supplies from government stores that were already covered in the terms of the surrender. But the leaders of the mutiny, whose effort to defend the fort had earned them a promise of amnesty, had no sooner returned to France than they were handed over to the executioner.

An attempt to retake the anchor-fortress the next year failed, when a powerful French fleet was wrecked by a storm at sea.

When a peace treaty was signed in 1748 at Aix-la-Chapelle, the New Englanders learned to their fury that London had handed back Louisbourg, their prize, to the French in exchange for a trading post at Madras, in India. In order to redress in some measure the strategic balance in Acadia (as well as to assuage the outraged feeling of the New Englanders) the British in 1749 established a naval and military base in Chebucto Bay: it was given the name of Halifax.

For the rest, the outcome of the war was a draw. Britain extracted from Spain the renewal of the iniquitous slave-trade monopoly. In North America, neither the English nor French colonies were strong enough on their own to decisively defeat the other. Only full-scale involvement of the rival imperial powers could bring about a decision. It was not long in coming.

The new outburst of conflict flared first around the forks of the Ohio. Here, where the Monongahela and Allegheny rivers meet, Virginia merchants and land-speculators of the Ohio Company had set about establishing a fort. The French evicted them and built an outpost of their own: Fort Duquesne. When the Americans tried to capture it, their entire war-party (led by a young officer who was also a shareholder in the Ohio Company—George Washington) was taken prisoner.

In 1755, without a declaration of war, the British launched a major campaign to seize the forks of the Ohio. British red-coats and colonial troops under Gen. Braddock laboriously hauled a ponderous siege train (including naval guns!) across the Alleghenies—only to be ambushed and mowed down by the French, Canadian and Indian forest fighters. The attacking force lost two-thirds of its number, including the commander. Discovered among the booty was Braddock's correspondence, revealing British plans for a thrust toward Lake Champlain.

This new offensive was aimed at the vitals of New France. In command was William Johnston, landowner and chief liaison man of the British with the Six Nations Indians. Early in the campaign his army ambushed and defeated an enemy force strengthened by fresh reinforcements from France, capturing its commander, Baron Dieskau. However, the British proved unable to exploit this victory. Wrangling among the colonial authorities, friction between Britishers and colonials and lack of decisive leadership stalled the planned invasion of Canada: the expedition got no farther than Lake George.

To the eastward, meanwhile, the British took the French fort of Beauséjour on the Chignecto isthmus leading to Nova Scotia. Charged with negotiating a too-easy surrender was a corrupt crony of Bigot's named Vergor. He was later court-martialed but acquitted: unluckily for French rule, as the sequel suggests.

With their base at Halifax now well established and Fort Beauséjour captured, the British were in a position to move once more against Cape Breton and its protecting fortress of Louisbourg. But before doing so they decided to eliminate a possible threat to their rear: the eight thousand or so French Acadian settlers who farmed the fertile marshlands of Annapolis Valley and Minas Basin. The crime of these people was that they sought to remain neutral in a colony held by Britain as a base for war against their former compatriots. Moreover, their rich farmlands were much coveted by New Englanders: as early as 1710 the latter had broached the question as to "whether the said French inhabitants may not be transported out of the province of Nova Scotia, to be replaced by good Protestant subjects." The matter had long remained in suspense; but now, with a new war in the offing, Governor Lawrence of Nova Scotia decided on ruthless action. Early in September, 1755, all the male inhabitants of Grand-Pré, "ten years or older," were summoned to the parish church to be told of "His Majesty's intentions." There, over four hundred of them gathered; and learned that their lands and homes and livestock were confiscated, and that they and their families were to be "transported out of this province." The church doors were locked, and British colonial troops stood guard until the "prisoners" were herded aboard ship. They then rounded up and embarked the women and children before putting the homesteads to the torch. That autumn the British deported some six thousand Acadians, and thousands more in the years that followed. They were dumped, penniless, in various ports along the Atlantic seaboard. Some managed to get to France, whose government, after granting them six sous a day, abandoned them, in the words of one official, to "the most frightful indigence and despair."

A certain number of Acadians made their way to what is now New Brunswick—harried along the coast by British ships and driven up the St. John River.

The tragedy of the Acadians burned deep into the consciousness of the French Canadians on the St. Lawrence, and was not forgotten when later their own survival as a national community was at stake.

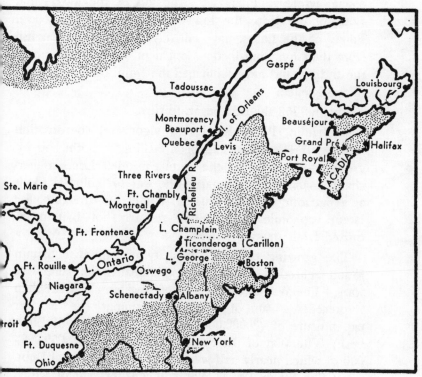

New France and the English Colonies. 1745.

Conquest of Canada: (II)

BRITAIN FORMALLY DECLARED WAR ON FRANCE IN MAY, 1756. That summer a combined force of French regulars, Canadian militia and Indians captured Oswego, taking a large number of prisoners and guns. Next year the French took Fort William Henry, at the head of Lake George. Things looked grim for the British; as one New England official wrote to Pitt: ". . . the loss of the waters and Country of Ohio, the loss of Oswego and the Naval Power of the Lakes, have entirely excluded the English from the Command in the Continent and all Power over the Indians and have confirmed the Dominion of America to the French."

But in 1758 the tide began to turn.

In Britain, Pitt infused new vigor and coordination into a war effort that had been lacking in both; this aggressive spokesman of the empire-minded London merchants managed to dramatize the war for colonial spoils as a patriotic national crusade. Under his direction, the latent economic and military resources of Britain acquired fresh striking power.

The growing economic capacity of capitalist Britain found reflection in soaring expenditures on successive wars. "The War of the League of Augsburg cost the then unprecedented sum of £18,000,000 (compare the total war expenditure of £5,000,000 for the whole reign of Elizabeth). The War of the Spanish Succession cost £50,000,-000 of which nearly half was added to the National Debt. . . . The Seven Years' War cost £82,000,000 of which

£60,000,000 was raised by loans." Of this process A. L. Morton observes, in his *People's History of England*: "The real history of the period . . . can be summed up in three words: accumulation of capital." The National Debt was one instrument of this accumulation; trade expansion, war industry and colonial plunder were others.

These operations built the fortunes of financiers, contractors, industrialists. Underpinning the feverish expansion of war finance was a steady growth of capitalist industry. British miners dug two million tons of coal annually in the early years of the century; by 1750 the figure was close to five million tons. Output of pig iron more than doubled during the second and third quarter of the century. A growing activity of arsenals and shipyards fed the widening maw of an economy periodically primed by war.

The monied and industrial power of Britain was growing at a tempo that her rival across the Channel could not match. The Anglo-American colonies also were developing their trade and manufactures.

New France, on the other hand, found itself in the grip of a long-ripening crisis that was closely connected with the crisis-symptoms of the regime at Versailles. The condition of the colony was marked by widespread hunger and privation among the people, corruption and debauchery among the ruling class. Bigot, the Intendant since 1748, headed an outfit of racketeering monopolists who cornered supplies of flour and other provisions and then sold them at prices inflated six- or seven-fold. Cadet, the commissary-general, at one time pocketed the money for 80,000 army rations that were never issued. Shortages were chronic. "Even in the midst of abundance," one observer remarked, "means have been found to engender frightful famine."

Wrote another: "Trade languishes, the habitant is harassed, but . . . those who have control of business, and their confidants, are making enormous fortunes." After the war ended, a Canadian wrote: "You know, it was tyranny and avarice that caused the downfall of Canada, our country (*notre patrie*)." Montcalm noted in his journal: "Peculation sheds its mask; it no longer knows any limits; . . . one company alone absorbs all internal and external trade, all the substance of a country which it devours: it is gambling away men's lives."

Toward the end, no carts were available for urgent work on the fortifications at Quebec: they were all being used in the building of a private bomb-shelter for Bigot's mistress.*

One winter the food shortage was so acute that Bigot was compelled to sell government provisions cheap: "Otherwise," he reported to Paris, "the people would have risen in revolt." That was in 1752. There was a crop failure in 1756 and again the year following, when "severe famine" was reported, Bigot took steps to reserve supplies of beef for himself and his rich friends, whose extravagant banquets and festivities were continued in the midst of famine. The populace, he decreed, might eat horsemeat. That year there were murmurings among the troops of the Montreal garrison; and at Quebec a mass deputation went to protest to Vaudreuil, the Governor. In the spring of 1758 the inhabitants' food ration was down to two ounces a day. According to one official, "The workers, artisans and day-laborers are so weakened by hunger they are utterly unable to work, and so feeble they can scarcely stand." Again, a protest demonstration

---

*Mme. Péan, wife of a subordinate official who controlled the supply of flour and vegetables. Her husband, it is recorded, consoled himself with the wife of a fellow swindler—until Chevalier de Lévis took her away from him. Such was the "little Versailles" at Quebec.

of women and children "assembled and demanded bread of the heartless intendant, who was not moved thereby in the least."

Small wonder that a prominent churchman in France voiced fears lest "some revolution" might break out in the colony. "In order to appease a discontent which seems to be universal, and ready to explode," Paris had, in 1755, for the first time appointed a Canadian-born governor: Vaudreuil.

The chief effect of the appointment was to emphasize (and sharpen) another crisis-element: the deep-seated and growing friction between the Canadians and French officialdom. The antagonism between Vaudreuil and Montcalm was only its most obvious expression.

Montcalm, the military commander, reproached the Governor with being "always partial, favoring the Canadians as against the French." Vaudreuil countered with the charge that the general "treated the Canadians harshly"; and went on to contrast the sort of defense that might be expected of "expatriate" troops from France with that of men "for whom the Colony is their resource, the site of their possessions, family and fortune." So deep was the cleavage between Canadians and Frenchmen that one of the latter, a lieutenant of Montcalm's, observed: "It would seem as though we belonged to a different, nay even to an enemy nation."

Relationships were not made easier by the attitude of the authorities in Paris. Their threat, in 1755, to "abandon the Colony" if its expenses of administration were not cut, was by no means the first. As far back as 1699, Louis XIV's ministers had warned that "His Majesty may well weary of a colony that costs him immense sums every year": a warning that had been repeated in 1709, 1712, 1727. Expenditures in the war years of the mid-century rose fantastically, helped in generous measure by the operations of Bigot and his accomplices in graft. Yet by and large, France spent less than one tenth as much on defending New France as the British spent on its capture. Voltaire expressed an opinion rather widely held in France when he spoke of Canada as a "wretched country" —"covered with ice eight months in the year, inhabited by barbarians, bears and beaver": in fact, not worth the cost of its defense.

The Canadians thought otherwise, and rallied to hold what they had come to look on as *their country* against the hated invader. Despite recurrent famine, despite corruption and discord in the high command, the Canadians and French braced themselves to face the onset of Pitt's grand offensive.

It opened, in the spring of 1758, with operations on three fronts: Louisbourg, Lake Champlain and the western forts. The Cape Breton fortress, manned by 8,000 men, fell in July, after two months' siege and bombardment by a combined military and naval force that outnumbered the defenders by more than three to one. British sea-power was able to pin the French fleet in home waters and thus prevent it from reinforcing Louisbourg.

In the centre, the French warded off the blow aimed via Lake Champlain. Here Abercrombie, with almost a five to one superiority in numbers, tried to break through Montcalm's position at Ticonderoga (Carillon) with a head-on, steamroller attack. The withering rifle fire of the well-entrenched defenders broke up the assault and the British recoiled, their offensive stalled for the rest of the year. But on the western flank, the British and colonial forces scored a series of successes; they captured Fort Duquesne, then Oswego, then Fort Frontenac itself. Now both the western and eastern bastions of New France were in enemy hands. The interior was cut off; the St. Lawrence gateway stood open to the sea.

In late May, 1759, an awesome British invasion armada of some 200 sail made its way up the river. It bore 8,500 soldiers commanded by Gen. James Wolfe; the naval force, numbering 13,500 seamen, was under Admiral Saunders.

The French failed to dispute the invaders' access to the river-narrows below Quebec, and later bungled an attempt to send fire-ships into the midst of the enemy men-of-war. The British were able to establish a camp on the Island of Orleans, and set up their guns across the river on the Lévis heights, from which they bombarded the city throughout the siege. The British commander-in-chief in North America, Gen. Amherst, had undertaken to launch a fresh offensive via Lake Champlain. He failed to get beyond preliminaries in his sector. Instead of joining forces with the invasion-force on the St. Lawrence, his role was limited to the fact that his army's presence held down part of the French force in the Montreal-Richelieu area.

After landing unopposed east of the Montmorency, Wolfe tried for over a month to find a way of breaking through Montcalm's main defensive works in the Beauport area, between the St. Charles and Montmorency rivers. A major British attack on July 31 suffered a heavy defeat with a loss of over five hundred men. Deadlock ensued, lasting all through August.

Meanwhile, Wolfe's troops ravaged the countryside. "It would give me pleasure," he had written earlier of French raids on the New England settlements, "to see the Canadian vermin sacked and pillaged . . ." Here was his chance, and his men reduced more than 1,400 habitant farms to ashes. The Canadians waged a determined guerrilla warfare of resistance. Wolfe, startled, recorded that "old men of seventy and boys of fifteen take up positions on the fringes of the woods, fire on our detachments, kill and wound our men."

But Quebec remained untaken, and autumn was closing in. Early in September a Council of War was of two minds about raising the siege. It was agreed to make one more attempt, however. Wolfe's brigadiers persuaded him to abandon the Montmorency lines, and try an attack up-river, above Quebec. The spot agreed on, twelve miles west of the city, would enable a landing force to cut Montcalm's supply-line from Montreal, and force him to move out of his entrenched position below Quebec.

Then, almost at the last moment, Wolfe altered the plan. With a recklessness that seemed close to folly, he decided on a night landing and scaling of the precipitous cliff just outside the city itself. This plan, which in the event of failure offered only the most hazardous line of retreat, and called for extraordinary coordination (and good luck) in the night movement of ships and troops, he kept secret till the eleventh hour from his own commanders. They protested at this (and were rebuked); later several of them criticized the desperate character of the gamble on which he had staked everything.

Yet perhaps it was less of an outright gamble than it seemed. On August 31 and again on September 10, Wolfe made reference to information received from French deserters. Gen. Townshend, one of his brigadiers, noted in his diary on the latter date: "By some intelligence the General has had, he has changed his plans as to the place he intended to land; heard we had some deserters from the enemy's camp at Beauport." On the 12th two more came over, "from one of the posts on the heights." They apparently told Wolfe that the Plains of Abraham were practically undefended, with one spot in particular most negligently guarded. This was the spot he picked for the landing and ascent. When the troops (set ashore in the darkness by the ships working in perfectly-timed coordination) scaled the 175-foot cliff they met no serious resistance.

The commander of the small French detachment at the top of the cliff was none other than the creature, racketeer and accomplice of Bigot, the one-time alleged betrayer of Fort Beauséjour: Vergor.*

The back door to Quebec stood open.

By dawn on the morning of September 13, some 4,800 British troops had climbed the cliffs and were drawn up on the Plains of Abraham to the west of Quebec.** The French, taken completely by surprise, were compelled hastily to transfer forces from the Beauport entrenchments on the east, across the St. Charles River, to the opposite (or west) side of the city. Here Montcalm managed to gather a mixed force of about 4,500 French regulars and Canadian militia. To the rear of the British, a couple of hours' march up-river, was a force of about 3,000 men under Bougainville, to whom urgent word was sent to hasten to Quebec. But instead of waiting for these reinforcements, whose arrival could have led to the British being caught between two fires, Montcalm ordered an immediate attack.*** It failed, being broken up by the

---

*Was Vergor in communication with Wolfe? In their six-volume work on the *Siege of Quebec*, Doughty and Parmelee express the opinion: "Of treachery, in connection with the post on the heights of Quebec, there certainly appears to be some reason to suspect Vergor." (Vol. III, p. 90.) There does indeed. But Wolfe was apparently the recipient of the intelligence that is referred to: and what he knew, he carried with him to his death in the battle. C. P. Stacey, in his excellent study: *Quebec, 1759, the Siege and the Battle*, dismisses the imputation against Vergor, for lack of specific evidence. G. Frégault's picture of Vergor, in *Francois Bigot*, leaves one somewhat less favorably disposed. The question-mark remains.

**The actual scene of much of the fighting has been built over. The British line was on or near the present de Salaberry St., the French close to Claire Fontaine St.

***Garneau cites the opinion of one of the French commanders, "that the precipitation with which Montcalm acted ... arose from his jealousies . . . His ambition was that his name alone should outshine all others . . ."

superior fire of the British, and the lack of unity and cohesion between French regulars and Canadian militia.

Vaudreuil, in a desperate appeal, sought to rally what was left of a national effort at resistance: "Finally, it is up to you, brave Canadians, to make your mark—you must try everything and risk everything, to preserve your religion and to save your country." It was chiefly the farmers and town working-people who responded, with an effort to keep up guerilla operations; the bourgeoisie, it is recorded, were busy seeing to their property.

There remained only Montreal, and against it were converging three British armies—from Oswego, Lake Champlain and Quebec. They outnumbered the defenders by about seven to one. Capitulation came on September 9, 1760, on Montreal's Place d'Armes.

New France became occupied territory, its fate to be settled only after three years of negotiations between the imperial powers.

In the bargaining that went on at the conference table it was evident that possession of Canada was only one of many items at stake. The prizes for which the contestants shed their people's blood (as well as other peoples') ranged over three continents, and included: dominance in Europe, mastery of India and of North America, control of the West Indies and access to the Spanish American empire, trade and maritime supremacy.

Britain had captured the French West Indies sugar island of Guadaloupe; whether to keep it or Canada (she could not get both, it seemed) was much debated. The French also were divided as to which should be surrendered. The shipping interests, merchants and bankers of Bordeaux were strong for keeping Canada: they had ten million livres invested in the trade with New France, and it had brought them two million livres a year in profit.

CONQUEST OF CANADA (II)

The bourgeoisie of La Rochelle likewise were loud in their outcry against giving up Canada. But the chamber of commerce of seven other coastal cities spoke up in favor of keeping Guadaloupe. After all, its trade in sugar was worth more than twice what the fur trade brought. Providing that fishing rights could be retained off Newfoundland, Canada could be let go: such was the consensus of opinion of the French merchant bourgeoisie, and Choiseul, the foreign minister, agreed with them.

In England some argued for holding the sugar-islands, but the British West Indies plantation-owners were opposed, fearing a fall in sugar prices if the supply were so suddenly increased. Benjamin Franklin and others in the Thirteen Colonies vehemently urged that Canada be annexed, preferably to the colonies but if not, then at least to the Empire. There were those in London who feared that removal of the French threat from the colonies' flank and rear would encourage unruly thoughts and the urge to independence. One pamphleteer argued, in 1761, that "Great Britain has no better guarantee against the revolt of North America than the presence on this continent of French positions capable of containing the Americans."* At Quebec, Gen. Murray was in favor of yielding Canada: "If we are wise we won't keep it. New England needs a bit to champ on, and we'll give her one to keep her busy by not keeping this country."

The warnings went unheeded. Pitt voiced the prevailing opinion of the bourgeoisie, who saw in the ousting of France from North America the brightest prospect of new markets for British manufactures, and a new base for ex-

---

*The same anonymous pamphlet warned Britain against allowing industry to grow in America "unless she has the intention of transferring her own power thither, and making her dependencies mistress of the world, while she, the poor old mother, becomes their slave." Quite a thought—for 1761.

panding empire. He pointed to Canada as "a country which will increase its power, trade, navigation and indemnify the country for vast expenditures in this war."

On all these grounds, the British ruling class came to the decision: let Guadaloupe go, and keep Canada.

NOTE: "CANADIANS," "FRENCH CANADIANS," "CANADA."

Early accounts occasionally refer to the aboriginal peoples as Canadians. With the establishment of a settled French community in New France, the growing distinction between permanent residents in the colony and "Frenchmen from France" found reflection in use of the term "Canadois," later "Canadiens," to describe those whose home and often birthplace was in Canada. (See pp. 95-6, 122, above; and 131, and passim, *above*.)

With the British Conquest, matters became complicated (and have remained so since, as the debate over the term "Canadian" in the 1961 Census has shown!). For some time after 1759, "Canadians" are the French-speaking inhabitants, as distinct from "British." (Even in 1807 we find the Quebec *Mercury* arguing that "it is evidently in the interest of the Canadians to learn English . . .") The term "French Canadian" only comes into use as the English-speaking settlers slowly begin to consider themselves also as "Canadian."

Hence to use the term "French Canadian" in reference to the settlers of New France would seem out of place. So, "Canadian" is employed —as it was by contemporaries. (Cf. pp. 201-14, 224-28, 280, below.)

Following the British Conquest the territory that had been known as "Canada" received the designation: "Province of Quebec" (1763-1791). Other British possessions in North America were the provinces of New Brunswick, Nova Scotia, Prince Edward Island, the colony of Newfoundland, and Rupert's Land or the Hudson's Bay Company territory.

Simultaneously with the passing of the Constitutional Act of 1791, a measure was adopted replacing the Province of Quebec by two separate provinces, Upper and Lower Canada (corresponding to the southern portions of what were later to be the provinces of Ontario and Quebec).

The Act of Union of 1840 reunited Upper and Lower Canada as the Province of Canada (1840-1867). It was this province that joined with the provinces of New Brunswick and Nova Scotia in the Confederation of 1867, at which time Quebec and Ontario were once more constituted as separate provinces. The new Confederation was designated in the British North America Act as "one Dominion under the name of Canada."

XXIII

Britain's New "Province of Quebec"

THE TRANSFER OF CANADA FROM THE FRENCH COLONIAL empire to the British posed a number of problems.

In the first place: What was to become of the Canadians themselves? Would there be an attempt to "make them over" into English-speaking Protestants? Would they suffer the same fate as the Acadians? (A remark of Gen. Murray's shows this was not excluded from consideration.)

Furthermore: What political and social changes would be engendered by the replacement of France's feudal-absolutist rule by that of a constitutional monarchy? The English bourgeois revolutions had resulted in the British colonies in America possessing parliamentary institutions in one form or another. What was to happen in the newly conquered colony?

It was widely claimed at the time that Britain had warred on France in order to spread what one contemporary described as "the inestimable benefits of political liberty and the Protestant religion." This idyllic view was stated afresh by Parkman with the resounding pronouncement that "England imposed by the sword on reluctant Canada the boon of rational and ordered liberty."*

What "reluctant Canada" got was something a trifle different. It took her people thirty years of struggle to secure the right to an elective assembly; over seventy years

---

*Variants on this theme by such present-day authorities as Burt, Creighton, Lower, McInnis are cited in an article by M. Michel Brunet in the *Canadian Historical Review* (June 1959).

(including a double-barreled uprising) to obtain a government answerable to parliament; and close to a century to get rid of the feudal burdens of seigneurial tenure (to say nothing of the privileged position of the Church in Quebec, which after two centuries is with us yet).

Is this to say that the change-over from French to British rule made no essential difference? Far from it. Three major changes resulted from the Conquest.

First: The existence in Britain of such democratic rights as were won in the 17th century English Revolution made it difficult for the authorities to refuse to their Canadian subjects (both "new" and "old") the right to assemble, petition and conduct political agitation: rights that had not existed in a like degree under the French régime, and which were exercised under the British with increasing vigor.

Second: Capitalist development in Britain (with the Industrial Revolution getting under way there) being much further ahead than was the case in France, the potentialities for economic and industrial growth in the colony were enhanced: as the example of the Atlantic colonies clearly showed.* (At the same time, as this example also indicated, capitalist growth in the colony had to assert itself against the restrictive efforts of the imperial metropolis.)

Third: The British Conquest created a new *national* question in Canada. European rule over the aboriginal

---

*Leading French Canadian historians have recently challenged this. M. Guy Frégault claims that France and England "assumed at approximately the same time a definite capitalist character" and that the bourgeois "upper middle class" held a leading position in New France just as in the English colonies. That capitalism was developing in both empires is undeniable; but the existence of feudal institutions hampered the one, while their elimination (by and large) gave the other free rein for industrial development. It was no accident that the Industrial Revolution occurred first in England, and only much later spread to the Continent.

peoples was the first such problem; now there was added the domination of one European nationality over another. The French Canadians had come under British rule: what would become of this national community, so firmly rooted in the St. Lawrence valley?

The answer to this question was to be affected profoundly by another: that of the relations between the Empire and the Atlantic colonies, which now were heading towards a decisive struggle for their rights and ultimately for independence.

At Quebec, Gen. Murray mused over the fate of the newly-acquired colony: as a matter of policy, he wrote, it "should perhaps be destroyed; but there may be reasons why it should remain, as it is a guarantee for good behavior of its neighboring colonies."

Here is contained, in germ, the subsequent British policy towards Quebec. Its value was to lie above all in its usefulness as a base of operations against insubordination to the south. To secure it for this purpose, there would be concessions—of a rather mixed sort.

First, however, its boundaries were cut down to size. In place of the ill-defined vastness of New France, reaching from Labrador to the Mississippi, the new "Province of Quebec" was delimited as a much smaller area, roughly oblong in shape, along the St. Lawrence. Labrador and Anticosti were attached to Newfoundland: it was expected that the naval force at St. John's would ward off French designs on the fishery.

More serious yet for the economy of Quebec was the severing from it of the entire western fur country: the western boundary of the province ran from Lake Nipissing to the St. Lawrence. The "pays d'en haut"— the Upper Country of the fur traders—was made into a closed reserve, under the control of the imperial authorities. This measure was likewise a blow to the American colonies. It appeared to block their expansion westward, and to hem them in along the seaboard just as New France had done; and it opened up the richest fur territory to the London merchants and their agents, to the disadvantage of American traders who had backed the war against France with every expectation of making the western country a profitable preserve of their own.

Before either could lay hands on it, however, a war of desperate Indian resistance rose to thwart them. Under the leadership of the Ottawa chieftain, Pontiac, there took place in May, 1763, a simultaneous rising of the tribes throughout the western fur country. One after another nine British-held forts on Lakes Erie and Michigan, on the Maumee and Wabash rivers, fell to surprise attack. At Michilimackinac, a lacrosse game between players of two tribes entertained the garrison—until the ball "accidentally" flew over the stockade, the pursuing players dashed in through the gate, took possession of the fort and captured or killed the soldiery.

Detroit was the only fort, west of Niagara, that proved too strong to take; Pontiac's forces besieged it from May until November.

The British command was slow in getting counter-action under way. There was no lack of ruthlessness, however, in their approach to the rising, which menaced the source of fur-trading profits. General Amherst, who earlier had threatened the tribes with punishment "if they do not behave properly," now proposed that blankets infected with smallpox be distributed to the Indian encampments. This fiendish measure of germ warfare was not implemented; it was felt that regular military operations would suffice.

Reinforcements only reached Detroit late in July. When orders came to raise an expeditionary force of three hundred Canadians, the greatest difficulty was encountered—

despite unemployment among the voyageurs at Montreal (the fur trade being at a standstill). After twenty years of it, the Canadians had had enough of war. It took a forced draft to raise even the small detachment that had been ordered.

Pontiac had counted on receiving help from the French, via Louisiana. None came. When he got word in October (1763) of the Peace of Paris, his supplies of ammunition were already running low, and British forces were moving into the interior in strength. Yet guerilla warfare continued for almost two years longer. In the summer of 1764 the Senecas made a separate peace, yielding to the British all land four miles on each side of the Niagara River. A year later Pontiac, "the Indian Spartacus," surrendered. The western fur country was in British hands at last.

During this time, in the "Province of Quebec," the new relationships of British colonial rule were taking shape. From 1760-63 it was a régime of direct military occupation. The royal Proclamation of 1763 (following the Treaty of Paris) continued military rule in modified form with an appointed council assisting the governor. Freedom of trade, the matchless "blessing of British liberty," was proclaimed; but the representative institutions that were expected to accompany it were strangely absent. The Proclamation provided for an elective assembly: but none was forthcoming. Were the promises of "popular liberty," loudly proclaimed during the war with absolutist France, to prove nothing but a hoax? The few hundred English and colonial merchants who had moved into the province on the heels of the British armies were vociferous in their protests.

In 1764 they were circulating leaflets which, in Governor Murray's view, spread "principles of sedition . . . notions of licentiousness under the mask of liberty." From

Quebec and Montreal, delegates went to London to plead for an assembly. There they got backing from the lord mayor, aldermen, M.P.'s and fellow merchants, who in a petition protested that "a military government is entirely incompatible with the spirit and genius of commerce"; and urged the granting of "a civil administration, with a regular house of representatives."*

The Quebec merchants had connections with London mercantile interests, but they were also closely linked with their American counterparts. Most had lived in the Atlantic colonies, and shared their aversion to "taxation without representation." Like their fellow merchants in Boston, those at Quebec refused to pay duties arbitrarily imposed by London.

Both Governor Murray and Carleton, his successor, firmly opposed the demand for an assembly. Fearful of colonial pretensions, hostile to the merchants as a group ("scum of the earth," Murray called them), the military governors allied themselves with the French Canadian seigneurs and upper clergy.

Contrary to a widely-held opinion,** most of the old ruling class stayed on after the Conquest. Those who went back to France were the small handful of top officials, including Bigot and his hangers-on.*** Of some two hundred seigneurs, about 140 remained in Canada.

---

*It must be recorded that there was a "catch" in the democratic protestations of these Protestant merchants: on the basis of the English Test Acts, which denied Catholics the right to vote or hold office, they visualized an "assembly" for themselves alone. At most, they *might* concede the Canadians the vote; but certainly not seats in the assembly!

**Repeated, mistakenly, in my *1837*, p. 31.

***Bigot and his associates—including Vaudreuil—were sent to the Bastille, and the "Canada affair" became a celebrated case in society and in the courts. Vaudreuil was acquitted of complicity in the thieving operations; the arch-culprit Bigot and his cronies were merely sentenced to fines and temporary banishment.

The change wrought by the Conquest was not a "social decapitation" due to an exodus of the seigneurs; it was, rather, the imposing of a new, Anglo-colonial ruling class on the conquered French Canadian nation.

The new rulers were at first made up in the main of the military and administrative officialdom; later on, their ranks were swelled by leading fur-traders and merchant-landowners.

The overriding concern of the British colonial authorities was to make Quebec a bulwark—and if need be a base of operations—against insubordination in the Atlantic colonies. To this end they decided to preserve feudalism and clerical privilege on the St. Lawrence: the best means, in Carleton's view, of securing for all time "a proper subordination of this province to Great Britain."

This policy of preserving intact the laws, customs and religious institutions of the Canadians meant in practice that their language was to be tolerated as well. The idea of any speedy anglicizing program had to be postponed.

Thus, on the one hand, the "new subjects" could thank the Atlantic colonists for the fact that the latter's rebellious pressure led London to make concessions to French Canadian national identity. On the other, they could blame the collaboration of seigneurs and clergy with the conquerors for the preservation of tithes and feudal burdens and absolutist rule, and the denial of democratic government.

As early as 1761, Murray was insisting on payment of seigneurial dues in hard cash. A few years later London decreed the granting of land on the basis of feudal tenure. For their part, the seigneurs strongly opposed the granting of elective institutions: the habitants, once given the vote, might get the upper hand in an Assembly! Already, there had been signs of popular opposition to the continuance of feudal impositions. At Chambly in 1762 it was reported "that several inhabitants of the place refuse to work on the king's road"— the hated *corvée* of enforced, unpaid labor. There were other incidents of refusal by habitants to carry out transport duties as demanded by the military. But the hatred of feudal oppression did no more than smoulder in the early years of the occupation; it flared up later, during the American Revolution.

The "Province of Quebec," established by the Proclamation of 1763, had yet to acquire a regular constitution. The authorities in London were under pressure from the merchants to grant elective institutions; they were under stronger pressure to refuse them. The arguments of Carleton, the seigneurs and the clergy gained ever-increasing weight as the tide of insubordination rose in the colonies to the south. True, in 1767 London toyed with the idea of granting an assembly of sorts, in which the French Canadians would get *one quarter* of the seats, with only seigneurs to qualify as representatives; and this proposal was embodied in the instructions to the governor the year following. But Carleton chose to ignore the instruction, and London did not press the point. Soon after, he went to London and took a leading part in drafting the Quebec Act of 1774. This measure simply carried forward and codified the terms of the class alliance that Murray and Carleton had forged: an alliance between the rulers of Britain and the old ruling element in Canada—the seigneurs and the representatives of the Vatican.

To make palatable an alien rule, Carleton urged recognition of the national identity of the Canadians: "Barring catastrophe shocking to think of, this country must, to the end of time, be peopled by the Canadian race . . ." Further, to secure their allegiance, representatives of the French Canadian ruling class should be accorded some share in the administration of the colony: "As long as Canadians are deprived of all places of trust and profit, they never can forget they no longer are under the dominion of their natural sovereign; . . . this . . . affects the minds of all, from a national spirit which (resents) the general exclusion of their countrymen."

Under the Quebec Act, feudal tenure and church tithes were to remain in force; French civil and English criminal law were to be in effect; habeas corpus was denied, as well as elective institutions.

In language that became rather worn with use by later British colonialists, Lord North told Parliament:"As soon as the Canadians shall be in a condition to receive an assembly, it will be right they should have one. They will naturally wish to get the government into their own hands. Though I would give the Canadians their laws; though I would give them their religion; I do not think it would be wise, at present, to give them an assembly."

In the non-elective council established by the Act to advise the governor, eight seats out of 22 were accorded to Canadians, all but one of them seigneurs.

The Quebec Act embodied Carleton's policy of making the new colony serve as a base of operations against revolution in the others to the south. He saw Canada as "the provincial scene, where the fate of America may be determined"; and as early as 1767 had urged that a series of fortified positions be built to link New York and Quebec, via the Hudson (later the scene of some of the decisive fighting of the revolutionary war). He was also worried lest France should support the Thirteen Colonies "in their independent notions," and seek to regain Canada.*

---

*Prof. A. L. Burt rejects both the idea that the Quebec Act was aimed against the rebellious colonies and that its drafters were influenced by fear of France's interfering in the quarrel. He does so on

The meaning of the Act was made clear by its framers: Lord North referred in the debate on it to the "very disorderly and ungovernable condition" of the Atlantic colonies. It was equally well understood by the opposition at Westminster and in America. One British parliamentarian said: "The measure carries in its breast something that squints and looks dangerous to the inhabitants of our other colonies." Its aim, wrote a Londoner, was to "hold the old colonies in terror." Pitt called it "a most cruel, oppressive and odious measure, tearing up justice and every good principle by the roots." To install clerical power and privilege at Quebec, said Samuel Adams in Boston, meant enthroning "the whore of Babylon."

The Anglo-American merchants at Quebec and Montreal joined in condemnation of the measure. When London in the autumn of 1774 set in motion the series of punitive measures that accompanied the Quebec Act—suspending the constitution of Massachusetts and ordering the closing of the port of Boston—the Quebec merchants sent Boston a gift of a thousand bushels of wheat, and those of Montreal sent funds. By the following spring, committees of correspondence in Montreal and Quebec were in regular touch with those in Boston, New York and Albany. This "subversive activity" evoked from the Attorney-General in London the comment that "sedition and treason, like tobacco and potatoes [are] the peculiar growth of the American soil."

When the First Continental Congress assembled in Philadelphia in September 1774 it registered a vehement

---

the curious ground that "there is too much to be said for both" of them. In his view the Americans' opinions of the Act were nothing more than "wild visions": their "imagination was . . . disordered by their own resistance to imperial measures." So speak the apologists of Anglo-American imperialist unity, out to purge the past of any suggestion of fundamental conflict. (*The Old Province of Quebec*, p. 155; and *U.S., Great Britain & British N. America*, in the Carnegie Foundation series on Relations of Canada and the U.S.)

protest against the Quebec Act, and adopted a Message to the Canadian People. This document explained the nature of democratic government, which the imperial authorities had refused to accord to Quebec: the "first grand right" of a British constitution, the Message stated, was to have "a share in their own government by their representatives chosen by themselves." It cited the French democratic philosopher Montesquieu on popular liberty; and as an argument in favor of Quebec entering a confederation with the American colonies, pointed to the example of the Swiss cantons, some of them Protestant, others Catholic, united in a federal state.

Two thousand copies of the Message were printed in French in Philadelphia by Fleury Mesplet (who later brought his printing press to Montreal and established the *Gazette*).* But even before they could be smuggled into Quebec, a correspondent of the time records that "handwritten copies . . . have been circulated among the French bourgeois"— explaining that at Quebec "our printer dare not publish anything of this nature."

The Message was widely circulated in Quebec: merchants who went out to the farms to "buy wheat" left copies of the appeal of Congress. The new ideas it contained made a deep impression. The animated discussions it evoked marked the awakening of a lively political consciousness among the habitants: a feature that this and subsequent struggles engraved in their national character. Among the active Canadian agitators in the countryside were such men as Clément Gosselin, Germain Dionne, Pierre Ayotte. With the exception of a few professional men, the partisans of Congress "were recruited from outside the governing classes."

---

*It is interesting to note that a German edition also appeared in Philadelphia in 1774, under the title: "Ein Schreiben an die Einwohner der Provinz Quebec."

XXIV

The American War for Independence

IN APRIL, 1775, THE GUNFIRE AT LEXINGTON AND CONCORD signalled the outbreak of the revolutionary war.* Almost from the start, Canada was involved. Spurred by the need to obtain arms, a border force led by Ethan Allen and Benedict Arnold on May 10 took Ticonderoga in a surprise attack and moved briefly against St. Johns. Congress at first was hesitant about authorizing an invasion of Canada: but after the battle at Bunker Hill (June 17) it decided to go ahead. Noting that at Quebec was to be found "the greatest store of munitions ever assembled in America," George Washington argued that it would be "folly not to do all possible to capture it." Canada in British hands was too serious a threat to the rebelling colonies: a second Message to the Canadians emphasized that not they, but the British forces of occupation were the enemy.

The effectiveness of the Quebec Act was now put to the test. The clergy proved to be, as Carleton had intended, "the most precious royalist agent." In May, a month before the Governor declared martial law, the Bishop of Quebec issued a mandate promising papal indulgences for all who should take up arms against the American rebels, and threatening refusal of the sacrament and even

---

*In his "Letter to American Workers" (1918) V. I. Lenin wrote: "The history of contemporary, civilized America opens with one of those great, truly liberating, truly revolutionary wars, of which there have been so few among the vast number of wars of plunder caused, like the present imperialist war, by squabbles among kings, land-owners, capitalists, over the partition of captured lands or plundered profits. That was a war of the American people against English pillagers who oppressed and held America in colonial enslavement..."

excommunication for those who refused to do so. The seigneurs, for their part, set about acting as recruiting agents for the British authorities.

The masses of the Canadians reacted to all this in a manner that shocked and startled their rulers. Parish after parish—Berthier, Joliette, St. Michel, St. Thomas— protested against clerical intervention. The business of the bishop, declared one resolution, was "to make priests": this was a conflict that "had nothing to do with religion." Hatred of the church tithe, reimposed by the Quebec Act, lent an edge to the opposition: and the bishop's subsidy of £200 from London was lampooned in ribald ballads. The mass resentment displayed in this crisis was the first expression of an opposition to clerical interference in political matters that later became an important part of the democratic tradition of the French Canadian people.

The attempts of the seigneurs to recruit volunteers for the British service met with an even more vehement rebuff. Asked to raise a force of 6,000 men, Carleton could not muster 300. At Berthier a roadside meeting of habitants took an oath not to take arms against the American colonists, nor to fight "to defend a pack of rascally pensioners of the Crown." At Terrebonne they defied the seigneur; another seigneur fled to Montreal to escape the wrath of his tenants. In some instances the repeal of the Quebec Act was demanded as a condition of support to the authorities.

In many parishes the women carried on an active agitation. A British commission which conducted an investigation throughout the parishes after the American withdrawal included in its report items such as these:

"St. Pierre, Isle d'Orleans: . . . The wife of Augustin Chabot . . . going everywhere from house to house, perverted by her seditious speeches almost all the habitants; it appears that this woman has a most eloquent tongue and according to several persons made a profound impression on their minds."

"Pointe-aux-Trembles: . . . The wives of Joseph and Jean Goulet went from door to door to blacken the names of those who last autumn urged the young fellows to march (with the British) . . . claiming that they were being led to the slaughter . . ."

From Montreal troops had to be sent to restore "order" in such "indocile parishes" as St. Martin, Ste. Rose, Vaudreuil. The farmers of the Richelieu valley in particular were strong in their sympathies with the revolution: six parishes there, with a muster roll of 1500 men capable of bearing arms, repudiated all allegiance to the British Crown. The merchants at Montreal refused to enrol in the militia; at Quebec they held illegal "town meetings."

As Carleton saw it, the trouble with the Canadians was that they had "imbibed" too freely of "the American spirit of Licentiousness and Independence." The feudal upper classes had shown themselves to be powerless. He was forced to appeal for large-scale help from London.

It was not until August that Congress gave its orders for a two-pronged move on Canada—via the well-trodden Richelieu route in the west and the ill-cleared, little known Kennebec-Chaudière trail in the east. Montgomery commanded the former, Arnold the latter operation.

Montgomery's advance on Montreal was held up for two months by the resistance of Carleton's main force of regulars at St. Johns. The capture of this fort by the Americans in November opened the gateway to Montreal. The inhabitants greeted the revolutionary army, declaring in an address that they accepted "the union offered by our brothers of the colonies," on the basis of "the same laws and prerogatives, proportional contribution, sincere union and permanent peace."

Carleton, escaping from Montreal just as the Americans were arriving, hastened downstream to organize the defense of Quebec. Arnold's men, after an exhausting trek through the bush, over a route never used by a large force, were laying siege to the town. They were soon joined by the force under Montgomery from Montreal. Cramahé, the Governor's deputy, reported that "the Rebels being in Force, have upon their side the Canadian Peasants, whom neither the zealous exertions of the Gentry, Clergy or Bourgeoisie could prevail upon to do their duty." Carleton moved to secure his position within the walls by expelling every one of 170 families suspected of sympathy with the rebels.

In the night of Dec. 31, under cover of a blizzard, the besiegers attempted to storm the Lower Town. The operation failed, and cost the life of Montgomery as well as of a large number of the attacking troops. Under Arnold, the siege continued, despite sickness, shortage of supplies and ammunition, until the spring. When, on May 6, a British fleet arrived with a powerful body of reinforcements under Gen. Burgoyne, the siege could be maintained no longer. Arnold withdrew his men to the Richelieu and thence southward.

The invasion of Canada had failed.

Militarily, one important cause of failure at Quebec was the lack of siege artillery and supplies for an operation conducted at a vast distance from the main base of operations in Massachusetts; another was British naval superiority, which forced the raising of the siege.

But the fundamental causes lay deeper.

True, there was widespread anti-feudal agitation and strong sympathy with the American revolt; yet something was lacking. No general uprising took place on the St. Lawrence. Quebec was far from being at the same advanced stage of social and economic development as the

Atlantic colonies: capitalist manufacture scarcely existed there. The main issue on which the Canadians *might* have risen in alliance with the Americans was that of national independence from alien rule. But the American colonies themselves had not yet taken a stand for outright independence. Their Declaration of Independence was adopted only *after* the invasion of Canada had failed. "If this declaration had been made nine months earlier," ruefully commented the revolutionary democrat Samuel Adams, "Canada would be ours today."

The fact is that due to the influence of the ruling propertied classes in the colonies, the war was not yet being waged in a revolutionary way. Their hesitations were reflected in the failure to combine a political offensive with the military one. Commissioners sent by Congress in November 1775 to assure the Canadians that their religious and other rights would be safeguarded,* and to organize the holding of elections in liberated territory, ventured no farther than Ticonderoga. Another, which included Benjamin Franklin, came to Montreal in May of '76; but its pledge that "the government of everything relative to their religion and clergy shall be left entirely in the hands of the good people of the province"— was given only on the eve of the evacuation of Montreal, when Arnold was in full retreat from Quebec.

These weaknesses in the political conduct of the revolutionary war made it easier for the British and their clerical helpers to neutralize important sections of the population who, while ready to assist the American troops in various ways, were not prepared to join them in military operations. (At no time were more than 500 Canadians enrolled for service with Congress.) This attitude

---

*The simultaneous violent denunciations by Congress of the Roman Catholic Church can hardly have reassured the French Canadians, however.

was reinforced by French Canadian distrust of the English merchants, among whom were some of the most active supporters of Congress; by the feeling that the quarrel was simply one between two groups of Englishmen, colonial and imperial, both of whom had been traditionally hated enemies of the French in Canada; and by resentment at the widespread pillaging to which the ill-supplied American forces resorted in the latter stages of their campaigning and retreat.

The arrival of Burgoyne's army at Quebec led the masses of Canadians to adopt an attitude of neutrality. As one of his officers sized up the situation in the summer of '76: "The clergy and better class of people are strongly attached to the government; as to the body of the inhabitants, they seemed to wish to remain neuter, or at any rate to join with the strongest side."

From Canada Burgoyne's army drove south, taking Ticonderoga and moving to link up with an army under Howe, based at New York. But Howe, instead of moving north, marched off in the opposite direction; and Burgoyne found himself bogged down and then surrounded at Saratoga. Here for the first time a revolutionary militia force took prisoner a whole army of European regulars.

In a military sense, this first major defeat of the British in the war vindicated the revolutionaries' invasion of Canada: by drawing Burgoyne's large expeditionary force to the St. Lawrence, they diverted it from the crucial New York-Philadelphia theatre, where it might have struck Washington's army a decisive blow.

It was the victory at Saratoga that decided Louis XVI's ministers to enter into an open alliance with the Americans against the British. Even before Bunker Hill, French volunteers had crossed the Atlantic to lend assistance to the fighters for colonial independence. But until 1778, it was official French policy to do the utmost to weaken

Britain, without becoming embroiled in open war. Now
the prospects looked more favorable: alliance with Congress could—in the event of military victory—both cancel
out some of the losses of 1763, and enable France to capture the rich trade of the American colonies, formerly
monopolized by Britain.

True, there were serious risks for feudal absolutist
France in aiding and abetting a revolutionary power. The
French ambassador in London had warned his government: "Such is the situation of Europe that she has no
less to fear from a revolution in England's colonies than
has England herself." His successor assured the British
that "all Europe is deeply interested in ensuring that
there should not be in America a new, flourishing, free
and independent government likely to encourage ideas of
liberty." When, despite these assurances, the alliance
was proclaimed, one French aristocrat warned lest it lead
to "the creation, perhaps, of a country vaster than our
own, and one which might, one day, subjugate Europe."
But neither ruling class fears of revolutionary contagion
nor anxieties about eventual American might were enough
to outweigh considerations of imperial rivalry. First
France, then Spain, joined forces with the Americans; and
their combined naval power outweighed that of the
British. This, together with military aid on land and a
large subsidy, was of decisive importance in helping to
turn the scales in favor of the Americans.*

The entry of France into the war caused the British
rulers of Canada considerable anxiety. Gen. Haldimand,
on succeeding Carleton in the military command, report-

---

*"In their difficult war of liberation the American people entered
into an 'agreement' with certain exploiters against others, in the interests of weakening oppressors and strengthening those waging a revolutionary struggle against oppression, in the interests of the *masses* of
the oppressed. The American people utilized the division among the
French, Spanish and English . . ." (Lenin).

ed "an inconceivable change in the minds of the Canadians": the clergy, it seemed, were growing lukewarm, the seigneurs less grateful for their blessings; should a French force enter Canada, the habitants, he thought, "most likely would take up arms against us."

Had he but known it, his fears were in scant danger of being put to the test, True, there were forces in Congress and in the north-eastern states that pressed repeatedly for a new invasion attempt; and Lafayette was actually named to head it. "The idea of a revolution in Canada holds charm for every good Frenchman," he wrote; it offered the opportunity "to restore freedom to our oppressed brothers while regaining the fur trade, Indian commerce, and all the profits of our erstwhile establishments.'"

But the expedition never got started. Not only was George Washington against it so long as English troops still held New York and other points in the colonies; but France as well secretly opposed any attempt at a conquest of Canada. Louis XVI's ministers felt that Britain's retention of the colony would act as a curb on American ambition: "Canada remaining in the power of England," wrote Louis XVI's first minister Vergennes, "that frontier alone would suffice to keep up anxiety in the colonies . . . " An ever-present threat from Canada would both cause the Americans to lean more heavily on the alliance with France, and keep them at loggerheads with London.

So there was no second invasion of Canada. The French forces (which played a major part in the final crushing British defeat at Yorktown in 1781) never approached the boundary of Quebec. Their sole operation in the northern half of the continent was a brief naval expedition to Hudson Bay in 1782, which raided and burned Forts Churchill and York. At the peace negotiations in 1782-3 the French continued the policy of playing their enemies against their allies, siding with the British on a number of points, and giving no support to American demands that Canada and Nova Scotia be accorded the status of independent republics. The British, for their part, sought to detach the Americans from the French by making large concessions to them in matters of trade and the fixing of boundaries.

XXV

The Maritimes and the Revolutionary War

THE COURSE OF EVENTS IN NOVA SCOTIA DURING THE revolutionary war was quite different from that followed in Quebec.

No large-scale effort was made by Congress to oust the British from the "fourteenth colony." But in two of its outlying areas the inhabitants themselves raised the banners of revolt, only to meet with defeat.

Unlike Quebec, Nova Scotia possessed an assembly, won in 1758 chiefly by the pressure of the inhabitants of Halifax, in the teeth of stubborn opposition by Governor Lawrence. Following the conclusion of the Seven Years' War large numbers of New Englanders, taking over the lands of the expelled Acadians, had settled in the province; they numbered some 14,000, or two thirds at least of its population. The traditions of local self-government they had brought with them were not appreciated by the colonial officialdom. Thus in 1770 the governor and his executive denounced "the proceedings of the people in calling town meetings for discussing questions relative to law and government." Such gatherings they held to be "contrary to law," and threatened prosecution if they were persisted in.

Some years earlier, when the Stamp Act was passed, Henry, the printer of the Halifax *Gazette,* had joined in the protest against the Stamp Act, and a demonstration took place on Citadel Hill. (In reprisal, Henry lost his contract and his apprentice, Isaiah Thomas, suffered banishment.)

Halifax, as a major military and naval base, was a strongpoint of imperial authority; and its leading merchants and officials, waxing rich on government contracts, were firmly tied to the imperial interest. But they had scant confidence in the attachment of the mass of the people to their cause. When the revolutionary war began, they decided not to call up the militia —"in view of the sentiments of the people of many of the settlements."*

The admiral commanding the North Atlantic Squadron at Halifax in October 1775 reported his fear of strikes among the dockyard workers, in the event of an invasion of the province by the revolutionary forces. The latter, he wrote, "would be sure of Assistance not only from the Town and Country people but even from the Artificers of the Yard . . . It is indeed a very serious Consideration that those employed in the King's Yard are so intimately connected with the Rebels that barely by not working they might throw us into many difficulties."

Sizing up the situation in the province, delegates from Nova Scotia who had gathered at Machias on the Maine border in the summer of 1775 judged that military aid would be needed to back any move that they might undertake. From Congress came promises of arms and assistance; but George Washington, engaged in the siege of Boston, pleaded insufficiency of available ammunition. Further, he raised a larger question of policy: noting that the province, while not adhering to the cause of Congress, showed no signs of resorting to hostilities against it, he observed: "To attack it therefore is a measure of conquest rather than defense, and may be attended with very dangerous consequences."

---

*The chronicler adds: "Where so large a proportion of the people was disloyal, great zeal and much energy were required to preserve Nova Scotia to the Empire." (Hannay, *History of New Brunswick*, pp. 98, 107).

No large-scale help, then, was forthcoming from the colonies to the south. But radical-democratic forces nonetheless took the path of rebellion in two areas of the province: on the St. John River* and the Chignecto peninsula. In the former district, in May of '76, the settlers gathered at Maugerville and by a vote of 125 to 13 declared their solidarity with the people of Massachusetts, and their readiness "to share with them . . . the present struggle for liberty." Apart from a small quantity of ammunition, they received no further aid from Massachusetts; yet the insurgents on the St. John held firm to their position of independence for the better part of a year. It took the arrival of the British warship *Vulture* the following summer to restore imperial authority by a show of superior force.

A larger outbreak occurred in the same period on the Chignecto peninsula.** In June of '76 a force of 200 British regulars had been sent to occupy Fort Cumberland (formerly Beauséjour): and a move was set on foot by inhabitants of the area to capture the fort for the revolution. A revolutionary committee was organized to direct operations, recruit reinforcements from other centres, and maintain liaison with the Massachusetts Congress. Its leaders were John Allan, Jonathan Eddy, Sam Rogers, Zebulon Rowe and Obadiah Ayer. In addition to the Cumberland area, men were recruited from Machias and Passamaquoddy, Maugerville and Sackville; they included a number of Acadians, who were in "wholehearted sympathy" with a stroke for independence, and some Indians. On November 12 they tried to take Fort Cumberland by

---

*The area that later became New Brunswick (1784) was at this time still part of the province of Nova Scotia.

**An article on this episode by W. B. Kerr in the *Canadian Defense Quarterly*, vol. XIII, is entitled "The American Invasion of Nova Scotia"; yet the author himself concedes (p. 434) that "the affair was rather an insurrection than an invasion."

storm, but were repulsed. For a fortnight thereafter there
was sporadic fighting. The fort's commander, though dis-
posing of a regular force at least as large as that of the
untrained and ill-armed besiegers, dared not risk a sortie,
but sent to Halifax for help. The commanding general
there despatched a body of marines and infantry to rescue
him; but in answer to an appeal for 100 mililitamen to
join the expedition, not one volunteer was forthcoming.

With the arrival of the contingent from Halifax the
insurgents faced overwhelming odds; yet they stood their
ground and fought until overwhelmed. With extreme difficulty they made their way southwestward through the
forest country to the St. John River, which they reached
only at the end of December.

The military defeat at Cumberland resulted from lack
of artillery and naval support. The rebelling American
colonies—lacking an effective navy—were not in a position
to intervene in strength; thus British naval superiority
proved decisive in holding the province in the period of
the emergency.

The relationship of forces changed, however, once
France and Spain came into the war on the side of Congress. Franklin then urged the French to move against
Halifax and St. John's, Newfoundland; but despite the
opportunities that offered—the main British fleet being
tied down elsewhere—the French fleet busied itself in the
Caribbean. Versailles feared that northern operations
might lead to involvement in a campaign for Canada,
which Congress was urging; and this ran counter to the
calculated Franco-Spanish policy of curbing the spread of
the revolution beyond the bounds of the Thirteen Colonies.

So nothing further developed in the Maritime-New-
foundland area, except a continuation of the inconclusive
sea-raiding operations that were started earlier by Ameri-

can privateers. They had raided Prince Edward Island in
'75, attacked Canso and Yarmouth in '76. English fishing
vessels were hunted down on the Grand Banks; and in
1778-9 there were raids on Placentia, Bay Bulls and other
settlements on the Newfoundland and Labrador coasts.
This type of warfare, compounding the ancient rivalry between Newfoundlanders and New Englanders, made it
certain that the former would go on siding with the
British in the contest with Congress.*

---

*In Newfoundland ". . . The republicans were few and scattered,
the loyalists were in an overwhelming majority; there were four or
five men-of-war always on the coast, a strong garrison, and at least ten
thousand sturdy West Countrymen." (Prowse, *History of Newfoundland*, p. 338).

XXVI

Canada and the American Revolution. Lower Canada and the French Revolution

In their "grand design" for crushing the American Revolution the British authorities had counted on strong support from Quebec as well as Nova Scotia. In this they were disappointed. Both Maritimers and French Canadians displayed reluctance to serve as imperial catspaws. Thereby, however indirectly, they were a factor in the outcome of the contest. Herbert Aptheker, in *The American Revolution*, comments on the fact that Carleton's attempt to raise a large force in Quebec encountered vigorous resistance. "Had this not been so, had instead several thousand Canadian men joined Burgoyne and fought . . . it is hard to see what the American forces would have been able to do to prevent the junction of Clinton and Burgoyne." Thus by their attitude at a crucial point in the conflict the Canadians helped frustrate the imperial policy. "To a considerable extent," writes Aptheker, "it was [the Canadians'] courageous refusal so to be used that defeated the policy and helped save the American Revolution."*

The revolutionary war established the national independence of the United States. It left in British hands the colonies of Quebec, Nova Scotia, Newfoundland. In none of them were the social forces developed that could offer a direct challenge to imperial rule.

Yet the impact of the American Revolution on British North America was immense.

---

*"Canadians," here in the sense of French Canadians. See Note, p. 198.

In the first place, it led to the introduction of elective institutions in Quebec: the institutions that the British Conquest had seemed to promise and then denied. In the areas taken over by the revolutionary army in 1775 the Canadians had begun for the first time to elect their own militia officers.

The popular agitation, the widespread opposition to enrolment in the British forces, the signing of petitions, all stimulated "the tendency of the lower classes to rally to the idea of freer government, tending to the establishment of a legislative assembly." For its part, Westminster was acutely aware of the ferment that was at work.

In 1785 the English Secretary of State wrote Pitt that "The Province of Quebec in its present situation is a dominion of very precarious tenure to Great Britain." In October, 1789, the Colonial Secretary outlined to Carleton (now Lord Dorchester) the plan of a new constitution for Quebec, *including an assembly*. It was sound policy, he argued, "to make these Concessions at a time when they may be received as a matter of favor, and when it is in Our own power to regulate and direct the manner of applying them, rather than to wait till they shall be extorted from us . . ."

The democratic pressure for an assembly in Quebec acquired added weight from an unexpected source. The leaders of the Loyalist migration were wealthy counter-revolutionaries to whom the very word "democracy" was an abomination. Yet even they were accustomed to representative institutions (however hedged about with qualifications of property and royal prerogatives); and the mass of their followers were by no means disposed to put up with the kind of modified military dictatorship that was in operation at Quebec.

Thus the Loyalist migration, while it represented primarily a transfusion of conservatism, buttressing the colonial officialdom, at the same time brought with it the makings of a contrary tendency.

A further major consequence of British defeat in the revolutionary war was the way it modified the national composition of the population in British North America.

Thanks to the Loyalist influx, Nova Scotia and New Brunswick (established in 1784 as a separate province) received an additional 30,000 inhabitants; another 10,000, moving into the upper St. Lawrence and lower Great Lakes regions, joined Pennsylvania German and other American pioneers in what is now southern Ontario. This migration changed fundamentally the national character of the then "Province of Quebec"; and laid the groundwork for the establishment in central Canada of two national communities. The English-speaking Maritimes and predominantly French Quebec, retained by Britain, already constituted a bi-national colonial community. Its extension westward, as a result of the Loyalist migration, both created the need and laid the basis for an eventual federation. The creation of "Upper" and "Lower Canada" in 1791 was one stage in this process.

In 1791, thirty years after the Conquest, the British parliament enacted the Constitutional Act, providing the people of Upper and Lower Canada with their first elective assemblies. (The Nova Scotians had secured theirs in 1758.)

The winning of representative, elective institutions in British North America was in the first place the fruit of stubborn struggles by the people of those provinces. Their democratic strivings were lent further strength by the traditions of the English Revolution of the 17th century, and by the inspiration of the American and French revolutions of the 18th.

When the Constitutional Act was proclaimed, in 1791, banquets to celebrate the winning of an elective assembly were held in Quebec's Upper and Lower Town. The toasts that were drunk at the celebration in the Lower Town have been recorded: they bear witness to the democratic and national sentiment of the participants, both "old" and "new" subjects (English and French Canadian). They included:

"The Revolution in France and true liberty throughout the world; abolition of the feudal system; may the distinction between old and new subjects be consigned to oblivion, and the name of Canadian subjects endure for ever (a toast drunk with wild enthusiasm: thrice acclaimed, thrice repeated, all joining hands); let liberty extend as far as Hudson Bay; may today's event strike a mortal blow at prejudices that are contrary to civil and religious freedom and to trade."

Such were the high hopes that accompanied the introduction of parliamentary government in the Canadas. Their fulfilment was another matter. The new constitution concealed a deep-seated contradiction, rooted in the relationships of colonial rule.

While the territory of the old Province of Quebec was divided, by a separate order-in-council, into the two provinces of Upper and Lower Canada (corresponding to present-day southern Ontario and Quebec)—the main change wrought by the Constitutional Act of 1791 was in the structure of government. It amended the Quebec Act to provide each of the provinces with an elective assembly.

At first sight, the Canadian colonists appeared to have obtained—with relative ease—the parliamentary rights won in hard battle by the British people in the bourgeois revolution of a century and a half before. As Lieut. Governor Simcoe told the members of the first Upper Canadian Assembly, they were to enjoy "the very image and transcript of the Constitution of Great Britain."

It was a bit of an overstatement. For the Canadian provinces were still *colonies*. Over their assemblies, granted as a concession to popular pressure, were set non-elective officials: an appointive Legislative and Executive Council, Lieutenant-Governor and Governor-General. These were answerable, not to the elected representatives in the colony, but to the British government overseas. Any divergence between Canadian interest and imperial policy would inevitably lead to a collision. Durham, a half century later, marveled at the illogical mixture of "representative and irresponsible government." But it was logical enough in the eyes of Pitt and his associates (who had just embarked on a similar experiment in their oldest colony, Ireland). In the words of the law officers of the Crown, it was out of the question for a colonial assembly to claim for itself the attributes of Parliament: to grant such a claim would be "to give subordinate bodies the mighty power of supremacy."

From the outset, the Canadians showed signs of challenging this imperial attitude. The Lower Canada Assembly asserted its full right to "the freedom of speech and generally all the like privileges and liberties as are enjoyed by the Commons of Great Britain." In Upper Canada, the Assembly at its second session successfully upheld the right of its members to freedom from arrest in civil cases.

However, the full unfolding of the conflict over the rights of colonial parliaments came only later. The first sharp struggles arose over a related issue: that of the national rights of the French Canadians. The Act of 1791, while preserving the old concessions accorded by the Quebec Act to feudal and clerical interests, at the same time emphasized afresh the implied recognition of French Canadian national identity. It did this by providing for an assembly in a province with a predominantly French-speaking population; in Pitt's words, "In Lower Canada, as the residents are chiefly Canadians, their assembly, etc., will be adapted to their peculiar customs and prejudices."

Creating Lower Canada and giving it an assembly, he argued, was "the best means of conciliating the French inhabitants, as they would, by this measure, be made sensible that there was no intention to force British laws upon them." At the same time he openly expressed the hope that this would in the long run lead to the complete anglicizing of the French Canadians. Its effect was just the opposite. Parliamentary struggles raised issues involving national rights. Attacks upon the latter soon led to encroachments on the rights of the elected representatives. Democratic and national struggles became one.

The first Assembly of Lower Canada had thirty-four French-speaking and sixteen English-speaking members. Considering that the English-speaking population was no more than a fifteenth of the total in the province, and that they did not comprise the majority in any constituency, their share of representation was more than equitable. Yet when it came to the election of a Speaker, the English members, headed by a group of leading merchants, vehemently contested the right of the French-speaking majority to elect one of their number to the post. They were over-ruled; but shortly thereafter a similar conflict arose over the use of French equally with English as an official language. In practice, the majority got their way; but in law, English remained the sole official language for the next half-century.

The creation of an Assembly provided a new arena of struggle, a new means of educating and drawing the people into political action. It was not long before grievances arising from colonial rule called forth struggles on a broader scale, outside the Assembly; and in this development the influence of the great French Revolution played its part.

During the summer of 1793 in Philadelphia a young Canadian, Henri Mézières, met with Citizen Genêt, the first envoy of revolutionary France. Together they drafted an eight-page pamphlet entitled: "Free Frenchmen to their Brothers the Canadians." It was a call to struggle for liberty and independence. It charged that London had accorded Canada no more than "a shadow of a constitution," and even that only out of fear lest the Canadians follow the example of France and America in "founding its government on the inalienable rights of man" . . . "This land is yours. It must be independent." . . . "The hour is propitious, and Insurrection is for you the most sacred of duties." The pamphlet closed with a "Summary of the Advantages the Canadians can obtain by freeing themselves from English domination"; they included:

"1. Canada will be a free and independent State.

2. It can ally itself with France and the United States.

3. The Canadians will choose their own Government, themselves naming the members of the legislative body and of the executive power . . ."

Other points were: abolition of the *corvée* and all other seigneurial rights; no privileged company to dominate the fur trade; no hereditary titles; freedom of worship, the priests to be chosen by the people and the tithe abolished; "Schools to be established in the parishes and towns. There will be print-shops, and institutions for the higher sciences, medicine, mathematics . . ."

This pamphlet, circulated in Lower Canada in both printed and hand-written copies, aroused intense interest. Read and discussed in clandestine meetings at Montreal and Quebec, and sometimes openly on market squares and at church doors, it came to be humorously called "the Catechism."

The influence of the French Revolution merged with and added fire to struggles that were born of bitter grievances in Canada itself. The "Catechism" listed them correctly. In 1794 the introduction of a new Militia Act, and in 1796 new measures to impose the *corvée* on French Canadian farmers, were met with violent resistance. Riots and demonstrations took place in the districts of Quebec and Montreal. At Charlesbourg, just north of Quebec City, over three hundred inhabitants massed to prevent the call-up by lot of men for the militia. They elected their own leaders "in the name of the public, which is above the law." Armed with muskets, pitchforks, flails, they pledged agreement "to defend ourselves, and let no one be taken from our villages." Two of the leaders, Pierre Chartré and Jérôme Bédard, were arrested and imprisoned.

Hoping to stamp out the widespread agitation, the old alliance of imperial officialdom and the clergy went into action. Warned the Bishop of Quebec: "The astonishing agitation into which the revolution in France has thrown the minds of the peoples, renders more necessary the unison of the empire and the priesthood." For his part, Dorchester put into operation the repressive Alien and Sedition Acts (which were being employed in England against those who supported the cause of the French Revolution), and began to make widespread arrests. In Montreal an armed attempt was made to set free political prisoners taken under the repressive Acts. On the Place d'Armes a prisoner was seized from the hands of the sheriff. At Quebec, riots broke out in the St. Roch district and across the river at Lévis. In 1797 the authorities arrested and sentenced to death for treason a leader in the agitation, David McLean. He was hanged, then beheaded and disembowelled, in a public spectacle intended to terrorize opposition.

Contrary to a well-established myth, French Canada was not cut off from all outside contact and influence in the period of the French Revolution. Not only was the tide of Canadian popular struggle at the time strongly affected by the mighty storm in the old motherland; but the ideas of revolutionary France entered into the quickening stream of democratic and radical thinking in Lower Canada.

Mézières, co-author of the French revolutionary government's appeal to the Canadians, was a student of the French materialist *Encyclopédie*. The ideas of the Encyclopedists, Diderot, D'Alembert, Voltaire, were widespread among the intellectuals and professionals who were leaders in the Canadian democratic movement.

In 1791, following the arrest of three Canadians who refused to serve in the militia, a pamphlet in French was printed in Three Rivers under the title: *The Northern Bastille or the three oppressed British subjects*. In style and argument its denunciation of arbitrary persecution and its appeal to the tribunal of public opinion bore the clear imprint of the influence of Voltaire's celebrated *Treatise On Tolerance*.

In 1792 the Bishop of Quebec complained bitterly to Rome of the "prodigious quantity of evil books" coming into the country, encouraging "a spirit of philosophy and indifference." A couple of years later he speaks of their "flooding the country, causing ravages even among Catholics." Another clerical writer reported later: "Around 1800 there was much unbelief in the country, and the evil books of Voltaire were, I believe, widely circulated." The bishop rounded up all the copies he could lay hands on and had them burned on the public square in Quebec.

By 1799 the mass movement had subsided; although there were still indications two years later of activity in Montreal by a secret revolutionary group.

XXVII

Indian and Negro Slavery. The Theft
of Indian Lands

THE KEEPING OF CAPTIVES TAKEN IN WAR AS SLAVES IN-
stead of adopting them into the victor's tribal family was
an occasional occurrence among the Indians of northeastern North America. It remained for the European
merchants, fur-traders and officials to turn the practice of
slavery into an established institution. They were unable
to introduce into Canada the plantation system of slave
labor such as flourished in the West Indies or in Virginia:
the character of the fur-trading economy and the relationships of feudal agriculture stood in the way of attempts
in that direction. But ownership of house-slaves was widespread among the wealthier families of New France.

Among the members of DeMonts' expedition to Port
Royal in 1606 was a Negro slave: possibly it was Mathieu
D'Acosta, whose ownership was the subject of a law-suit at
one time in Rouen.*

The sale of a young Negro was recorded at Quebec in
1629: Louis, a native of Madagascar, was purchased for
50 *écus* by one Le Bailly from David Kirke, the English
commander who that year took Quebec.

In 1688 the question was raised at Quebec of obtaining the king's permission "to have in this country Negro or
other slaves, as has been allowed in the Islands" [West

---

*He acted as an interpreter for the French among the Acadian
Indians. It is suggested that he may have learned the Micmac lan-
guage while in the service of Portuguese fishing-masters. (M. Bishop,
Champlain, p. 98).

Indies]. This, it was argued, "would be the best way to succeed in all manner of manufactures."

A royal decree of the following year authorized the possession of African slaves in New France. But this was something of a luxury. More common was ownership of a *Pani* or Indian slave (from the name Pawnee: many were bought by traders in the Ohio country). An ordinance of Intendant Raudot in 1709 decreed "that all Panis and Negroes who have been purchased, or shall be hereafter, shall belong in full property as slaves to those who have purchased them."

A decade later his successor Bégon was arguing that large-scale employment of slave labor was the reason for the prosperity of the West Indies. "If there were Negroes," he urged, "the establishment of the Colony would soon expand, the habitants would no longer have to find day-laborers for hire . . ."

However, this "solution" for the difficulties of New France was not practicable. Slavery was limited in the main to domestic servants. These, however, represented a large enough investment to warrant coverage in the conditions of surrender of New France. Number 47 of the Articles of Capitulation signed at Montreal in 1760 read: "Negroes and Panis of both sexes shall retain their status as slaves in the possession of the French and Canadians to whom they belong; these shall be free to keep them in their service in the Colony or to sell them."

Some indication of the number of Indian slaves in Montreal at that time is provided by the fact that they accounted for one-tenth of all burials registered there in 1761.

The prevalence of slave-ownership among the Anglo-Canadian merchants is reflected in numerous advertisements in the English-language press during the 1760's.

Thus, at Quebec in 1765 John McCord offered a reward of $4 for the capture of a runaway Negro slave. The *Quebec Gazette* two years later carried an advertisement for the sale of "some Negroes, of both sexes, chair, saddle and work-horses, with oxen, cows, sheep, etc." Another advertisement, in 1768 announced: "TO BE SOLD, a very healthy Negro Girl, about Eleven Years of Age . . ."

Following the American War, many of the well-to-do Loyalists brought Negro house-slaves with them to Canada. A census of 1784 reported that there were 304 slaves in the province, of whom 212 were in the Montreal district and 88 in the Quebec City area. In Upper Canada in 1791 there were said to be some 300 Negro slaves in the Niagara district. In New Brunswick it has been estimated that the greater part of the 441 "servants" of the wealthy Loyalists (listed in 1784) were in fact Negro slaves. A New Brunswick historian says of the institution of slave ownership: "The sentiments of the people were not in its favor."

At the time of the founding of Halifax (1749) the English had brought slaves to Nova Scotia. The trade in slaves was actively pursued there for the next half century. A Boston paper in 1751 carried the notice: "Just arrived from Halifax to be sold, ten strong hearty Negro men, mostly tradesmen, such as caulkers, carpenters, sailmakers and rope-makers." Male slaves in 1770 were selling at about £30, women at £20; ten years later the price appears to have doubled. Records of sale and rewards for capture of runaways occur in these years at Windsor, Annapolis and Falmouth, Nova Scotia.

According to Haliburton "there were a number of free Negroes, who emigrated to the Country, at the conclusion of the American Revolutionary War." They had been promised grants of land, but the promise proved deceptive: it was not "strictly fulfilled," as Haliburton puts it. So wretched was their condition that when in 1787 the colony of Sierra Leone was established in West Africa (partly as a result of anti-slavery agitation and partly as a missionary and commercial enterprise), many Nova Scotia Negroes applied for removal thither. Close to 1200 were shipped from Halifax, 65 of whom perished during the passage.

Shortly thereafter, a large group of "the insurgent Negroes of Jamaica" arrived in Nova Scotia. These were the survivors of the awe-inspiring struggle waged in the mountains of Jamaica by hundreds of escaped slaves. Known as the "Maroons," their forefathers had taken to the mountains following the English conquest of the island from Spain in 1655. For a century and a half, they had conducted an intermittent guerrilla warfare against the white plantation owners. A quarter of a million pounds sterling was spent on efforts to suppress them. Entire regiments of regular troops, using bloodhounds, were sent against them; yet the Maroons kept up their heroic resistance. Finally, in 1795 they were driven to surrender: a condition of their capitulation being that they be permitted to remain in Jamaica. As soon as they laid down their arms the British government broke its promise and deported 600 of them to Nova Scotia.

Some of the deportees were employed on the construction of the Halifax Citadel (the "Maroon Bastion erected by their efforts, remains as a monument of their active industry," writes Haliburton). Most of them were removed to the township of Preston, where during two severe winters they suffered bitter privation, ill-sheltered and lacking firewood or adequate food supplies. In 1800 a number of the Maroons were shipped to Sierra Leone; others remained in the province, later to be joined by Negro refugees from the slave-owning Southern States.

Opposition to the institution of slavery was widespread among the people of Canada and the Maritimes. It was re-inforced, in the business community, by hard-headed considerations of profit. Wrote Haliburton: "Independent . . . of political and moral considerations, such a system is by no means suitable to a Colony like Nova Scotia, where there are few branches of business requiring a regular body of laborers, and where their clothing and provision is attended with so much expense."

Similar considerations entered into the thinking of legislators in the first assemblies of Lower and Upper Canada. Panet in 1793 introduced a "Bill for the Abolition of Slavery in Lower Canada," but opposition from slave-owners blocked its passage. However, a series of court decisions in the years 1797-1803 undermined in effect the legal right to possession of slaves. These decisions were vigorously protested in a petition circulated by certain citizens of Montreal who stated that they "have purchased at great cost a considerable number of Pani and Negro slaves . . . the which . . . have become refractory through a spirit of disobedience with which they are imbued, under the pretext that no slavery exists in this country." The last public sale of a slave took place in Montreal in 1797; he was sold for £36, but the courts annulled the transaction.

In Upper Canada in 1793 the Assembly passed a measure "to prevent the further introduction of slaves and to limit the contract for servitude within this Province." Governor Simcoe reported "the greatest resistance . . . to the Slave Bill, many plausible arguments being brought forward in respect to the dearness of labor and the difficulty of obtaining servants."

Its preamble read: "Whereas it is unjust that a people who enjoy freedom by law should encourage the introduction of slaves, and whereas it is highly expedient to abolish slavery in the Province so far as the same may gradually be done without violating private property, be it enacted . . . in order to prevent the continuation of slavery within this Province" children born of slaves should be supported until they reached the age of twenty-five years, when each should be entitled to discharge from further service, while "any issue born of such children shall be entitled to all rights and privileges of free-born subjects."

How slow was the process envisaged by the Act may be seen from the fact that in 1806 the Hon. Peter Russell, a member of the ruling officialdom, was advertising for sale "a black woman named Peggy, aged 40 years, and her son named Jupiter, aged about 15 years"— for $150 and $200 respectively.

In Nova Scotia and New Brunswick, the legal basis of slave ownership was gradually removed by court decisions. In 1808 slave-owners at Halifax demanded legislation "securing them their property or indemnifying them for its loss": in response the Assembly passed a Bill to Regulate Negro servants, but it was never officially proclaimed.

The iniquitous institution of slavery was thus in effect in French and English Canada for at least two centuries. The stain of it is not so much to be measured by the extent of its application in the economy, as by its fostering of the bestial prejudices of "white chauvinism" and deep-rooted delusions of racist superiority.

Following the close of the Seven Years' War in 1763 the British by a royal proclamation closed the Ohio country to European settlement—in order to further the interests of imperial trade. "Let the savages enjoy their deserts in quiet," ordered the Lords Commissioners. "Were they driven from their forests the peltry trade would decrease." The Treaty of Fort Stanwyx in 1768 solemnly pledged that the lands northwest of the Ohio River should remain in Indian hands.

As long as the British needed Indian help in successive wars against the French and the Americans, they pretended to deal with them as sovereign, independent peoples. "It was British policy," states one authority, "to acknowledge the Indian title to his vast and idle domain, and to treat for it with as much gravity as if with a sovereign power."

At the same time as they were negotiating with them as "allies," the British rulers were passing legislation that treated the Indians as subject peoples. Sir William Johnson, agent of the British among the Six Nations Indians, observed in his official correspondence that the latter would be "startled" should they learn that at Westminster they counted as "subjects." For they held themselves to be "Allies and Friends, and such we may make them at a reasonable expense, and thereby occupy our outposts and carry on a trade in safety, until in a few years we shall become so formidable throughout the country as to be able to protect ourselves and abate of that charge . . ."

The duplicity is unmistakable, and shameless.

Involved was a twofold trickery. The Indians were led to believe that their status as equals and allies was being given recognition; and that the lands of which the treaties guaranteed them possession were indeed theirs. It assuredly never occurred to them that what was ceded to them by treaty was at one and the same time, "in law," vested in the Crown—and hence "not really theirs at all."*
To the British rulers, the treaty rights to land were no more than "a sort of precarious title," something existing "merely as a policy"— in other words, as an expedient deception.

---

*This only began to become clear long afterward; to this day, the Indian people cling to their lawful Treaty rights, and assert in Canadian courts their status as allies, not subjects, of the Crown: as in the Six Nations' case, in April 1959.

Once the war with the American colonies was ended, the British—who had relied on and been aided by the support of Indian allies—secretly and behind their backs surrendered to the United States the lands pledged to the Indians at Fort Stanwyx. When the Indians found out (despite an unblushing British effort to fool them into thinking that no such betrayal had occurred) they protested bitterly:

"The King surely would not pretend to give the Americans that which was not his to give; and would not believe the Americans would accept that which the King had not the power to give. They [the Indians] were allies of the King, not subjects, and would not submit to such treatment . . . They would look for favors from neither [side], nor would they be aggressors, but would defend their own. If England had done so, it was an act of cruelty and injustice and capable only of Christians." So ran the words of protest of the Mohawk chief, Thayendanegea—Joseph Brant. To appease the protests, the British accorded his people of the Six Nations Confederacy the land lying six miles on each side of the Grand River, which empties into Lake Erie.*

It was not long before a swarm of land-sharks got their teeth in it. Playing on Brant's last hope of securing some measure of financial security for his People of the Long

---

*While fighting to retain possession of their lands, the Indians upheld at the same time their right to political independence. Joseph Brant in the 1780's had succeeded in organizing a far-flung coalition of the Six Nations and nine of the western tribes, in defense of the lands west of the Ohio; this development "produced a profound sensation in Congress." An act was passed authorizing the negotiation of treaties with the Indians; when tested in the U.S. courts, it was upheld, and an Indian tribe was declared to be "a state, and uniformly treated as such since the settlement of the country" . . . and to be "a distinct political society." (This did not save the Indians in the U.S. from being dispossessed and decimated in the century that followed. Its interest lies in the recording of recognition of nationhood.)

House, they filched from them all but a fifteenth of the original grant.

How precarious was the Indians' title to their lands (according to British law of land-tenure) is shown by the following:

When, long after Brant's death, his son was elected in 1832 to the Upper Canada Assembly, his election was declared null and void on the ground that the settlers who elected him held leases obtained from the elder Brant, and "the courts had decided that the title in fee simple (i.e., outright ownership) was not held by the Indians."

The "opening up" and settlement of Upper Canada was carried through by a massive expropriation and eviction of the Indian peoples dwelling there.

To cite only the example of the Missisauga (an Ojibwa people):

On Dec. 7, 1792, in exchange for a promise of £1,180 in annuity-money, the Missisauga tribe surrendered to the British some three million acres of land, embracing the counties of Norfolk, Haldimand, Brant and Wentworth, and portions of six others.

On Aug. 1, 1805, they yielded "a portion of York County"— 250,850 acres of it—for the sum of ten shillings.

History, dead-pan, records that "large portions of Upper Canada were thus relieved of the burden of the Indian title," the lands being "sold for their benefit"! The fact of the matter is that the Indians were dispossessed of their lands by a colossal operation of fraud, misrepresentation and legalized theft.

XXVIII

Rise of the North West Company

WITH THE CONQUEST, BRITAIN HAD GAINED POSSESSION of the rich North American fur empire of the French. But instead of the Hudson's Bay Company taking it over (as might have been expected), something quite different happened. A swarm of "free traders"— Scots, English and American merchants who had moved into Montreal on the heels of the British army—set about organizing "ventures" of their own. With such capital as they brought with them, and some backing from business connections in London or Albany, they quickly took over the Canadian trading machinery and labor force.

Alexander Henry (from Albany) at Michilimackinac in 1761, James Finlay on the Saskatchewan a few years later, moved into the old French trading posts and made contact with the western Indian tribes. To begin with, they made use of Canadian traders, men like Cadotte, Blondeau and others. "The French having acquired a thorough knowledge of the trade of the Northwest countries, they were employed on that account after the reduction of Canada, by the English traders there, in the establishment of this trade with which they were themselves quite unacquainted." Thus wrote Jonathan Carver, who was at Grand Portage in 1767. The French Canadian "partners" were for the most part soon elbowed aside; but as guides, interpreters and canoemen, their compatriots made up the main body of employees of the newly established English-speaking merchants.

Before the Conquest, La Vérendrye and the other traders of New France had challenged the Hudson's Bay Company's claim to possession of the vast northwest territory, drained by the rivers flowing to the Bay. Now the challenge was renewed, but this time by British-Canadians. At first, complacently relying on the legal bulwarks of their ancient charter, the London monopolists were content to sneer at the "pedlars from Canada." The company factors, secure in their posts on the rim of the Bay, waited each spring, as was their custom, for the Indian trappers and hunters to bring in their harvest of pelts. Meanwhile the more enterprising "pedlars" were reaching out to capture the supply at its source, deep in the interior. By 1772 the men on the Bay were complaining to London that the trade at their posts was "greatly diminished"; the Indians, "who are the Support of it, being intercepted by the Canadian Pedlars who are yearly Gaining fresh Influence over them."

The Company began to bestir itself. In 1769 it had sent young Samuel Hearne to explore northwest of the Bay. Guided by the Chipewyan, Matonabee, he crossed the Barren Grounds, reaching the Coppermine River and the Arctic Ocean; turning south, they got as far as Great Slave Lake; then made their way eastward, back to Fort Churchill. The hope that this expedition might result in drawing the Copper Indians to the Hudson Bay trading posts did not materialize. But in 1774 Hearne was sent south, to establish the Company's first important trading post in the interior, at Cumberland House on the Saskatchewan. Others were added soon after at Brandon and near the present Prince Albert.

It was not long before the Montreal fur-trading interests began to combine their efforts and merge their resources in order to compete more effectively with their London rivals. The first such merger took place in 1775 on the Saskatchewan. James McGill, the Frobisher brothers and, later, Alexander Henry, decided to pool their stock of provisions and trade goods, in order "when the season was over, to divide the skins and meat." Henry had found his fellow traders "in a state of extreme reciprocal hostility, each pursuing his interests in such a manner as might most injure his neighbors." Such is "free enterprise." But combination had its advantages: "This arrangement," says Henry, "was beneficial to the merchants, but not directly so to the Indians, who, having no other place to resort to, nearer than Hudson's Bay, or Cumberland House, paid greater prices than if a competition had existed." Thus was launched the forerunner of the first Anglo-Canadian monopoly.

From the start, monopoly meant higher profits for the merchants and more ruthless exploitation of the native trappers. "Taught by experience," wrote one of the Frobishers some years later, "that separate Interests were the Bane of that Trade, we lost no time to form . . . a Company." This was the famous North West Company, which had its beginning in 1775 on the Prairie, and was consolidated in 1779 and 1784 by agreements in Montreal. The merchants Simon McTavish and the Frobishers acquired a dominant position in it by 1787.

Formation of the North West Company did not, of course, eliminate all competition. Fierce struggles with other groups of traders ensued, greed for fur profits resulting on more than one occasion in the murder of competitors. (The trader Peter Pond was implicated in two such cases.) A rival concern, the XY Company, put up a stiff fight before it was finally absorbed by the Nor'Westers in 1804.

For more than a decade after the American War of Independence, Montreal traders continued to operate in the rich fur country of the upper Mississippi, Michigan and Wisconsin, where the British retained hold of their forts until 1796. By a sort of agreement on "spheres of influence," the Nor'Westers concentrated on the country to the north and west, while a rival Montreal group (McGill, Forsyth, Richardson) operated from Michilimackinac, exploiting the tribes of the southwest. The latter was the richer area; but British withdrawal from the posts in American territory opened the way to the advance of U.S. traders, headed by John Jacob Astor, and the Montrealers were finally ousted. (For a time a joint U.S.-Canadian enterprise was in operation, but the war in 1812 put an end to it.)

Dominant in what is now the Canadian West was the North West Company; it had its advance base first at Grand Portage then, after 1803, at Fort William—the surveying of the international boundary having revealed that the old post was on the wrong side of the line.

The structure of the North West Company was that of an association of partnerships: it was never actually incorporated. The profits of each year's trading venture were distributed among the partners, no reserve of capital being built up. (This set-up later proved a source of fatal weakness in the struggle with the Hudson's Bay Co.) There were cases of partners retiring in affluence on the proceeds of two or even one year's trading.

Since the associates were required to contribute only trade goods and not cash capital, a key position was held by those appointed to deal with the London supply houses and to manage the credit and banking transactions of the firm. It was this role that enabled the Frobishers and McTavish (and later his nephew, William McGillivray) to constitute themselves in effect the management of the North West Company.

The labor from which this first Canadian monopoly drew its fabulous profits was primarily that of the native Indian tribes of the northwest. Their hunters and trappers tracked down the beaver, otter, mink, marten and fox; the women scraped and prepared the pelts and, with their children, carried the burdens on the long trek to the trading posts. In the 1780's it was estimated that the annual shipment of beaver to England totalled more than 100,000 pelts. Often, wrote the trader and explorer Alexander Mackenzie, they suffered "intolerable fatigue" and "innumerable hardships, and were sometimes even starved to death." The Plains Indians, hunting the buffalo and making the pemmican on which the Company's whole trading and transport system in the West depended, bartered this "pounded meat and grease . . . for liquor, tobacco, powder, balls, knives, awls, brass rings, brass wire, blue beads and other trinkets" (Alexander Henry). "Their friendship and cooperation," a Company statement noted, "is necessary to the support of the trade . . . *They alone supply all the food on which the company's servants subsist;* without which they would be compelled to abandon three fourths of the country, and all the valuable part of the trade."

Reduced to dependence for their survival on European trade goods, the tribes were not only fleeced by the Company, but also were incited to fratricidal strife. "The Indians with whom we trade," reported Joseph Frobisher, "are frequently at war with distant nations to the Westward which the Traders generally encourage, because on their return they come over a vast tract of country and bring with them large quantities of fine furs . . ."

Rarely were the tribes able to offer any effective resistance to their exploiters. There was one instance in 1780 when a band in the Eagle Hills north of the Saskatchewan revolted and attacked the traders, putting them to flight.

(This act of resistance was the sequel to a trader's poison-
ing an Indian with laudanum—in order to steal his furs,
presumably.) In the same year two posts on the Assiniboine were attacked. "It appeared," wrote Mackenzie,
"that the natives had formed a resolution to extirpate the
traders . . . and nothing but the greatest calamity that
could have befallen the natives, saved the traders from
destruction: this was the smallpox, which . . . destroyed
with its pestilential breath whole families and tribes..."

The disease struck hardest at the Crees and Chipewy-
ans. One tribe that had formerly numbered five hundred
lodges was left with only ten survivors. Hearne reported
that in 1780-82, nine-tenths of the Northern (Athabaskan)
Indians were exterminated.

If exploitation of the Indian peoples through swindling
and extortion was the main foundation of the trade in
furs, the exploitation of wage-labor in the work of transport between Montreal and the "pays d'en haut," or
Upper Country, was an essential part of the business.
Some twelve hundred hired servants of the Company—
French Canadian voyageurs or canoemen, interpreters,
guides—carried the trade goods and the traders to the distant posts, and brought back the great loads of pelts. These
men toiled across the greater part of a continent, by way
of hazardous watercourses and over back-breaking portages or "carrying-places." (There were 36 of these between Lachine and Georgian Bay alone.) "I have known
some of them," wrote Mackenzie of the voyageurs, "set off
with two packages of ninety pounds each, and return with
two others of the same weight, in the course of six hours,
being a distance of eighteen miles over hills and mountains." "A labor," comments another trader, "which oxen
cannot conveniently perform." And a third observes:
"The Indian trade . . . is carried on at great expense,
labor and risk; every year furnishes instances of loss of

men and goods by accident or otherwise." The supply of provisions being kept to a minimum (in order to load up with trade goods or pelts), the voyageurs had to depend on getting additional supplies from such Indians as they might encounter on the way. "When this fails . . ." wrote the Frobishers, "they are exposed to every misery that it is possible to survive."

The working force of voyageurs was divided roughly into two equal parts: one group paddled the big *canots du maitre* (master's canoe), which carried a burden of about four tons and were manned by a crew of eight or ten, travelling between Montreal and Grand Portage or Fort William; the others, in crews of four or five, took the *canot du nord* (of one and a half tons' burden) over the narrower streams and precipitous portages of the distant interior. The latter group, "northmen" or "winterers" tended to look down on the "mangeurs de lard" (pork-eaters) of the former category. Such division and friction between groups of employees was doubtless to the advantage of the Company. The wages picture would seem to bear this out.

One account gives wages paid between Lachine and Michilimackinac as £25 for two "end men" (bow and steersman) and £66.13.4 for eight middlemen. The French traveller La Rochefoucauld described the pay-arrangement thus: "All employees, except 40 guides and 1,400 men working between Montreal and Grand Portage who are paid half in cash and half in merchandise, are paid entirely in merchandise, which at Grand Portage yields a profit of 50 per cent. As a result of profit, 900 servants in 1791 owed the Company more than the amount of ten or fifteen years' pay." In that same year the Company sold in London, for £88,000, furs that had cost them about £16,000.

The Company's partners were famed for the sumptuous feasts they held at the Beaver Hall in Montreal, and on occasion at Grand Portage; but there was no extravagance when it came to the "keep" of their canoemen!*

Regarding the men's provisions on the Lachine-Grand Portage route, Mackenzie remarked that they had "no other allowance than Indian corn and melted fat . . . Corn is the cheapest provision that can be procured... A man's daily allowance does not exceed ten-pence."

Mackenzie also commented on something that has to do with the nature of the *state* in a society where a minority lives off the labor of the rest. He marvelled that the Company managed to keep its hundreds of servants in the west in a fitting "degree of subordination," despite the fact that the proprietors or their representatives at Grand Portage were "comparatively but few in number, and beyond the aid of any legal power to enforce due obedience."

Actually, it was not long before a prison for "refractory voyageurs" was added to the establishment at the Lakehead. But the authority of the employers was reinforced by other means as well. No man could get work as a voyageur without a reference from his parish priest. Another factor in the Company's hold on its servants was the establishment of a fund for disabled canoemen, made up out of the deductions of one per cent of wages. While there was division amongst categories of employees ("northerners" vs. "pork-eaters"), it is probable that there also existed among the European employees a sense of common interest with the Company in the exploitation of the Indians.

---

*"The evidence points very directly to the conclusion that a monopoly control of the trade made possible substantial reductions in wages . . . After the amalgamation (1804) of the XY Company and the North West Company, clerks' salaries were reduced from £100 per year to £60 . . ." (H. A. Innis, *The Fur Trade*, 1956, p. 241).

Yet there were clashes between the men and the Company. The trader Duncan McGillivray in 1794 reported on a strike of voyageurs at Rainy Lake. The tone of his account has the familiar ring of company news-releases on such occasions:

"A few discontented persons in their Band, wishing to do as much mischief as possible assembled their companions together several times on the Voyage Outward & represented to them how much their Interest suffered by the passive obedience to the will of their masters, when their Utility to the Company, might insure them not only of better treatment, but of any other conditions which they would prescribe with Spirit & Resolution . . . They all declared with one voice that unless their wages would be augmented, and several other conditions equally unreasonable granted them they would immediately set off to Montreal." Threats and intimidation induced some to "return to their duty"; but "a few of the most resolute were obstinate enough to hold out . . . and were therefore sent down to Montreal in disgrace."

Only rarely was the authority of the Company thus directly challenged. Its wealthy partners wielded a power equivalent to that of rulers of the colony. Backed by British garrisons, they were able to carry through, by means of voyageur and Indian labor, the profitable commercial conquest of a sizeable portion of the continent. These "Lords of the lakes and forests" were the precursors of the modern Canadian capitalist class.

XXIX

The North Pacific. Russian and British America

OPERATING FROM THEIR BASE ON THE ST. LAWRENCE, the traders of the North West Company gradually extended their network of posts throughout the West. Outflanking their English competitors on Hudson Bay and their American rivals to the south, the Montrealers reached the shores of the Arctic in 1789 and of the Pacific in 1793. By so doing they blazed the trail for a Canada that would one day span the continent.

Their efforts in pursuit of trading profits need to be seen in the larger setting. The fur company empires were themselves the outgrowth of a historic process: the striving of the West European capitalist powers to reach the Pacific and subjugate the countries of East Asia. The search for a short-cut through the land barrier of North America dated back to the days of Cabot and of Frobisher. The explorations of the Nor'westers, extending their trading territory to the Rockies and beyond, came to be interwoven with the ancient and still-continuing search for "a North-West Passage."

Maps made in the mid-1700's left blank the whole of northwestern North America; or else filled in the unknown with imaginings, such as the fabled "Strait of Anian," said to link Hudson Bay, southwestward, with the Pacific. (On some maps, America was joined to Asia—a continuation of the ancient theory that pictured Labrador as an extension of Siberia.)

Beyond Lower California, little was known of the west coast. (California, moreover, was depicted as an island as late as the 18th century.) Drake in 1579 had sailed perhaps as far north as Oregon; he looked in vain for the western entrance to the alleged "Passage" for whose eastern approaches Frobisher was probing from the North Atlantic. Juan de Fuca claimed in 1592 to have found the "Strait of Anian"— it may have been the strait since named for him. Soon after, Vizcaino was off the Oregon coast, and de Fonte reported reaching 53 degrees north—the latitude of the Queen Charlottes.

Then came a lull in the search. Spain had her hands full, consolidating her empire in Mexico and South America; and the territory to the north held no such promise of loot as did the realms of the Aztec and the Inca. The English, for their part, were balked in efforts to find a western exit from Hudson Bay; and Baffin's report, that his bay likewise was closed on the north and west, served to discourage further attempts in that quarter. Then came the English Revolution and the founding of the Hudson's Bay Company, with the search for a northwest passage as a condition of its charter. But the Company's obstruction of any probing in its domain, due to its opposition to having a "through" route to the Pacific traverse its monopoly preserve, placed a roadblock in the way of fresh discovery.

Northwest America, as it turned out, was to be reconnoitered from quite another direction.

While West European mercantile, political and military energies were focused elsewhere, a new power appeared on the Pacific. In the years when Montreal was being founded and Huronia destroyed, Russian fur traders were moving eastward through Siberia.* In 1648 a

---

*T. A. Rickard (*Historic Backgrounds of British Columbia*, 1948, p. 29) in referring to the traders and frontiersmen who ranged over

party led by the Cossack Simon Dezhnev made their way
to the Arctic Ocean and sailed along its coast to the
easternmost tip of Siberia (now called Cape Dezhnev).
After coming south through the strait that eighty years
later was explored by Bering, they returned by an overland route to their starting point, Yakutsk. This feat was
long kept secret among the fur traders: the account of it
did not become known for over a century.*

Just as the French monarchy had taken over from the
trading companies the direct administration of the colony
on the St. Lawrence, so the Russian state toward the end
of the reign of Peter I ("the Great": he reigned from
1682 to 1725) undertook to bring Siberia under its control
—as a source of tribute for the imperial treasury. In 1697
the German philosopher-scientist Leibnitz raised with the
tsar the question of geographical exploration in the Far
East. Of the relationship between Asia and America he
wrote, some years later, that "Only in one place has that
frontier not been investigated, and that place lies within
the tsar's domains." In 1716, Leibnitz, after an interview
with Peter, voiced the hope "that through him we shall
learn whether Asia and America are joined together."

One of the tsar's last acts was to plan the expedition to
the Pacific that was led by the Dane, Vitus Bering, in
1725-28. After crossing Siberia, Bering and his men sailed
north from Kamchatka. It was known from the reports
of the Siberian Chukchi (kin to the Arctic peoples of this
continent) that there was a "Great Land" (Bolshaya Zem-

---

*F. Golder, in his *Russian Expansion in the Pacific 1641-1850,*
(published in 1914) disputes the claim that Dezhnev reached Bering
Strait; it is upheld, however, by Soviet historians and geographers, and
also by V. Stefansson, *North West to Fortune* (1958), and Marius
Barbeau, *Pathfinders of the North Pacific* (1958). The latter cites
the "Pacific Russian Scientific Investigations" (Leningrad, 1926) of
the USSR Academy of Sciences.

Siberia, notes that "the *promyshlenniki,* or freebooters . . . played
much the same part as the *coureurs de bois* in Canada."

lya) lying to the eastward. But Bering's expedition, though it sailed northward through and some distance beyond the strait that now bears his name, never got sight of the American mainland.

The first Europeans to reach northwest North America were a party of Russians led by the navigator Fyodorov and the geodesist Gvozdev in 1732. Sailing northeast, they reached what is now Cape Prince of Wales, Alaska. Gvozdev's report, compiled from his observations and information obtained from Chukchi on the nearby islands, was the first record of the physical aspect, inhabitants and wild-life of northwestern America. It has been described as "an outstanding event in the history of cartography."

Now at last the great blank spaces in the maps of the north Pacific began to be filled in. A joint expedition of Bering and Alexei Chirikov in 1741 charted the approaches to Alaska and some of the Aleutians. Bering sighted the St. Elias Mountains (they include Mt. Logan, the highest peak in present day Canada). Chirikov went further south and reached the coast in the area of latitude 55°— north of the Queen Charlotte Islands. Thus, at the very time when La Vérendrye and his sons were advancing across the Prairies in search of the "Western Sea," the Russian navigators were visiting its northerly coasts.* The French explorers were, like the Russians, fur traders. The way for the expeditions of Gvozdev and Bering-Chirikov was prepared by the Russian fur traders: the discovery of sea-otter, reported by Chirikov's men, led to the swift

---

*A map in the author's possession, entitled "Northerly Parts of the Globe" (1758) by the French geographer, Bellin, shows most of northwest America and the north Pacific as a blank; but a short stretch of shore-line opposite easternmost Siberia bears the notation: "Land seen by the Russians in 1728" (a mistake in date—it was first visited by Gvozdev in 1732); and considerably to the south-east is another bit of shore-line marked: "The Russians saw land here in 1741, but knew not whether it was island or mainland": the reference being to Chirikov's voyage.

growth of a new, maritime branch of the fur-trade. From the 1740's on, the Russian traders reaped a rich harvest of profit from the sale of sea-otter pelts to the merchants and mandarins of China. Conducted overland, the trade centred at Kiakhta, near the Chinese-Russian border, south of Irkutsk.

First Spain, then England, reacted to the expansion of Russian trading operations. Madrid learned in 1767 of further expeditions being organized by the Russian empress, Catherine II. A dispatch of the year following stated: "It is well-known that the Russians have familiarized themselves with the navigation of the sea of Tartary, and that they already carry on trade in furs with a continent, or perhaps island, distant only 800 leagues from the western coast of the Californias." Soon there were Spanish missions in Upper California, and a post in San Francisco Bay (1776). In 1774 the navigator Perez Hernandez reached the Queen Charlotte Islands, and on his way back anchored in an inlet just north of Nootka Sound, on the west side of Vancouver Island. Later he landed near Point Granville, on the mainland, (47° 20' n.) and claimed the country for Spain.

The English were not far behind.

Victory in the Anglo-French wars of the mid-century had given Britain possession of both India and Canada; her navy was now directed to conduct exploration in the Pacific, to counter the challenge of Russian and Spanish expansion. Leadership in these operations was entrusted to Capt. James Cook; in 1776-78 he carried out his third voyage of exploration in the Pacific. The son of a Yorkshire farm-laborer, Cook as a lad had worked on colliers, then joined the navy; he had served at Louisbourg in 1758, played an important part in the navigation of the St. Lawrence when the Wolfe-Saunders expedition moved against Quebec, and in 1763 had charted the Newfoundland coast. In 1778 he reached the west coast of North America with instructions from the Admiralty to look for an entrance to a possible North West Passage. He missed the mouth of the Columbia, gave Cape Flattery its name, and paused at Nootka Sound (which he believed to be part of the mainland). The expedition then continued north, up to Cook's Inlet (which he mistook for a river, an error that was later to be of some consequence); then on past the Aleutians and through Bering Strait. His further probing was brought to a halt by an ice-barrier at Icy Cape, on the north coast of Alaska.

Cook met his death on the voyage homeward, in the Sandwich (Hawaiian) Islands. His men, who had traded for sea-otter pelts when at Nootka, sold them at sensational prices when they reached Canton. According to one account, "Skins, which did not cost the purchaser sixpence, sold in China for a hundred dollars." All in all, the crew's "take" was around $10,000. When word of this reached England and the United States, traders of both countries headed for the north Pacific.

The Russians then had been trading in the area for close to half a century. They had established the first European settlements in northwest America, on the islands and—in 1784—at Sitka. A couple of years later, English merchants active in the India and China trade visited the West Coast; in 1788 one of them, John Meares, set up a trading post at Nootka. Having brought over a work-force that included a number of Chinese laborers, he had them build a sloop—the first modern ship to be launched in the northwest. A year earlier, traders from Boston and New York got into the race for sea-otter pelts.

Spain, which had reacted to Russian expansion by claiming Nootka and the surrounding territory some two years before Cook reached the area, was stirred to fresh action by these new incursions. In 1789 a naval force under Martinez occupied Nootka, expelled the British traders, and began to fortify the post.

Both powers mobilized their fleets, and Pitt was ready to declare war when a sudden shift in the relation of forces in Europe forced the Spanish to back down. The ally on whose support they had depended—the Bourbon monarchy in France—was overthrown by the storm of revolution. Spain surrendered Nootka and acknowledged British claims to territory and trading rights (1790).

The opening up of the maritime fur trade with China gave new impetus to the search for a short sea passage through or around North America. Cook's efforts in this respect had met with failure. He had, however, on his way north noted "the affinity we found subsisting between the Greenlanders and Esquimaux, and those of Norton's Sound and Oonalaska"; and concluded that "there can be little doubt of there being a Northern communication of some sort, by sea, between this West side of America and the East side, through Baffin's Bay; such communication, however, may be effectually shut up against ships, by ice, and other impediments." The ice did in fact prove to be "an insurmountable barrier to any attempt we can possibly make." Despite two attempts, his ships did not get beyond Icy Cape.

Soon after the Nootka incident, the British were at war with revolutionary France and then with Napoleon. They set aside the search for a north-west passage by sea for another quarter of a century. Moreover, Cook's *Journal* (published in 1784) indicated that the long-sought "Strait of Anian" was nothing but a myth. By an extraordinary coincidence, the map with which the publishers adorned his *Journal* contained the first public record of another, earlier feat of exploration that was to have an important bearing on the whole question of the "Passage." This map showed the route that Samuel Hearne had taken in 1771-72 in his journey overland from the western shore of Hudson Bay to the mouth of the Coppermine River on the Arctic coast: an achievement which Hearne felt should "put an end to all disputes concerning a North West Passage through Hudson's Bay."*

Instead of a sea-passage through the continent, it was an overland river-and-portage route that was finally discovered. And the ones who did it were the trader-explorers of the North West Company from Montreal. At first, they had no such intention, but were simply trying to outflank to westward their northern rivals on the Bay. The year that Cook was at Nootka, Peter Pond (and then Alexander Henry) was busy establishing a fur-route over Methye Portage: crossing the height of land that divides the two great river systems of the Saskatchewan and the Mackenzie. The new district of Athabaska thus opened by the Nor'westers soon became the base for wider explorations. Henry drafted a plan in 1781 for seeking an overland route to the Pacific. Pond relayed Indian reports of a Russian trading post located on the northwest coast. He knew of a river that flowed out of Great Slave Lake and surmised that it was a tributary of "Mr. Cook's River" emptying into the north Pacific. (This "river," as already noted, was in fact only an inlet.) By following it, Pond believed one would arrive at "Unalaska and so to Kamschatka and thence to England through Russia."

----

*Hearne had been taken prisoner by the French when they captured Fort York in 1782; the French naval commander was the renowned navigator La Pérouse, who insisted as a condition of Hearne's release that the latter publish the narrative of his journey to the Coppermine. Publication took place, actually only after Hearne's death; and was carried out by the same person as arranged for the editing of Cook's *Journal*: hence the inclusion of Hearne's findings in the same work.

The attempt to follow this route was made by a youthful Scots trader who had wintered with Pond on Lake Athabaska: Alexander Mackenzie. Of striking appearance and outstanding ability, he was, as he says of himself "endowed . . . with an inquisitive mind and enterprising spirit; possessing also a constitution and frame of body equal to the most arduous undertakings, and being familiar with toilsome exertions in the prosecution of mercantile pursuits, I not only contemplated the practicability of penetrating across the continent of America, but was confident in the qualifications, as I was animated by the desire, to undertake the perilous enterprise."

Early in June 1789 Mackenzie set out from Fort Chipewyan (on Lake Athabaska) with a party that included four French Canadian canoemen—Barrieau, Ducette, Landry, Delorme, and the Indian wives of two of them; J. Steinbruck, a German; an Indian known as "English Chief," two Indian women and two others of his followers. After a fifteen-hundred-mile journey down a mighty river that persisted in flowing north (instead of turning to the west, as Mackenzie had hoped), they reached the open sea. It was covered with ice-floes; and Mackenzie, on taking reckonings, had to conclude that he had reached the wrong ocean. It was the Arctic, not the Pacific. Turning homeward, he called the great stream the "River of Disappointment." Posterity, however, named it the Mackenzie.

The river he had explored was the second longest on the continent (next to the Mississippi). Unknown to him, it possessed another peculiarity: only a short distance from its mouth a portage route led westward to the head-waters of the Porcupine River, this in turn being a tributary of that "Great River of the West" of which Pond had heard reports: the Yukon, flowing into the Pacific well to the south of Bering Strait.*

Back in Montreal old Simon McTavish ("more interested in profits than in the advancement of Science") was not overly impressed by Mackenzie's devotion to exploration. The latter, however, determined to keep up the search, returned to England for a year to study science and improve his mastery of the instruments of navigation.

Once again, in 1792, Mackenzie led an exploring party from Fort Chipewyan; this time they moved up the valley of the Peace, setting up a base camp at the point where that river and the Smoky meet. Two Indians, six French Canadians—two of them veterans of the journey to the Arctic—and a Scots assistant made up the expedition. In the spring of the following year they started: upstream through the redoubtable Peace River canyon; overland to the forks of the Finlay and Parsnip rivers; thence through the mountains to a new "Great River" (the Fraser); after traversing four hundred miles of its winding, rock-bound course, overland again on a two-weeks march to the Bella Coola—and so to Dean Channel and an arm of the Pacific. They had conquered a 450-mile-wide mountain barrier; they were the first to have crossed the continent north of Mexico. On a rock by the sea, using vermilion mixed with grease, the leader and organizer of the expedition inscribed the words: "Alexander Mackenzie, from Canada by land, the twenty-second of July, 1793."

Just seven weeks earlier, the self-same spot had been visited from the sea by Capt. George Vancouver, then engaged on a survey of the coast. Vancouver had been sent

---

*V. Stefansson points out, in his latest work, how close Mackenzie came to finding this water-route to the Pacific; and notes that the course of the two rivers, the Mackenzie and Yukon, lie almost exactly along a "great-circle" route to Asia. (*North West to Fortune*, p. 132).

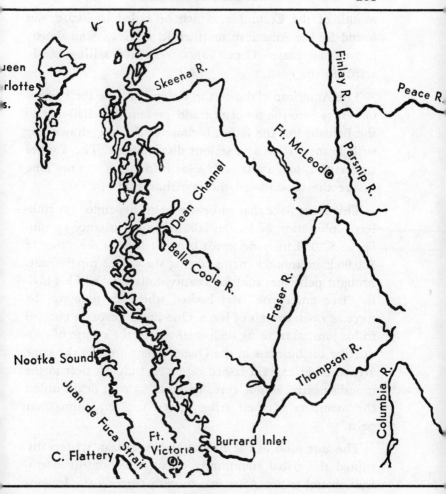

Areas of exploration on the West Coast at the turn of the century.

to take over from the Spanish commander when Nootka was surrendered to the British; he then undertook a survey of the whole coastal area. In the course of it he entered Burrard Inlet, where the city of Vancouver now stands; and established the fact that the island which bears his name was in fact unconnected with the mainland. The mouth of the Columbia, which he failed to locate, was found by the American mariner R. F. Gray, who shortly before had passed Capt. Vancouver, then sailing northward up the coast.*

The American claim to the Columbia, like their vigorous entry into the sea-otter trade, presented a challenge to the British; but the latter, because of the long-drawn war with France, were at a serious disadvantage. The Yankee traders thus had a relatively clear field and it was not long before they dominated the maritime trade in furs.

This trade, like that in beaver pelts, depended on ruthless exploitation of Indian labor. In one instance an outlay of $3,000 in trade goods brought furs to the value of $20,000; in another, items costing the trader ninety cents brought pelts that sold for twenty dollars each. This idyllic "free enterprise" was backed whenever necessary by force or open threats of force. One Boston captain boasted in his journal of using such methods, in the course of conducting his business in the Queen Charlottes; in the same area another captain lashed captured Indian chiefs to the mouths of his cannon, threatening them with death unless the members of their tribe agreed to "sell" him their pelts.

The intrusion of the British and American traders disrupted the tribal community organization of the northwest coastal tribes. After first forcibly turning the Indians into suppliers of sea-otter pelts, the traders then conducted operations with such rapacity that within the space of a few decades the sea-otter were all but exterminated. The trade collapsed, and the disorganized Indian community

---

*It is worth remembering, in this matter of finding the entrances to rivers and straits, that sailing vessels cannot usually cruise parallel to a shoreline, as can steamers: they have to tack.

was left to shift for itself: until a new form of European exploitation should arrive to replace the old.*

The traders frequently met with vigorous resistance on the part of the Indian population. (It was no accident that it took three attempts before a post could be established at that strategic point, the mouth of the Columbia.)

First Russian, then English and American merchants had thrown themselves into the cut-throat scramble for profit in the sea-otter trade. The Nor'westers, in spite of Mackenzie's successful crossing of the mountains, were left out of it. For one thing, they had yet to occupy and organize communications and transport in the new fur country west of the Saskatchewan and Mackenzie watersheds. Moreover, their energies were absorbed in internal rivalries, including a break with Mackenzie and a fierce struggle with his XY Company.

It was only after the merger of the XY and North West companies in 1804 that the Montrealers once more turned their attention to enlarging their empire in the west. In 1805 Simon Fraser was sent to establish new posts west of the Athabaska district. On the upper Peace River, the Parsnip and the upper reaches of the Fraser the district of New Caledonia took shape. It included the first post west of the Rockies—Fort McLeod.

At the same time, to the south, David Thompson was mapping the expanse of country between Rocky Mountain House (on the North Saskatchewan) and the Kootenays. A former servant of the Hudson's Bay Company, he had joined the Nor'westers in order to have a better oppor-

*That the sea-otter trade was "of a predatory character" and "amounted to little more than a looting of the coast" is conceded by even such zealous apologists for capitalism as the authors of the Carnegie-endowed work, *British Columbia and the United States*, (1942) pp. 12, 14.

tunity to work as a geographer and surveyor—a field in which he made a massive contribution.

Alexander Mackenzie had thought that the "great river" he traversed on his way to the Pacific was the Columbia. Now Simon Fraser set out to follow it to the sea. In 1808 he led a party of twenty-three (including two Indian guides and nineteen voyageurs) down the turbulent stream. Its Hell's Gate canyon and other hazards compelled them to make repeated and precipitous portages, showing conclusively that this was no route for the trade. It also turned out, on arrival at the river mouth, that this could not be the Columbia: it was several degrees too far north. David Thompson later gave this river its name: the Fraser.

Thompson, meanwhile, was systematically working over the upper basin of the Columbia; he established Kootenay House, and in 1811 explored the middle and lower reaches of the Columbia, "in order to open out a passage for the interior trade with the Pacific Ocean." At the forks of the Columbia and Snake rivers he claimed the surrounding territory for Britain and the North West Company. But when at last he arrived at the mouth of the Columbia, he found an American post already there, established some months earlier. John Jacob Astor's men had got there first.

While the men of the North West Company were gradually extending their operations westward beyond the Rockies, the government of the United States had entered the contest for control of the north west. President Jefferson—voicing the fear that the British "have thoughts of colonizing in that quarter"— took a direct part in organizing an expedition to explore the head-waters of the Missouri and an overland route to the Pacific. This was the Lewis and Clark expedition of 1805. With the help of an Indian woman, Sacagawea and her Montreal voyageur husband, Charbonneau, the party made their way over the Lembi Pass to the Columbia.*

In 1811 Astor's Pacific Fur Company established its post at the mouth of the Columbia, and a struggle with the Nor'westers got under way for control of the fur-rich country upstream.

On the American side the northwestward thrust was an early expression of the expansionist drive that followed the successful revolutionary war and the coming to power of the youthful U.S. bourgeoisie (in alliance with the southern slaveowners). It is interesting to note that the American Major Pike, who carried on intelligence work inside the Spanish territories of the southwest prior to their seizure by the U.S., also published a claim that the territory of the United States extended as far north as Queen Charlotte Sound. (He was later killed in the course of the attack on Fort York—Toronto—while in command of the invading U.S. troops.) In 1811 a pamphlet published anonymously in London, entitled *On the Origin and Progress of the North West Company of Canada,* warned that "the ambitious and encroaching disposition of the [U.S.] government is well known." It went on:

"The Government of the U.S.,—stimulated, in part, by an avarice of territorial acquisition . . . and still more by the anxiety to destroy the British Fur Trade, the political —as well as commercial importance of which they well know;—have long affected to consider the river Columbia, and the adjacent coasts, as part of their territory, and have lately encouraged an expedition to be fitted out at New York by a *chartered* commercial company, the object

---

*Brebner observes that "Sacagawea almost deserves the credit for the first Missouri-Columbia-Pacific traverse." (*Explorers of N. America,* p. 390).

of which is *to take possession of and form settlements upon the coast*."

The British had successfully asserted their claim to a position on the northwest coast, at Nootka in 1790; but the Montrealers' efforts to obtain naval backing for a challenge to the Americans at the mouth of the Columbia were ignored — until after the outbreak of the Anglo-American War of 1812.

The staking out of a Canadian claim to the Columbia watershed and to that of the Thompson and Fraser to the north, was entirely the work of the Nor'westers. In this respect they prepared the way for the creation, a half century later, of a transcontinental British North America. Their motives were those of commercial profit; even the passionate scientific interest of David Thompson was perforce pursued within the framework of Company operations—even though the significance of his work transcended by far that of the traders' balance-sheets.

The contribution of the leading traders of the North West Company to Canada's national emergence was hardly a conscious policy. When they looked beyond Company concerns, men like Mackenzie thought in terms of British imperial interests. He spoke of his work of "penetrating across the continent of America" as a means to "add new countries to the realms of British commerce." The prize to be grasped was the China trade—and more: "By opening this intercourse between the Atlantic and Pacific oceans . . . the entire command of the fur trade of North America might be obtained, from latitude 48° North to the pole, except that portion of it which the Russians have in the Pacific. To this may be added the fishing in both seas, and the markets of the four quarters of the globe. Such would be the field for commercial enterprise, and incalculable would be the produce of it, when supported by the operations of that credit and capital which Great Britain so eminently possesses."

It was as a "field for commercial enterprise" that the northern half of the continent attracted both fur-traders and architects of empire. Only belatedly, and then in a minor key, did any distinct Canadian consciousness find voice. Yet the Nor'westers of Montreal and the *pays d'en haut*, pitted against the London monopoly of the Bay, were forerunners of a British North American challenge to imperial dominance. Out of the Anglo-American war that began in 1812 came a further defining of Canadian interests and identity. But the follow-up to Alexander Mackenzie's journey to the Pacific lay a long half-century in the future.

XXX

Anglo-American Conflict.
U.S. Expansionists and Canada

BRITISH NORTH AMERICA AT THE CLOSE OF THE 18TH CEN-
tury consisted of several loosely-connected colonial provinces (Upper and Lower Canada, the Maritimes, Newfoundland) and the widely-scattered trading posts in the
North-West. The fur trade, based on exploitation of the
Indian peoples, had, together with the Atlantic fishery,
provided the initial framework. Settlement, agriculture
and the beginnings of local manufacture were now providing a firmer economic base for the colonial community.
The key word is *colonial*. Shaped by the outcome of the
Anglo-French War and then of the American War of Independence, British North America was the dependent
possession of the imperial metropolis. The Canadas and
the Atlantic provinces alike were offspring of a warring
Empire. And at the turn of the century they lived in the
shadow of a persisting conflict of interests that divided
imperial Britain and the republican United States.

The roots of the conflict went deep. In the War of Independence American capitalism had successfully asserted its
claim to independent existence. Now, with England locked in bloody struggle with Napoleonic France,* the new
ruling class in the United States saw a chance to consolidate the newly-won independence, weaken their old an-
tagonist and extend their own sway to the whole of the
North American continent.

---

*England was at war with France from 1796 to 1814-15, with a
brief truce intervening in 1802.

For their part the British imperial rulers, who had embarked on war with France in an effort to throttle the French Revolution, still nursed hopes of annulling as well the victory of the American Revolution. Should it not prove possible to reduce the erstwhile colonies to a "proper subordination" to the metropolis, at least the pretensions of an upstart commercial rival might be checked.

The conflict between Anglo-American capitalist interests had been a mainspring of the Revolution; it now was entering upon a new phase—that of a contest between capitalist powers. On the British side, the aims were unmistakably predatory and counter-revolutionary. On the American, they were more complex: for the U.S., this was a period of *transition* from a national-revolutionary struggle, historically progressive in character, to one that was aggressive and expansionist. The element of fighting to uphold and consolidate the gains of the Revolution, to free North America of European colonialist domination was still present (particularly in the thinking of large masses of the American people). Yet the role of the industrial capitalist expansionists was not only present, but was growing and in the process of becoming decisive.

Even before 1776, British port entries had shown the ratio of American-built ships to British-built as almost two to three. By the end of the century, with a shipping that was second only to the British in tonnage, U.S. merchants and industrialists were in a position to challenge Britain's trade with the West Indies and Europe. Between 1795 and 1806 U.S. foreign trade (including tens of millions of pounds of sugar and coffee from the Indies) increased two and a half times.

Writing home from London in 1785, John Adams remarked of his hosts: "A jealousy of our naval power is the true motive, the real passion which actuates them.

They consider the United States as their rival, and the most dangerous rival they have in the world."

The British struggle with Napoleon over the mastery of Europe led to a crisis in Anglo-U.S. relations. While Napoleon's Berlin Decrees (1806) put British ports out of bounds for U.S. merchantmen, Britain's orders-in-council in turn denied them access to the Continent. The U.S. countered with an embargo cutting off supplies of cotton, tobacco, flour and wheat to Britain. Forcible seizure ("impressment") by British men-of-war of seamen aboard U.S. vessels strained relations still further.

President Jefferson on the eve of war declared the issue to be "fair and equal access to market with our productions, [and] our due share in the transportation of them." He complained: "Our commerce has been plundered in every sea; the great staples of our country have been cut off from their legitimate markets, and a destructive blow aimed at our agricultural and maritime interests."

Oddly, though maritime issues were the theme of argument, and "Free Trade and Sailors' Rights!" the favored war-cry, the merchants and ship-owners of Boston and New York were not the ones who pressed for war. On the contrary: hard hit by Jefferson's embargo, they opposed his entire course of policy. From Philadelphia in 1809 one of their correspondents had written plaintively: "What is that huge forest of dry trees that spreads itself before the town? You behold the masts of ships thrown out of employment by the embargo."

Jefferson and Madison, in steering towards war, were impelled by broader interests. In the new United States, merchants' capital no longer held decisive sway. Out of the revolutionary war and the industrial revolution, new forces had thrust their way to the fore. Industrial capital was starting on its way to power. Even before 1775, ironware and tools had been exported to the West Indies from Pennsylvania and Massachusetts. During and after the Revolution, foundries and furnaces multiplied, manufacturing increased. War in Europe lent added impetus. Shipbuilding tonnage trebled in the last two decades of the 18th century. In 1790 the first American textile mill was opened; others followed, in Rhode Island, Connecticut, Massachusetts, New York. Pittsburgh became a manufacturing centre of some importance. In the last decade of the century, two hundred and ninety-five corporations were established in various branches of business and industry. By the close of the century the factory system was taking hold. In 1807 there was a steamboat on the Hudson, in 1811, one on the Ohio. With the expansion of capital went the drive for wider areas of profitable investment. Northern businessmen reached out for the rich lands of the Northwest, and cast a covetous eye on the St. Lawrence outlet to the sea.

The industrial capitalists of the North were not yet strong enough by themselves to determine national policy. But in alliance with the Southern planters, they could.

So the deal was made. The Southerners agreed: "We consent that you may conquer Canada; permit us to conquer Florida."

Grundy of Tennessee graciously conceded: "I am willing to receive the Canadians as adopted brethren."

Said Hunter of Rhode Island: "The declaration that Canada should be conquered and retained was the exacted pledge of the Northern men who voted for the war." There was to be "an enlargement and [rounding out] of the territory at the two extremities: a fair division of the spoil."

What, in all of this, had become of the Rights of Man, the pursuit of Liberty?

Just as, in France, the people's war in defense of the revolution had given way to a war of imperial conquest and aggression, once the bourgeoisie were firmly in the saddle—so in the United States, the winning of independence was followed by a turn towards aggressive expansionism.*

Thus the patriots of '76 gave way to the "War Hawks" of 1810.

"All North America," said Gouverneur Morris with foreboding of the expansionist aims, "must at length be annexed to us—happy, indeed, if the lust for dominion stops there."

For close to a decade, the expansionists' clamor had risen in raucous crescendo.

The first great target: Canada.

Its conquest Burwell of Virginia declared in 1809 to be "an object of first importance to the peace of the United States."

Johnson of Kentucky had it on the very highest authority that the St. Lawrence should by rights be awarded to the owners of the Mississippi; said he: "The great Disposer of Human Events intended those two rivers should belong to the same people."

Harper of New Hampshire thought so too: "This great outlet of the northern world should be at our command for our convenience and future security. To me, Sir, it appears that the Author of Nature has marked our limits in the South, by the Gulf of Mexico; and on the north, by the regions of eternal frost."

---

*Lenin, writing of the change that took place in the character of the wars waged by France, states: "It was not in 1792-1793, but many years later, *after* the victory of reaction within the country, that the counter-revolutionary dictatorship of Napoleon transformed the wars on France's part from defensive wars into wars of conquest." The development in the U.S.A. presents, if not a parallel, at least an analogy.

The Nashville *Clarion* (April 28, 1812) kept the argument on an equally high plane: "Where is it written in the book of Fate that the American republic shall not stretch her limits from the Capes of Chesapeake to Nootka Sound, from the Isthmus of Panama to Hudson Bay?"

Behind these flights of eloquence lay a small matter of business. Congressman Porter from Buffalo "had been creditably informed that the exports from Quebec alone amounted during the last year (1811), to near six millions of dollars, and most of these too in articles of the first necessity . . . by carrying on . . . a war . . . we should be able in a short time to remunerate ourselves tenfold for all the spoliations [Britain] had committed on our commerce."

Andrew Jackson was no less businesslike. Said he: "We are going to vindicate our right to the fur trade, and to open a market for the productions of our soil."

Thanks to British wartime needs, Canada was enjoying its first boom. Imports from Britain to the North American colonies doubled in fifteen years; tonnage in the trade with the West Indies increased fifteen-fold. In 1802, over a million bushels of wheat, and 28,000 barrels of flour were exported from Canada. A few years later the trade in timber soared, Napoleon having cut off supplies to Britain from the Baltic. Over a hundred thousand tons of oak and pine timber were shipped from Canada in 1810. That year, 661 ships were cleared by the Quebec port authorities. In 1809, the first steamer on the St. Lawrence, the Canadian-built *Accommodation*, made the trip from Montreal to Quebec in 36 hours' travelling time.

In April, 1810, the *Upper Canada Guardian or Freeman's Journal* carried a significant item: "With a view to encourage the infant manufactures of this Province, a contract has been made to supply His Majesty's ships and vessels on these Lakes with cordage of our own manufacture."

For some years already, the British colonies to the north had been eyed by enterprising and acquisitive Yankees. The Maritime market had long been flooded with U.S. goods, cotton, iron, leather, etc. "You can scarce enter a House, but you see an American package," lamented one Nova Scotian in 1787.

In 1799 Philemon Wright of Massachusetts had gone up to the Ottawa to Hull. "I should think that we climbed to the top of one hundred or more trees," he reported. "By this means we were enabled to view the country and also the timber . . ." Both were found to "answer our expectations."

Without his having to bother climbing trees, John Jacob Astor's eye took in an even wider sweep. From his base in Montreal, established in 1794 (the building stood till 1923, at Vaudreuil Lane and Ste. Thérèse St. by the river) he set up a land company which schemed (unsuccessfully, as it happened) to lay hands on some twenty-four townships in Lower Canada. Meanwhile, his American Fur Company, reaching into the Northwest, acquired an extension, in his Pacific Fur Company, with a trading post at the mouth of the Columbia.

The struggle for the northland was taking on continental proportions.

XXXI

Imperialist Policy and Democratic Struggles in British North America

WITH U.S.-BRITISH RELATIONS NEARING THE BREAKING-point, the rulers of the Empire had perforce to give thought to their straggling North American possessions.

For London, the Canadas and the Maritimes were of importance in several respects. Not only were they all that was left of the imperial domain in North America, a source of fur-profits and a potential market for British manufactures. They were also a valuable supply-base—especially in timber. But most immediately important: they were the base of operations for any effort to re-conquer the lost colonies and re-establish British domin-ance in North America.

In any war with the United States, the British would face the problem of conducting operations in a distant theatre, secondary to that of the decisive struggle with Napoleon; and of concerting the efforts of a colonial population deeply divided both politically and by nation-ality.

As their principal allies, the British counted on the Western Indian tribes, whose survival was threatened by the relentless pressure of U.S. land-grabbing. In the words of fur-lord James McGill: "The Indians are the only Allies who can aught avail in the defense of the Canadas. They have the same interest as us, and alike are objects of American subjugation, if not extermination."

That the British colonizers would encompass their ruin just as surely, if more slowly, the Indian tribes may well have suspected; the betrayal of 1783 was clear enough notice of what they could expect. But here it was a matter of making the best of a bad business, of joining forces with the lesser threat against what appeared to be the greater and more pressing. Even so, the support was given with reluctance, and the Six Nations on the Grand River held out, at first, for neutrality.

Among the colonial population, London could count on the firm support only of the "Loyalists," the landowner "aristocracy" and officialdom, the Church, and the fur barons. Most zealous for aggressive action were the magnates of the North West Company, the McTavishes, McGillivrays and Frobishers, who saw in war with the United States the opportunity of reconquering a vast fur territory on the Ohio and Mississippi, and beyond. Six months before war broke out, they offered to put their eight hundred servants, transport and communications at the service of the War Office. They urged action to seize Michilimackinac, at the gateway to Lake Superior, and Astoria at the mouth of the Columbia.

Significantly, when war was declared, it was through the "grape-vine" of the North West Company, long before official dispatches arrived, that Governor General Prevost learned the news. And Major General Brock, commanding in Upper Canada, got word of it on the same day, through one of Astor's agents. As Brock's biographer observes: "Mr. Astor had extensive fur interests in Canada, and obtained early and private information from Washington in order to prevent his store of furs being sent from their depots."

In terms of military strength, the British had at their disposal several thousand regular troops, and naval forces based at Halifax. Discipline in the army and navy was maintained by a regime of ruthless brutality. A regimental court-martial was empowered to inflict 999 lashes (the "cat" being customarily steeped in brine). Desertion was prevalent, mutiny not rare. One of Brock's first acts in Upper Canada was to quell a mutiny at Niagara, provoked by his predecessor's extreme severity. Brock's relative humaneness was a factor in the morale of the forces under his command, in which desertions were less frequent than elsewhere at the time.

Recruitment for the navy was carried on by the press-gang. Haliburton's chronicle of Nova Scotia (1829) contains numerous entries such as these:

"Nov. 16, 1795. A warrant of impress granted to Capt. Murray, for forty-eight hours.

"Dec. 16, 1796. Press warrant granted to Captain H. Mowgate for four days.

"Oct. 17, 1797. A warrant to impress seamen, not inhabitants of Nova Scotia, granted to Admiral Vandiput, for two months.

"May, 1805. Press warrant granted for fourteen days.

"Dec. 8, 1808. Edward M'Crae and Matthew Allen, two landsmen, having been impressed and forcibly carried off from their labor on shore at Pictou, and put on board of one of his Majesty's ships and sent to the West Indies, the house voted the same oppressive and illegal."

In 1797, seamen of the British Fleet had mutinied at Spithead and the Nore, in a desperate protest against low pay, bad food and brutal treatment. That the spirit of resistance was not lacking among the men on this side of the Atlantic is indicated by the warning issued in August of that year by the admiral commanding the Halifax station; he stated his readiness to take "the most vigorous measures for Counteracting any attempt that may be made by ill designing persons to excite a spirit of Mutiny amongst the Crews of His Majesty's Ships."

An inquiry resulting from insubordination on board a ship of war in St. John's harbor in the same month revealed that there had been talk of mutiny on shore "under the Fish Flake near the sign of the Romney Sunday last between the hour of one and three o'clock."

In many instances, discontent among the seamen led to desertion and shipping aboard U.S. vessels where the pay was higher. In other cases, there was insubordination and mutiny. Haliburton reports, for the one year 1807, instances of both types:

"Aug. 26. A Court Martial held at Halifax, on board his Majesty's ship Belleisle . . . for the trial of John Wilson . . . lately taken from the American frigate Chesapeake, on charges of mutiny, desertion and contempt, when sentence of death was passed upon him; he was executed on the 31st.

"Oct. 15. Two seamen executed on board of his Majesty's ship Jason . . . for mutiny.

"Dec. 31. A Court Martial assembles at Halifax, on board of his Majesty's ship Acasta, for the trial of forty-four seamen and one marine, charged with mutiny, ten of whom are found guilty and one executed."

What was the condition and state of mind of the rank and file of the civilian population in these years?

In Lower Canada the first decade of the new century was marked by deep-going unrest that culminated in a political crisis. The new English-speaking merchant aristocracy raised the rents on their seigneurial estates, called for the anglicizing of the French Canadian community, and strove (with active help from the colonial governors) to impose their own minority rule in defiance of the elective Assembly. The response to this was a wave of French Canadian national resentment, the emergence of a national-democratic party and the founding (in 1806) of the newspaper *Le Canadien* as organizer and agitator for the popular cause.

As compared with the situation in the early 1790's, there were now much more clearly defined political groupings in the Assembly: political *parties* were emerging as the spokesmen of class and national interests. The "Tory" or "British" party was that of the Anglo-colonial merchants, the most powerful of whom were the fur lords of the North West Company (established in 1784, reorganized in 1804); several of them—Benjamin Frobisher, Richardson, Alexander Mackenzie—held seats in the Assembly. Although a minority in the lower chamber, these men and their associates dominated the appointive council and executive. Their organ was the rabidly imperialist *Quebec Mercury*.

The majority formed the "Canadian" or "democratic party." Mainly French Canadian in make-up, it included also a number of English-speaking democrats, including the Irish radical, Thomas Lee. Most of its elected members were notaries or lawyers; there was one blacksmith, and a few habitant farmers.*

Their organ was *Le Canadien,* launched in November 1806. Pierre Bédard, a leading member of the Assembly, was its editor, and Thomas Lee was one of its owners. As the publishers of the paper were strongly influenced by Voltaire and the Encyclopedists, the bishop was soon complaining bitterly: "You cannot conceive of the ravages caused by this wretched sheet among the people and the clergy."

---

*It would be interesting to know what was the effect on popular representation, of the property qualification for voters, established by the Constitutional Act. It was fixed at property bringing in annually 40 shillings net, in rural constituencies; and town property bringing in a minimum of £5, or payment of rent at least to the amount of £10 per annum.

Le Canadien was founded just when a new campaign of British chauvinism was being waged by the Quebec *Mercury*: the province was "much too French for a British colony," and the supreme aim should be "to unfrenchify it." *Le Canadien* undertook to answer this diatribe in its first issue, and not at all in a spirit of narrow national exclusiveness: "Are not all the inhabitants of the province British subjects? The English here should no more continue to be called Englishmen than should the Canadians be called Frenchmen. Are we never to become known as one people, as British Americans?"

The democrats' rejoinder projected the idea of a British North American identity: a step towards that of a Canadian identity. At the same time *Le Canadien* vigorously defended the equal rights of the French Canadians with their English-speaking compatriots. The paper conducted a systematic campaign of enlightenment on parliamentary practices and rights: it was a political educator which did much to speed the rapid mastery of elective processes and institutions by a people who now enjoyed them for the first time in their history.

Le Canadien in one of its early issues exposed the fact that "the Ministerial Party has constantly sided with the Montreal merchants, in opposition to the Assembly"; and asked: "Does not this circumstance seem to reveal how the influence of the North West Company is dominant in the country?" The question (however unwittingly) touched on the key feature of a bourgeois democracy: despite elective institutions, it is the economic power of capitalist wealth that is dominant in the state. As Adam Smith put the matter, in *The Wealth of Nations*: "Civil government, so far as it is instituted for the security of property, is in reality instituted for the defense of the rich against the poor, or of those who have some property against those who have none at all."

*   *   *

With the arrival of Sir James Craig as Governor in 1807 the Tories received open and vigorous backing for their offensive. A military autocrat, the new governor had no sympathy whatever for the democratic leanings of the Assembly.

In 1809 *Le Canadien,* quoting Locke and other English constitutional authorities, had the audacity to assert that "the executive power, as such, is inferior to the legislative power . . ." Craig, outraged, refused to accept the Assembly's claim that his Executive was in fact a ministry, and that "in imitation of the Constitution of Britain, that Ministry is responsible to them for the Conduct of Government." Here was the crux of the dispute that raged from this time onward over "responsible government": the demand of a colony for a government controlled by itself—a position whose logic led to a demand for outright independence.

At first, however, the quarrel was limited to control of the public purse. A resolution of the Assembly of Lower Canada in 1810 insisted that the province was quite capable of paying all the expenses of civil government: the matter was referred to London for decision.

When the Governor deprived several leaders of the "Canadian party" of their commissions as officers in the militia, the Assembly responded by electing one of them, Panet, as Speaker. Twice Craig dissolved the Assembly, and each time what he described as the "violent and numerous democratic party" was returned with a strong majority. The governor complained bitterly of the decline in influence of the "Noblesse and Seigneurs": only seven of these held seats in the Assembly, as against fifteen lawyers and notaries and fourteen farmers. Leadership was in the hands of "a new order of men . . . and with these has sprung up at the same time, a spirit of insubordination among the People that is entirely adverse to the ancient System of the Country."

The popular-democratic forces in Lower Canada were by now learning to utilize the parliamentary institution of the Assembly as an instrument of struggle against oppression. But the state machine was firmly in the hands of the ruling colonial oligarchy.

Following the dissolution of the Assembly in 1810, Craig decided on more drastic measures—starting with an attack on freedom of the press. Craig had reported earlier to London that the publishers of *Le Canadien* took "the utmost pains to disperse their paper over the Province, to every part of which it was sent and distributed gratis, and that it already began to have an effect in many parts, that in consequence a new language seemed to be springing up among the People among whom the words *Revolution and Reform* had been heard . . ."

In March 1810, a body of soldiery raided the printshop of *Le Canadien* and seized its press. The printer, Lefrançois, was thrown into prison, and two days later three of the editors, including Bédard, suffered a like fate. All three were members of the Assembly: they were imprisoned without benefit of trial. (*Le Canadien* did not resume publication until 1817.)

But this attempt to silence opposition by intimidation and violence did not succeed in cowing the electorate. The elections that followed gave a resounding victory to the majority. Among the new members was the son of one of the leaders of the majority: young Louis-Joseph Papineau.

Craig, thrice rebuffed by the electors, turned to London with an appeal for a more extreme measure than any he had yet contemplated. He began by denouncing the "spirit of independence, of total insubordination" of inhabitants; and complained that "it seems to be a favorable object with them to be considered as a separate Nation: *La Nation Canadienne* is their constant expression." Then he came out with the proposal that seemed to him the only solution left: *abolish the Assembly*. He staked everything on getting London's agreement to this measure of desperation: a reform of the Constitutional Act that would eliminate elective institutions in the province.

In reply, the British Secretary of State assured him that "we are all fully convinced of the Evils which have arisen from the Act of 1791, and of the absurdity of attempting to give what is falsely called the British Constitution to a People whose Education, Habits & Prejudices, render them incapable of receiving it." But the imperial government, occupied with the war against Napoleon, was not prepared to embark on so risky a course as cancelling the concessions of 1791. It did not even endorse Craig's high-handed arrest of Bédard and his colleagues. While agreeing that "in Canada, the Executive is not dependent on the Assembly," and that such dependence "would be incompatible with the character of a colony and its connection with the metropolis," the policy London recommended was one of temporizing and conciliation. The Governor was forced to beat a retreat.

Bédard, after a year's illegal imprisonment (the others were released earlier) was set free. Shortly thereafter Craig left for England, to be replaced as governor by Sir George Prevost.

Craig's recall in 1811 somewhat lessened the tension in the province; but a remark of the British military commander Isaac Brock indicated the temper of popular opinion on the eve of the impending war. He spoke of "the spirit of insubordination lately manifested by the French Canadian population of this colony." "It is but too evident," he wrote, "that the Canadians generally are becoming daily more anxious to get rid of the English." Any indiscriminate handing out of arms to the militia in the Lower Province he considered "highly imprudent and dangerous."

The rioting in the Montreal district that followed the declaration of war bore out his forebodings. Hundreds of men resisted a forced draft of the militia, and their resistance "grew into an organized insurrection"— which was only quelled by military action involving regular troops with artillery.

Contrary to a well-established legend, those who founded Upper Canada were neither exclusively British nor predominantly Loyalist. Large numbers of American settlers entered the province in the course of the general westward movement of population. Among those who cleared the bush and started farms and mills in the Niagara district, on the Grand River, and north of Toronto, a considerable number were German-speaking settlers from Pennsylvania.* Many of them were pacifists, who had taken little or no part in the revolutionary war.

The actual Loyalists were a minority in Upper Canada: they probably accounted for about one quarter of the pre-1812 settlement. Moreover, they too were of diverse national origins: predominantly British, with Germans the second largest group (former Palatine troops in the British forces, many of them) ; but also French Huguenots, Dutch (the Ryersons, for instance) and Swiss.

Yet the social structure reflected the imperial aim of

---

*Abundant evidence thereof is provided by the Jordan Museum and by the Dalziel Pioneer Museum north of Toronto (in the great barn built by Johannes Schmidt in 1809). G. Reaman in *The Trail of the Black Walnut*, and *Waterloo Review* (Summer 1959: "A Revisionist Looks at Canadian History") tellingly refutes the "exclusive Anglo-Saxon settlement" myth.

erecting in Upper Canada a Loyalist bulwark against republican subversion. Loyalists and British officials formed the ruling oligarchy. With a view to establishing a "frontier aristocracy," the post-revolutionary land-grant system gave 200 acres to rank and file soldiers who had served in the war against the American Revolution—and 5,000 acres to field-officers. With this as a starting-point, the officialdom at York went on to cultivate a luxuriant growth of land-jobbing, speculation and favoritism that evoked angry resentment among the settlers (and not only among the non-Loyalist portion of them).

With a view to curbing unrest the authorities in 1804 passed an "Alien Act." This measure threatened radical-minded new arrivals with jail, banishment or the gallows should they so much as give grounds for suspicion that they were: "about to endeavor to alienate the minds of His Majesty's subjects of this Province from his person or government, or in anywise with a seditious intent to disturb the tranquility thereof."

This odious measure had the dual purpose of intimidating independent-minded immigrants and implanting among the population generally the idea that radicals were by nature alien, "foreign agents" and the like. (It was used against British-born democrats as much as against those from other lands.)

With a government whose members were engaged in tranquilly appropriating to themselves, their relatives and cronies vast expanses of the public domain, it was not surprising that even before the tenure of the first governor ended, "murmurings had become loud."

The settlers soon found spokesmen for their grievances —men like Judge Robert Thorpe, the organizer of an "Upper Canada Agricultural and Commercial Society." Elected to the Assembly as member for York, Durham and Simcoe, Thorpe denounced the Alien Act and exposed the legalized theft of Crown lands by the "Shopkeeper Aristocracy."

No sooner was he elected than the ruling officialdom intrigued to secure his suspension from office and his recall to England. Lieutenant-Governor Gore charged that Thorpe was seeking "to erect an independent Republic." The efforts of the reactionaries to force him to leave the province were successful.

An associate of Thorpe's was Joseph Willcocks, who had come to Canada from Ireland after the Rising of 1798. Willcocks founded at Niagara the first independent newspaper in Upper Canada, *The Guardian*. It became (as had *Le Canadien* in the lower province) the rallying point for the popular opposition forces. In the eyes of Gore and the authorities, it was an "Engine" designed for "an attempt to revolutionize the Province."

With revolt smoldering in Ireland, her exiles in North America were a constant source of anxiety to the British authorities—and ready allies of every movement of colonial protest or resistance. Willcocks was said to be a member of the organization of the United Irishmen, and to be in communication with Emmett* and other Irish exiles in New York.

The charges of "subversion" did not deter the electors of Lincoln from sending Willcocks as their representative to the Assembly in 1808 and again in 1812. Clearly, there was widespread sympathy with the ideals of the American Revolution among rank-and-file settlers in Upper Canada. On the outbreak of war Benjamin Mallory, till that year member for Oxford-Middlesex, and two sitting members, Abraham Markle (representing West York, Ancaster and Saltfleet) and Willcocks (Lincoln County) declared them-

---

*Robert Emmett: leader of an unsuccessful rising in Ireland in 1803.

selves for the United States; and Willcocks organized, from among hundreds who crossed over to the American side when hostitilies began, a force of "Canadian Volunteers."

The proclaimed American objective: to break the grip of British imperial rule on the remaining portion of the continent—found a response in a section at least of the Upper Canadian community.

In the Atlantic provinces the power of colonialism was firmly maintained, thanks to the presence in force of the British naval arm, the commercial ties of the merchants with London, and—in the Maritimes—the mass influx of Loyalists at the close of the American Revolution.

If Newfoundland's position was in any way exceptional, it was only in the extreme degree of its economic and political subordination. The institutions accompanying "colonial status" elsewhere were yet to be achieved. One observer writes: "Nova Scotia was a flourishing colony with a representative legislature sixty years before a resident of Newfoundland could procure legal title to his own house or obtain permission to have his own garden." "Newfoundland," declared Secretary of State Grenville in 1789, "is in no respect a British colony." And as though to underline the point, the commanding admiral that year ordered the destruction of every building that possessed a chimney. The fishing-station was to be that alone—no settlement permitted!

Yet settlers there were. True, they had no civil rights, no legal existence. What they did have, however, was an abundance of debts: they were hog-tied with debt, owed to the English West Country merchants and shipowners. Finally in 1792 a Judicature Act established courts on the island (the judges being such naval officers as might be available). A popular demand for representative institions was sternly repressed: William Carson, a doctor at

St. John's who advocated their introduction, was promptly dismissed from his post. (Not until 1819 was the settlers' right of occupancy of their homes recognized as legal. Five years later the British Parliament yielded to popular agitation and recognized the existence of Newfoundland—*as a colony*.)

The period around the turn of the century in Nova Scotia witnessed the emergence of a Reform movement. Its targets were the maladministration of justice, the restrictions on democracy in the militia and in the localities.

The reactionary character of the ruling military-landlord-merchant clique at Halifax was reinforced as a result of the Loyalist invasion. But as in Upper Canada, cleavages on class lines appeared among the Loyalists themselves. The poorer settlers found common ground with the former New Englanders who had entered the province in the pre-revolutionary years, and who chafed under such restrictions as the denial of the right to hold town-meetings.

Two Loyalist attorneys, Sterns and Taylor, in 1788 campaigned against judicial abuses—and were refused the right to practice law. A petition against this arbitrary act was signed by "a few Merchants of their Party, & near two hundred Tinkers, Taylors, Dray Men, Servants, &c." The working people, in Halifax and in the countryside, were becoming active opponents of reactionary rule.

A new impetus to reform agitation came from the campaign conducted by the naval officer of the province, Cotnam Tonge, to democratize the militia. In 1797 he called together a convention of militia officers for this purpose: a step which the authorities saw as a challenge to the whole system of colonial rule. Elected Speaker of the Assembly in 1805-6, Tonge led a struggle over the control of provincial revenues by the executive. The lieutenant-governor thereupon refused to recognize him as Speaker, and the following year removed him from the post of naval officer.

Attempts by his supporters to organize protest meetings were sternly put down, the law against town-meetings being invoked to justify suppression of the right of assembly.

From 1807 on, popular opposition in Nova Scotia was in the main confined to citizens' harboring deserters from the naval press-gang or from the army, and indulging with more than accustomed gusto in smuggling activities.

The reluctance of the New England merchants to sharpen the growing conflict with Britain led to their adopting a stand of practical neutrality: this meant that the province faced far less of a threat than did Upper Canada; and the British naval "presence," combined with measures of repression, kept opposition elements firmly in check.

Land-monopoly, which had given the whole of Prince Edward Island to sixty wealthy proprietors, was also the main issue in what is now New Brunswick. Prior to the revolutionary war, one Alexander McNutt had secured for himself land grants in Pictou, Colchester, on the St. John River and the Miramichi, totalling some two million acres. With the coming of the Loyalists, the system of granting estates received a fresh impetus.

Of the 30,000 Loyalists who came to Nova Scotia about one third settled across the Bay of Fundy in the valley of the St. John River. Here lived Acadian farmers, many of whom had returned after the dispersal of 1755. Once more they suffered eviction at the hands of British authorities. Wealthy Loyalists seized their lands and forced them ever farther back into the uncleared forest country.

In 1784 New Brunswick was accorded the status of a separate province: a measure intended to strengthen Tory

Loyalist control and isolate the population of the area from Nova Scotia radicalism.

It was not long before land-grabbing by Loyalist grandees engendered a New Brunswick radicalism also. The taking over by a few well-to-do individuals of the townsite of St. John, the decision to make Fredericton the provincial capital (as more convenient to the landed proprietors than the populous centre of St. John)—these were but two of many grievances.

An early critic of abuses was the Loyalist attorney Elias Hardy, who organized "Committees for Obtaining Redress of Grievances." The ruling group responded by withholding land grants from some militant settlers, arresting others, denying the right of petition, and intervention by the military (at St. John) to defeat opposition candidates.

From 1789 to 1805 the leading spokesman of the small settlers was the Scot, James Glenie—a mathematician, member of the Royal Society, a vigorous writer and speaker and courageous champion of popular rights. Starting with the defense of ex-soldiers' land-claims against a cheating, grasping officialdom, Glenie went on to challenge the whole system of colonial administration.

In the interest of developing the province, Glenie in 1791 urged the construction of a canal through the Chignecto Isthmus that connects Nova Scotia and New Brunswick (a project that to this day awaits fulfilment). He opposed the burdening of the tax-payers of the province with the costs of elaborate and useless fortifications (charge them to the English army estimates! he urged). The big landowners sought endowment of a college for the education of their sons; Glenie called for the building of parish schools for the settlers' children: a college, he said, "without them is only calculated for the accommodation of a few individuals, and has a tendency to monopolize education."

At the heart of his agitation was the demand for a change in the structure and system of government. As member of the Assembly for Sunbury he led the struggle for control of public funds by the elected representatives. The non-elective Executive Council argued that the House could not dispose of money for any purposes other than those indicated by the government. That, said Glenie, "is a proposition to which I hope in God no House of Assembly will ever give its assent."

In 1795 he secured the adoption by the Assembly of a bill "Declaratory of what Acts of Parliament are Binding in this Province." Its purpose was to eliminate in large measure the arbitrary prerogatives of the Executive and make possible a democratic administration responsible to the electorate. The Council rejected the bill after its passage by the Assembly; it was roundly condemned as being "a compleat declaration of independence."

Glenie returned to Britain in 1805, and died there twelve years later at the age of 67. It is noteworthy that his reactionary opponents in New Brunswick had linked his name with those of the Scottish and English supporters of the French Revolution. One Tory voiced the wish that Glenie might be deported to Botany Bay along with such Jacobins as Skirving, Muir and others.*

The entrenched power of the New Brunswick land-owners stubbornly blocked the pressure of the popular movement. With the growth of the timber trade a mercantile group emerged at St. John, allied with the land-owners and further reinforcing Toryism in the province.

Such was the situation in the scattered colonies when Anglo-U.S. conflict reached and passed the breaking-point —embroiling British North America once again in war.

---

*See Reference Notes.

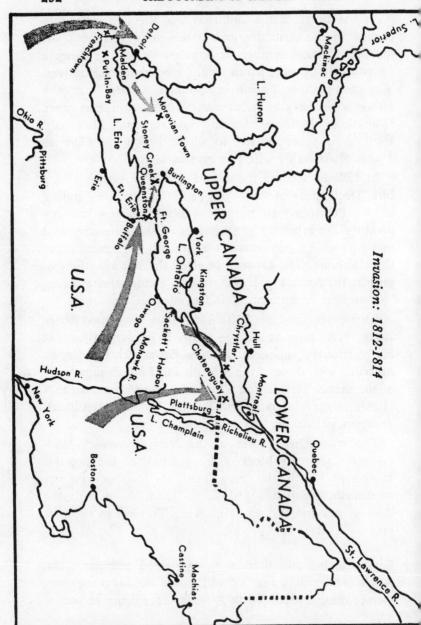

Invasion: 1812-1814

XXXII

Invasion of Canada

T OWARD THE END OF JUNE, 1812, WORD SPREAD THROUGH
the homesteads of Upper Canada, the parishes on the St.
Lawrence, the settlements by the Atlantic: the United
States had declared war on Britain. Although they had
had no voice in the quarrel, it was the settlers in British
North America who were to bear the brunt of it.

The immediate aim of the United States was to take
possession of Canada while the main British naval and
military forces were tied down by the war with Napoleon.
The Emperor, now in command of all western continental
Europe (except Spain, whose people were waging a fierce
war of national resistance), was preparing to move against
Russia. The U.S. acted in concert with him. By declaring
war on Britain on June 18, 1812, she opened a new front,
thereby lessening the British pressure on the French. Six
days later, without any declaration of war, Napoleon's
Grand Army crossed the Niemen, on the road to Smo-
lensk.

When the U.S. expansionists came to consider the matter of taking over Canada, they were not burdened with
undue modesty. Said Mr. Eustis, the Secretary for War:
"We can take the Canadas without soldiers, we have only
to send officers into the province and the people . . . will
rally round our standard."

Said Henry Clay, Speaker of the House of Representatives: "We have the Canadas as much under our command as Great Britain has the seas." "The conquest of

Canada is in your power. I trust I shall not be deemed presumptuous when I state that I verily believe that the militia of Kentucky are alone competent to place Montreal and Upper Canada at your feet."

Jefferson said it would be "A mere matter of marching."

The relationship of military forces certainly lent color to the boasts. In Upper and Lower Canada (with a population of less than half a million, as against the U.S. eight million) were 4,500 regular troops, and perhaps half that number of militia in some state of readiness. The U.S. establishment numbered 35,000, with a potential militia pool of over 450,000.

In addition to political disaffection, Brock noted at the onset of war an almost universal disbelief in the possibility of successful resistance to the U.S. colossus. In July, he wrote from York: "My situation is most critical, not from anything the enemy can do, but from the disposition of the people. . . . A full belief possesses them that this Province must inevitably succumb—This prepossession is fatal to every exertion—Legislators, Magistrates, Militia Officers, all have imbibed the idea."

From this, Brock concluded not that the situation was hopeless, but that it was essential to go on the offensive.

Brock's plan was to defend Upper Canada "by a series of offensive strokes with limited objectives." First of these was the capture, by a surprise action on the part of a small mixed force of regulars, North West Company voyageurs and Indians, of the U.S.-held post at Michilimackinac.

Meanwhile, on July 11, a U.S. army of 2,500 under General Hull had crossed the Detroit River and invaded Canada. A U.S. cavalry detachment penetrated as far as 110 miles east of Sandwich (now Windsor); some five hun-

dred settlers went over to the invaders. But Hull now gave
a first indication of that incompetence which loomed large
in U.S. military leadership throughout the war. He failed
to take the key British position at Fort Malden (near Amherstburg) which, on his right flank, threatened his line
of communication and supply, both in relation to any advance he might make into the interior, and to his rear,
across the river, as well. After a couple of ineffectual
thrusts in the direction of Malden he withdrew to Detroit.

Brock meanwhile with all possible speed was moving a
body of 300 York militia by water to Burlington, then
overland to Long Point on Lake Erie, and thence in boats
provided by local farmers, to Malden. Here they joined
forces with a body of 600 Indians under the Shawnee
chief, Tecumseh.

Although Hull occupied a well fortified position across
the river, with superior artillery and double the number
of troops, Brock took the offensive—crossed the river and
advanced on Detroit. After a preliminary bombardment,
and terrified by the rumored approach of "Indians [from
Michilimackinac] . . . swarming down in every direction"
—Hull capitulated. With his 2,000 men and thirty cannon,
he surrendered the fort and command of the Michigan
Territory. Brock paid tribute both to the Canadian
militia and the Indian allies; of Tecumseh he wrote: "A
more sagacious or a more gallant warrior does not I believe exist."

Having smashed the U.S. base of invasion in the West,
Brock now transferred his force to the central, Niagara
sector, where the enemy was massing a considerable force.

The American objectives in an invasion via Niagara
were summarized thus by Van Rensselaer, the general in
command: "Should we succeed, we shall effect a great discomfiture of the enemy by breaking their line of commu-

nication, driving their shipping from the mouth of this
river, leaving them no rallying point in this part of the
country, appalling the minds of the Canadians, and opening a wide and safe communication for our supplies."
They would also, he expected, obtain "excellent barracks
and winter quarters." Yet a correspondent wrote to him
from Canada: "A determination now prevails among the
people to defend their country."

The U.S. forces numbered 6,300, two-thirds of them
regulars. The British-Canadian defenders totalled 1,200,
half of whom were militia, and 200 Six Nations Indians.
But Brock was determined, as one of his officers said, to
"neutralize numbers by activity and vim."

The invaders crossed the river at Queenston early in
the morning of October 13. At the outset they were successful in gaining command of the heights; but on the arrival of reinforcements from Newark, they were dislodged
and driven back across the river, several hundred being
taken prisoner. Early in the action Brock was killed while
leading an assault.

Not only was Brock's military leadership outstanding;
but the political effect of his successes strongly affected
the subsequent course of the war. Unlike some imperial officers, he appreciated at their worth the citizen-
soldiers, and welded them and the regular troops into an
effective fighting force. As the Upper Canada Assembly
declared in 1815: "By the wisdom of his counsels, the
energy of his character and the vigor with which he carried
all his plans into effect, the inhabitants of this Province,
at a time when the country was almost destitute of regular
troops, were inspired with the fullest confidence in him
and in themselves."

On the frontier of Lower Canada General Dearborn was
threatening the approaches to Montreal with a massed

force of ten thousand men. What was to be the position of the Reform movement, whose newspapers had been suppressed by Craig, and their spokesmen imprisoned? While the new administration of Prevost had been marked by concessions and a lessening of repression, there were big questions still, of national and democratic rights. The historian F.-X. Garneau tells of "a secret conclave held at Quebec, in Mr. Lee's house, whereat L.-J. Papineau, Borgia and some other members of the Assembly attended, to deliberate on the question whether a neutral position should be taken by them; but M. Bédard and his friends opposed that intent and it was finally renounced."

The Assembly thereupon unanimously voted credits for the defense of the province from invasion.

In November, Dearborn crossed the frontier and started a tentative advance on the Odelltown-L'Acadie road, parallel to the Richelieu. As news of the invasion spread, militia units from Vaudreuil, Pointe Claire, Longue Pointe and Montreal crossed the St. Lawrence to support the outposts. They were joined by voyageurs of the North West Company, who formed a corps of rangers. Dearborn found his advance blocked by roads made impassable by fallen trees, broken bridges, *abatis*; and at La Colle his advance guard of 1,400 men was repulsed by two companies of Major de Salaberry's Voltigeurs (light infantry), three hundred Indians, and militiamen from the neighboring parishes. Disheartened at so inhospitable a reception, Dearborn halted his army, then withdrew to winter quarters, south of the border.

In the spring of 1812 the spokesman of the "War Hawks," Calhoun, had boasted to Congress: "In four weeks from the time a declaration of war is heard on our frontier, the whole of Upper Canada and a part of Lower Canada will be in our power."

In four months of trying, the invaders had thrice suffered failure in their attempts to conquer Canada.

In December, expansionist Henry Clay took comfort from imagined victory of the Americans' mighty ally in Europe: "Perhaps at this moment," he exulted, "the fate of the north of Europe is decided, and the French Emperor may be dictating the law from Moscow."

Alas, for Mr. Clay and his friends: at that very moment the Emperor, abandoning his routed army in its nightmare of retreat from Moscow, was posthaste heading homeward. The Russian people, led by Kutuzov, were waging a victorious war of national resistance against the hated invader. With the shattering of Napoleon's dream of conquest, the hopes of the U.S. expansionists suffered a blow also.

Two weeks before he met his death, Brock had written Prevost urging the speedy destruction of Sackett's Harbor, the U.S. naval base at the eastern end of Lake Ontario, across from Kingston. He warned: "The enemy is making every exertion to gain a naval superiority on both lakes, which if they accomplish I do not see how we can retain the country."

The proposal was sound, but Prevost rejected it. At the time of Brock's letter Chauncey, the U.S. naval commander, was having 140 ships' carpenters sent up to Sackett's from the New York navy yards. In the shipbuilding race that ensued, all the advantages lay with the Americans: in skilled manpower, availability of supplies, superior roads.*

---

*Mahan observes: "From York to Niagara by land was eighty miles of road impassable to laden wagons; by lake, thirty miles of water facility." And he quotes Prevost's rueful comment, much later in the war: "The command of the lakes enables the enemy to perform in two days what it takes the troops from Kingston 16 to 20 days of severe marching."

They made full use of them in order to gain naval superiority on Lake Ontario. One of its first fruits was the successful attack on the capital of Upper Canada.

On the morning of April 27, 1813, the inhabitants of York saw sixteen sail anchoring off the harbor, just east of the mouth of the Humber. To meet the arrivals—some two thousand U.S. troops under Chauncey and Dearborn—were three hundred regulars, two hundred militia, and forty Indian warriors. Nothing had been done to put the fortifications in a state of readiness; even the guns were half-mounted. After a sharply contested resistance in the woods of what is now Parkdale, the defenders were beaten back. After blowing up a powder magazine at the fort, they surrendered the town. The U.S. troops thereupon burned to the ground the buildings of the Legislative Assembly (at the foot of what is now Parliament St.) sacked the library, and pillaged the homes of citizens. Shortly thereafter the invading force departed.

A month later Prevost made an irresolute attack on Sackett's Harbor. It failed, because he ordered a retreat just at the moment when success was in his grasp. Meanwhile, Chauncey and Dearborn with 4,000 men had moved on Niagara, captured Fort George at the mouth of the river, and compelled the retreat of a force of 1,700 under Vincent to Burlington Heights.

The victorious American force now in command of the Peninsula and advancing on Burlington was in a position to sever the British land link with Lake Erie, and thereby to gain control of all of western Upper Canada. Vincent's small force, outnumbered five to one, was reduced to 90 rounds of ammunition to each gun. He decided on a daring stroke.

At eleven-thirty in the night of June 23, his men marched by way of what are now York and King Streets,

Hamilton, and at 2:00 a.m. stormed the enemy encampment at Stoney Creek. Taken by surprise, the invaders were thrown into confusion. Four guns and a hundred prisoners were taken—including two generals, Chandler and Winder. The attacking force withdrew before daybreak. Dearborn then ordered a retreat, first to nearby Forty Mile Creek, then on the arrival of a British naval squadron on one flank and Indian fighters on the other, all the way back to Fort George.

By the bold stroke at Stoney Creek, the way was opened to combined naval and ground offensive actions which by the year's end retook Fort George, captured Fort Niagara across from it on the U.S. side of the river, and swept as far as Black Rock. Politically, this operation electrified the inhabitants of Upper Canada, arousing a new spirit of confidence and combativity. A military analyst of the time estimated the results of the engagement in these terms: "The preservation of the Niagara district, and of Kingston, may . . . with the strictest justice, be attributed to the attack upon the enemy at Stoney Creek. The nature of the war seems instantly to have changed after that most manly and energetic affair."

In the course of the operations which followed, on the approaches to the Niagara River, word of an impending attack on one of Vincent's outposts was overheard by the wife of a wounded militiaman, Laura Secord. At great risk to herself, this mother of five children crossed the American lines and made her way for twenty miles through the bush, to give warning.

The battle that ensued was fought at Beaver Dam, near St. Davids. A force of nearly 600 U.S. troops was defeated and taken prisoner by combined detachments of Mohawk and Caughnawaga Indians. These were only half as numerous as their opponents. Leading the Indian fighters

were John Brant and Dominique Ducharme. Of their feat
of arms the British officer Fitzgibbon wrote: "Not a shot
was fired on our side by any but the Indians. They beat
the American detachment into a state of terror." The
Beaver Dam victory had the important effect of paralyzing
for some time enemy offensive efforts against the Niagara
Peninsula.

While the picture in the Burlington-Niagara sector was
changing from one of reverses to success, that on Lake Erie
and in the southwest followed an opposite course. Here
everything hinged on command of the lake; and this was
secured by the enemy, based at Erie, just at a time when
Procter's force at Malden was running out of provisions.
On September 10, at the western end of the lake, the
British-Canadian naval squadron under Barclay was compelled to engage a more powerfully armed force under
Perry. In a fiercely contested battle, the latter was victorious. The Americans were now able to ferry across an
invasion army of 4,500 men in eighty vessels to the Canadian side.

Procter, whose initial success early in the year at French-
town, on the American side of the river, was followed
by ineffectual attempts to take the U.S. forts on the south
shore, now decided to abandon his position. This despite
the fact that his force, including the Indians, equalled that
of the enemy under Harrison; and that he had pledged his
word to Tecumseh to hold his ground. When the Indian
leader discovered that Procter had deceived him and was
avoiding battle, he declared: "You have always told us
that you would never draw back or take your foot off
British ground; but now, father, we see you are drawing
back, and we are sorry to see our father doing so without
seeing the enemy. We must compare our father with a

fat dog that carries its tail high when all is peaceful, but when frightened it drops it between its legs and runs off!

"Father! You have the arms and ammunition which our great father sent for his red children. If you intend to go away, give them to us, and you may go, and welcome so far as we are concerned. Our lives are in the hands of the master of life. We are determined to defend our lands, and if it be his will, we wish to leave our bones upon them."

When Procter, after repeatedly promising to make a stand against the advancing Americans, left it to the Indians to fight the rearguard actions, Tecumseh made the bitter comment: "General Brock said, 'Tecumseh, *come* fight the Yankees.' General Procter says, 'Tecumseh, *go* fight the Yankees'!"

Thanks to his own gross mismanagement, with bridges left intact and his force burdened with excess baggage, Procter was finally overtaken and forced to fight at Moraviantown on the Thames. The British force broke before a cavalry charge; the Indians stood and fought until overwhelmed by the enemy. Tecumseh gave his life in battle; Procter saved his by ignominious flight.

Vincent, at Burlington, now occupied a key position. Should Harrison join forces with the U.S. army on the Niagara, there was a fair chance of their taking most of Upper Canada. Prevost, characteristically, ordered Vincent to abandon his position. He failed to comply with the order. Harrison, instead of following up the victory on the Thames, fell back on Amherstburg.

The boast of the Lexington *Recorder,* in October, failed to materialize. It had announced: "The loyal Canadians may lay in an additional stock of wood, for our troops mean to spend the winter with them."

Instead, the U.S. troops abandoned Fort George and withdrew across the Niagara.

*　　*　　*

Up to now, burdened with incompetent generals, the U.S. had been paying the price of a major flaw in its strategy. As Admiral Mahan observed long after: "To make the Western territory and control of the Indians the objects of the campaign was a political and military move perfectly allowable . . . but to make these things the objective of operations was to invert the order of proceedings, as one who, desiring to fell a tree, should procure a ladder and begin cutting off the outermost branches, instead of striking at the trunk by the ground . . . The Canadian tree was rooted in the ocean, where it was nourished by the sea power of Great Britain . . . In fact, the nearer the sea control over the water communications . . . [could] be established, the more radical and far-reaching the effect produced. For this reason Montreal was the true objective of American effort."

Now, in the fall of 1813, a massive attempt to strike at the heart, instead of the extremities of the Canadian position, was set under way. Two great armies, one from Sackett's Harbor under Wilkinson, the other from Plattsburg under Hampton, were directed to converge on the St. Lawrence, sever Kingston's communications and take Montreal.

Wilkinson moved downstream from Sackett's with 8,000 men in 180 great boats. At the head of the Long Sault, just west of Cornwall, a pursuing force caught up with the American rearguard. In a sharply fought engagement at Chrystler's Farm, the U.S. force was worsted and suffered serious loss. Wilkinson, however, proceeded with his main body to the appointed rendezvous with Hampton, at St. Regis, across from Cornwall. Here he learned to his discomfiture that his opposite number had not kept the appointment; he had met with an obstacle. Like Wilkinson, but on a more extended scale, Hampton was beset by what one dispatch described as "the active universal hostility of the inhabitants of the country."

General Hampton, a wealthy Virginia land speculator, and the owner of 3,000 slaves, had crossed the border into Canada on September 20 with an army of 4,000 regulars, 1,500 militia, and ten cannon. Bedevilled by ceaseless, sudden small-scale attacks on the part of militia detachments and Indians, led by Captain Joseph Mailloux, the invaders halted and cast about for a more favorable line of advance than that of the Richelieu. Hampton decided to try the line of the Châteauguay River. He moved westward to Châteauguay Four Corners, then downstream to its confluence with the St. Lawrence opposite La Chine. This movement to the Châteauguay took his army a month. De Salaberry, leading a couple of hundred militia and Indians, "constantly needling the enemy, harassed him, killed some of his men, impeded his advance."

Because Prevost, cautiously husbanding his main body of troops, gave little support to de Salaberry, the latter's handful of pickets were all that stood between the enemy and Montral. On October 26, at a spot on the river selected by the Canadian commander, the three hundred militia and Indians, with another couple of hundred in reserve, made a stand against the vastly superior invading force. By dint of good generalship, hard fighting, and a ruse which caused Hampton to think he was confronted by a much larger force than in fact he was—the Canadians caused the enemy to retreat. Once started on his homeward way, Hampton was encouraged to continue—all the way back to his starting point at Plattsburg.

At Châteauguay, a militia force made up overwhelmingly of French Canadians and Indians had stopped the invaders in their tracks and thrown them back. Thereby they had lifted the most serious threat the Canadas faced:

a major converging blow on the life-line of the St. Lawrence and Montreal. As C. P. Lucas observes in his history of the war: "This fight proved to be a demonstration that the war was a national war for Canada."

A song written in 1812 by a militiaman, J. B. Fréchette (a printer who worked with the Reform leader, John Neilson of Quebec City) voices the spirit of resistance which grew up in French Canada in answer to the invaders:

"Allons amis préparons-nous,
Puisqu'ils veulent faire la guerre
Que les Yankés sentent nos coups
Sachons vaincre comme nos pères . . .

"Le jour de gloire est donc venue,
Il vaut pour nous cent ans de vie
On a toujours assez vécu
Quand on a servi sa patrie.

Refrain

"Ne craignons pas ces fanfarons
S'ils entrent dans notre province
Ils y trouveront des lurons
Qui leur feront changer de ton."*

The war entered its concluding phase in 1814, the remaining major engagements being fought in the Niagara Peninsula, on Lake Champlain, and on the Atlantic seaboard.

In December, 1813, the U.S. troops had destroyed the village of Newark (now Niagara-on-the-Lake); over 400

---

*"Come friends let us prepare—Since they want to wage a war, Let the Yankees feel our blows, Let's conquer like our sires of yore . . . The day of glory has arrived, It's worth a hundred years of life; One has ever lived to the full, When one has served one's country. (Refrain): Let's not fear these boasters, if they step into our province They'll find some lads who'll make them change their tune!" (Sung to the tune: "Voulez-vous suivre un bon conseil?"—"Do you want some good advice?")

women, children and old folk were turned out of doors into the cold night of winter and, while they watched, 150 houses were burned to ashes. This atrocity, added to the wanton burning of York and the pillaging of the farmsteads, deepened the growing sense of national anger.

Having failed to get any sort of hold on their adversary's throat—the St. Lawrence lifeline—the Americans now made another try at the Niagara midriff. With Detroit and Lake Erie in their hands, and with naval superiority achieved on Lake Ontario, they were in a favorable position for a simultaneous pincers movement from west and east.

The issue was fought out in a "desperate and sanguinary engagement" at Lundy's Lane, just west of Niagara Falls, on July 16. The British and Canadians, under General Drummond, lost 878, killed and wounded; the Americans, under Brown and Winfield Scott, lost 860. Tactically, it was a drawn battle; but since it was followed by U.S. withdrawal to Fort Erie, and the abandonment of the offensive on the Canadian frontier, it must count as a victory for the defenders.

Shortly thereafter, following inconclusive engagements on the fortified lines at Fort Erie, the U.S. abandoned their position there and the whole peninsula was cleared of the invaders.

Just as they had failed to combine their invading armies against Montreal, so in the Niagara theatre the Americans failed to co-ordinate operations on land with a projected naval attack by Chauncey from Lake Ontario.

Brock's words, in a letter to his brother, proved prophetic: "Were the Americans of one mind the opposition I could make would be unavailing; but I am not without hope that their divisions may be the saving of this province."

Disunity in the enemy camp—plus vigorous offensive action by the defenders—decided the issue. Deficiency in the latter component could be disastrous, as Prevost soon demonstrated at Plattsburg.

In September Prevost's forces were strengthened by the arrival of four brigades from Wellington's Peninsular Army. He was thus able to advance with some 12,000 men against the American positions at the head of Lake Champlain. Despite his vast preponderance of strength, he insisted on waiting nearly a week before Plattsburg for naval support on the lake. When the naval squadron arrived and at considerable disadvantage engaged a U.S. force in the harbor, Prevost, who had been counted on to take the land guns which covered the American squadron, continued to stall; and when the British squadron was beaten, he used the defeat of those whom he had left in the lurch as justification for retiring without a fight.

Recalled shortly thereafter to face a court martial, Prevost died before it could be held. Politically, he had helped to rally French-Canadian support for the war, and to mend some of the damage done by Craig's repressive regime. But as a military leader he exercised a baneful influence; when an offensive was called for, he imposed a defensive; when defense was indicated, he proposed withdrawal. Lucas sums up his failing:

"As a leader in the field, he was wanting in nerve; he had none of that instinct which grips the occasion, strikes quick and hard, and extorts success."

Up to this time, two factors accounted for the relative immunity of the Maritimes. One was the naval weakness of the U.S., which ruled out the possibility of dislodging the British from Halifax, to say nothing of Newfoundland. The other was the *de facto* neutrality of the neighboring New England states, which were perfectly happy to enrich themselves by means of trading with the enemy, as they did during the greater part of the war, to the mutual profit of merchants in Boston and Halifax.

In November, 1812, an American in Halifax wrote that in the space of a fortnight twenty thousand barrels of flour from Boston had been unloaded from vessels flying Spanish and Swedish flags. This supply was of vital importance to the British forces in the Canadas. Prevost reported that two-thirds of his army were eating beef obtained from Vermont through U.S. contractors.

While Halifax was enjoying a boom, there were nonetheless periodic alarms and excursions. Haliburton's chronicle records some of them:

"July 1, 1812: His Majesty's ship Belvidera arrived at Halifax, and reports that she was chased on the 23rd ultimo by an American squadron, consisting of three large frigates, a sloop of war, and a brig, and fired into by the leading ship. The captain and eighteen seamen wounded, and two killed . . .

"July 31: An American privateer comes into Broad Cove near Digby, and is driven off by the militia . . .

"June 6, 1813: His Majesty's frigate Shannon arrives at Halifax, with her prize, the American frigate Chesapeake, which she had captured after a short but severe engagement of eleven minutes."

Yankee privateers preyed on merchantmen and fishing ships; over two-thirds of all their captures were made in the Bay of Fundy and off the Nova Scotia and Newfoundland coasts. Here were the busy crossroads of the sea routes from the West Indies to Canada and those from Canada and Nova Scotia to Britain. In return, privateers out of Halifax warred on the U.S. raiders, and by the end of the war had captured some two hundred of them.

In the last year of the war the provinces by the Atlantic were drawn more directly into the hostilities. With Napoleon beaten at Leipzig in 1813 and exiled to Elba, the full force of the British fleet could be brought to bear on the Atlantic seaboard.*

It applied a strong blockade of U.S. ports and conducted offensive operations against Washington, Louisiana and the Maine coast.

As it tightened, the stranglehold of close blockade stifled U.S. foreign trade. From over $100 million before the war, it was reduced, in 1814, to the neighborhood of $5 million.

In August, 1814, the British attacked Washington and put it to the torch in retaliation for the burning of York, Newark and Sandwich the year before. In the same month an expedition from Halifax took Castine and Machias in Maine, thereby securing a hundred-mile stretch of coastline and the tract of land lying between New Brunswick and Lower Canada.

By now, negotiations for peace were taking place.

In January, 1813, the Russian government had offered to mediate the conflict between Britain and the U.S. Although American commissioners went to St. Petersburg to enter upon negotiations, the British in effect rejected the proposal. Finally, direct negotiations got under way in 1814; after dragging on for months, they terminated with the signature, on December 24, of the Treaty of Ghent.

The treaty ignored the issues of maritime rights that had been most hotly in dispute on the outbreak of the war. In the main, as regards territory, it restored the situa-

---

*"[Madison] had counted on a Napoleonic victory over Russia to bring Britain to terms." . . . "The fall of Napoleon knocked the bottom out of the war of 1812." (A. L. Burt, *The U.S., Great Britain and North America, 1775-1820*, p. 345).

tion that obtained previously. The western fur country in the regions of the Illinois and upper Mississippi, regained in the course of the hostilities, was abandoned by the British negotiators. At the same time they dropped the demand (for which at first they had pressed) for a neutral Indian territory in that area. Thus once again the British reward for Indian support was betrayal at the peace. The U.S. claims over the Western Indian territories were acceded to: the Indian tribes were denied any recognition whatsoever, either as parties to the peace or as independent communities. It mattered little that they had made it possible for the British to hold all the Western fur country as far as the upper Mississippi. Their claim to a neutral western territory was dropped by the British negotiators, in what one historian has called "an abandonment of conclusive finality."

Some disputed points regarding the U.S.-Canadian boundary were left for subsequent negotiation. Two years after the Treaty of Ghent was ratified, an agreement was reached on naval disarmament on the Lakes. Because these waters were not accessible to the ocean fleets, command of them hinged on lake shipbuilding capacity. As the Americans had a decided edge in this respect, and as it was considered that British naval superiority on the Atlantic coast more than outweighed any local disadvantage in the interior, the British agreed in effect to "surrender to the United States the potential control of the Lakes in the event of war." This, the Rush-Bagot agreement, was signed in April, 1817.

If the Americans were hardly winning the war when it ended, they cannot be said to have lost the peace.

British North America, however, was preserved. On a medal struck by the Loyal and Patriotic Society of Upper Canada, together with the words "Presented by a grateful country" and "Upper Canada preserved," there appeared the following device: "A strait between two lakes: on the north side a beaver—emblem of peaceful industry—that ancient cognizance of Canada; in the background an English lion slumbering . . . On the south side of the strait an American eagle (circling), checked from seizing the beaver."

The Outcome of the War

As between Britain and the United States, the War of 1812 ended in a draw. The former retained possession of its North American dependencies but failed to break the power of the United States. The latter succesfully upheld its independence but failed in its attempt to conquer Canada. The military stalemate reflected the relation of forces between the major antagonists: it shaped the setting within which the British North American colonies were to evolve in the century that followed.

But if the outcome was a draw in terms of the war aims of Britain and the United States, it was a victory in terms of Canadian resistance to an American invasion. It is in this sense that the war has come to be known as "the national war of Canada" or even as "the Canadian War of Independence."

Challenging this interpretation, Professor S. D. Clark views the war as an unsuccessful effort by the United States to liberate Canada from British colonial rule.

Clearly, the interpretation of the character of the war involves two related problems: an assessment of the class forces and aims of the chief antagonists—Britain and the United States; and of the relation to the foregoing of the British American colonial population. Oversimplification invites pitfalls. One such consists in viewing the war solely in terms of Canada, instead of starting with the relationships of the major powers whose collision turned British North America into a theatre of war. Another does the opposite: focusing only on the Anglo-U.S. conflict, it ignores the distinct and peculiar Canadian component which, while secondary to the relation of forces of the major powers, was nonetheless of importance for the outcome of the contest, and was crucial for this country's subsequent history.

The first question, then, has to do with our assessment of the over-all character of the conflict. As has been suggested previously,* the Anglo-American war of 1812-14 was the armed collision of two bourgeois national states: the British, possessors of a colonial empire, allied with feudal-absolutist Europe in a struggle with post-revolutionary, Napoleonic France; and the recently established American Republic, whose expanding commercial interests conflicted with those of Britain, and whose national sovereignty was being challenged by British naval and military power. Because the United States was *in transition* from its era of bourgeois-democratic revolution to that of consolidation and expansion of bourgeois power, the war on its part possessed a dual, ambivalent character. To the extent that it was waged in resistance to British counter-revolutionary aims of annulling the gains of the American Revolution, there was a strong national-democratic element in the war. But to the extent that it expressed the new expansionist drive of the ruling classes in the United States (the coalition of emergent industrial capitalists and entrenched slave-owners), the character of the war was predatory and aggressive. In this contradictory amalgam of conflicting aims, the revolutionary-democratic element was in the process of receding in importance, while the bourgeois-expansionist element was growing more pronounced, foreshadowing the claim to "Manifest Destiny".

In this view, the war cannot be considered as basically a revolutionary, anti-colonial "liberation effort" on the

*Cf. pp. 270-274, above.

part of the United States. True, the element of "defense of the gains of the American Revolution" was present, and it was this that caused the most radical of the popular opposition leaders in Upper Canada to see the United States as the bastion of freedom. (Thus Joseph Willocks, the Irish democrat, member of the Upper Canada assembly, went over to the American side and organized a contingent of "Canadian Volunteers" to fight the British.) But the increasingly dominant element in the U.S. effort was predatory and expansionist.

On the part of the British ruling classes, the aims of the war were predatory and colonialist. They sought the disruption of the new-born Republic, the reversal of its victory in the revolutionary War of Independence. Sea-power and the colonial-military base in British North America were the chief instruments of this policy. In this imperial context, the regular troops and colonial militia in the Canadas were alike part and parcel of the machinery of a reactionary war. The war involved a certain strengthening of the colonial framework, confirmed with the retention of the colonial provinces in the Empire as a result of the war's outcome.

Yet the deep-seated conflicts of interest as between the imperial rulers and the colonial settlers (expressed in the agitation and refrom movements of the 1790's and early 1800's), while they might be repressed in some measure by the state of war, could not thereby be removed, and were in some respects aggravated and intensified. Thus, in October 1812 the governor-general, Prevost, complains to the Colonial Office of "a lukewarmness in the disposition of the Canadians." In May 1813 he writes of "the growing discontent and undissembled dissatisfaction of the mass of the people of Upper Canada in consequence of the effects of the militia laws upon a population thinly scattered over an extensive range of country, whose zeal was exhausted and whose exertions had brought want and ruin to the doors of many and had in various instances produced a considerable emigration of settlers to the United States, whence most of them originally came." He observes also that "the militia had been considerably weakened by the frequent desertion of even the well disposed part of them to their farms for the purpose of getting seed into the ground before the short summer of this country had too far advanced."

In June 1813 Lt. Col. De Boucherville reports that "the disaffection of the settlers is shocking."

Professor S. D. Clark observes: "Behind Brock was a population of divided loyalties, and a decisive American victory in 1812 would have resulted without much question in the defection of a large portion of it to the American side."

Yet the trend that increasingly asserted itself was one that worked in a contrary sense. A clue to what occurred is contained in a letter from a republican sympathizer in Canada to U.S. Major-Gen. Van Rensselaer in the fall of 1812, following the unsuccessful American invasion effort from Detroit:

"When Gen Hull's proclamation appeared it had its effect, there being a security for private property contained in it. Most of the inhabitants would willingly have submitted, but when it was found that private property was seized without (compensation?) the public sentiment entirely changed. The success of Gen. Brock established the change of sentiment . . . A determination now prevails among the people to defend their country."

It was the grim experience of invasion, of devastation and pillage by occupying troops, that called forth a sense of national solidarity among the Canadian settlers. Episodes like the burning of the parliament building at York and the ruthless laying waste of Newark stirred a mounting sense of national anger. A visitor to Upper Canada in 1816 bore witness to the misery brought by war to the settlers in the western districts:

"I was sensibly struck with the devastation which had been made by the late war: beautiful farms, formerly in high cultivation, now laid waste; houses entirely evacuated and forsaken; provision of all kinds very scarce; and where once peace and plenty abounded, poverty and destruction now stalked the land."

The fact that the British-Canadian war effort took the form of a strategic defensive, warding off an American drive for conquest, reinforced the feeling of the settlers that this was a war in defense of hearth and home. As Brock's biographer described it:

"The old men left their farms and their plowshares to bear arms for their beloved country. The wives and daughters supplied the place of husbands and fathers in the drudgery of agricultural life. The women during the war... could be seen sowing the land in the spring and reaping in fall. They thought no sacrifice too great to be made, so that their hearthstones might be protected from the ruthless hands of the invader. There were many Laura Secords in those days."

At the same time within the strategic defense, successful tactical offensive strokes (under Brock's leadership, and later at Stoney Creek) inspired a new sense of confidence.

Thus the war, in the words of one historian, "gave birth in Canada to that feeling of self-reliance and self-respect without which no strong national spirit can well exist."

The struggle, which had been thrust on the Canadians from without, became for them something of a national war. And this fact in turn played its part in deciding the military outcome.

It has become fashionable of late, as part of the process of "U.S.-Canadian integration" (i.e., Americanization), to play down, ridicule, or deny outright, the role of the Canadian people in past struggles. One expression of this tendency is the irrepressible urge of some historians to display their sophistication by sneers at the national past. "Except for the uninformed and for the professional patriots," writes Professor Lower of the 1812 war, "time has almost turned its melodrama into farce." Smart-aleck "cosmopolitanism" now finds common ground with professional military snobbery: it has long been customary for imperial-minded military writers to promote the myth according to which the war was really "fought by outsiders," that it was the British regulars alone who "saved the colony," that the Canadians played no significant part in determining the outcome of the war.

Facts speak otherwise. Of a total 8,000 regular troops, half were raised in the colonies themselves: e.g. the Canadian Fencibles, Canadian Voltigeurs, Royal Newfoundland Regiment, New Brunswick Regiment, Royal Veterans, and the Glengarries. Another 4,000 militiamen shared with the foregoing in the decisive engagements of the war.

In the words of F.-X. Garneau, this country's first historian:

"The courage of the colonists themselves, with the disciplined valor of the small amount of regular soldiery which the home authorities could spare, formed the living and almost sole barrier that was at first opposed to American invasion."

The American failure—despite vastly superior manpower and resources—to take Canada was due in part at least to internal disunity. Behind military incapacity lay political indecision. Opposition of the New England mercantile interests to any war with England put a brake on the American effort. In Vermont and up-state New York there was a current of popular resistance to war for the conquest of Canada. A bellicose military proclamation in 1812 calling for the subjugation of Canada elicited a vigorous "Answer of the Men of New York, inhabiting the Western District":

"Why appeal to our valor," they asked, "for the destruction of our own happiness or that of others?" War meant "desolation . . . fields strewn with carnage . . . the tears of the widow . . . the orphan perishing in want and disease." As against the folly of war, "our victories are (won) over the unproductive face of nature; our renown is in fertile fields, in peaceful homes and numerous and happy families."

This stand of American democrats in opposition to an expansionist war deserves an honored place in the tradition of international fraternity and solidarity. It was part of the popular-democratic striving that carried forward the revolutionary tradition of 1776, and that had its counterpart in the incipient radical and reform movements in the British North American provinces as well.

The war sowed the seed of a sense of Canadian identity. But it is well to remember that it did so within the cramping framework of British colonial rule: a framework that was strengthened—albeit temporarily—by the outcome of the war.

Moreover, the emergence of a "Canadian" consciousness was further slowed by the cleavage between two national communities, French and English-speaking, and by geographical dispersal and regional diversity.

In the Atlantic provinces, adjoining neutralist New England and dominated by the Halifax naval base, a sense of regional identity was interwoven with pro-British, anti-American feeling (the latter zealously stoked by the strong upper-class Loyalist contingent). In the absence of close communication, and sharing no common experience of invasion, the Maritimes and Newfoundland had little in common with the Canadas other than a like awareness of "being British."

It was in Upper Canada that the most marked change was effected by the war. Here the beginnings emerged of an Anglo-Canadian national consciousness. Yet here, too, the sense of "Britishness" was strongly interwoven with the incipient feeling of Canadian identity: most strongly, in the case of the Loyalist element. Brock's speech to the Upper Canada legislature in July 1812 fairly accurately expressed the amalgam of British loyalism and local patriotism that was taking shape:

"When invaded by an enemy whose avowed object is the entire conquest of this Province, the voice of loyalty as well as of interest calls aloud to every person in the sphere in which he is placed to defend his country. Our militia have heard that voice and obeyed it. They have evinced by the promptitude and loyalty of their conduct that they are worthy of the King whom they serve and the Constitution which they enjoy."

Invasion, the threat of conquest, defense of country, loyalty to British monarchy, attachment to parliamentary institutions as against American republicanism: all are alluded to as ingredients in a determination to resist the Americans. All played their part in the making of what eventually became a British North American, and then a Canadian consciousness.

Canadian—or Anglo-Canadian. For the French Canadians were already a compact national community. What the threat of U.S. conquest was beginning to do for English-Canadian attitudes in Upper Canada, the reality of British conquest had accomplished, a half-century before, for French Canada. Whereas Anglo-Canadian national feeling was in the first place anti-American (and only later took on an anti-British tone), French-Canadian national feeling was primarily anti-English. Now, in the war with the United States, an element of common resistance to conquest began to link the peoples of Lower and Upper Canada: the forerunner of a sense of common Canadian identity in the two national communities of British North America. Queenston Heights and Stoney Creek, Chrysler's Farm and Chateauguay: in these engagements, settlers belonging to both national communities perhaps for the first time became conscious of an attachment to a common country.

Reference has been made* to the decision of the French-Canadian reform leaders to support the war effort. In this they undoubtedly were influenced by the policy of conciliation pursued by Governor Prevost, which was in sharp contrast with the repressive regime of Craig, his predecessor. A dispatch of Prevost (cited in a recent work by Helen Taft Manning) sheds light on the way his concessions to the French Canadians strengthened the hand of the imperial authorities:

"The use which has been made of—and the confidence reposed in—the Canadian Peasantry . . . have materially changed their character and disposition—so much so that the best informed amongst the Canadians themselves have not failed to remark the circumstance with equal satisfaction and surprise. By putting arms into their hands and calling them forth for the defence of their country in conjunction with His Majesty's regular forces their former prejudices and distrust have been removed . . ."

Prevost exaggerated; but there was some truth in his assertion, as is shown by the tribute paid to him in an address of the Lower Canada assembly following the termination of the war:

---

*P. 297, above.

"The events of the late war have drawn closer the bonds which connect great Britain and the Canadas . . . the blood of the sons of Canada has flowed mingled with that of the brave soldiers sent for its defense . . . The inhabitants of this country can lay claim with more reason than ever to the preservation and free exercise of the benefits assured them by their constitution and their laws."

Worth noting is that the concluding words convey an unmistakable reminder of the French Canadians' resolve to preserve their civil and national liberties: a determination that was put to the sternest test in the quarter-century following the war. *Our language, our institutions and our laws* had been the motto of *Le Canadien* in 1806; it was the rallying cry of the Patriotes in the 1830's.

In both Lower and Upper Canada, then, the war heightened a sense of national consciousness and quickened the assertion of constitutional liberties.

It has been said in relation to the Decembrists' uprising of 1825 in Russia, that "the triumph of 1812 made not only serfdom but also continuance of autocratic despotism morally intolerable." In a like manner, those Canadians who had fought for hearth and home against the invader were less inclined to endure without challenge the combination of colonial yoke and Family Compact tyranny.

In the years that followed the War of 1812, colonial rule in British North America encountered a growing and ultimately revolutionary resistance. The mainspring of this resistance was the growth of a *local capitalism,* which the War of 1812 did much to stimulate. Britain's war with Napoleonic France had called forth a boom in the trade in timber, a rapid increase in wheat production, and new beginnings in local manufactures.* The War of 1812 enriched the mercantile and industrial capitalists of Montreal, Quebec and Halifax. One of the founders of the

*Cf. pp. 273-4, above.

Halifax Banking Company (est. 1825) was Enos Collins, who after making a fortune out of wartime privateering became an importer of "brandy, silks, spices and ammunition." The Molsons of Montreal, who had invested some of the profits from their brewery in a shipyard, launched their second steamer, the *Swiftsure*, in the summer of 1812. Used as a troop transport, she was the first steamship to serve in war: an operation from which the Molsons grossed the respectable sum of £40,000.

It was wartime profits, joined with those of the fur-traders, that furnished the capital for the founding of Canada's first bank: the Bank of Montreal, established in 1817.

A further by-product of the war was the impetus to road and canal building in the interior of Upper Canada: the vulnerability in wartime of the lines of communication on the Lower Lakes lent weight to pressure for projects like the Rideau Canal, the military survey for which was started in 1816.

While the provisioning of the war effort stimulated the early shoots of local capitalist industry, the peace settlement struck a blow at the power of the Montreal fur traders. Surrender by the British of the posts that had been captured in the Michigan-Illinois country (Michillimackinac, Prairie du Chien and others) was a calamity for the Nor'Westers. It was promptly followed by American action barring Canadian traders from that area. "The Treaty of Ghent destroyed the Southern trade," wrote William McGillivray later. Lord Selkirk's planting of a settlement on the Red River, in 1811-12, athwart the North West Company's lifeline to the Great West, was a blow from another flank.* These developments made the

---

*This development will be dealt with in the sequel to the present volume.

contest of the Nor'Westers with the Hudson's Bay Company even more murderous and intense than it had been in the years before the war.

All in all, the weakening of the North West Company—historically the first powerful group of "Anglo-Canadian" capitalist entrepreneurs—strengthened relatively the interests centred in the Hudson's Bay Company, and hence, metropolitan as against colonial capital. But the weakening of the Nor-Westers also had another consequence: it set the stage for the appearance of a new capitalist grouping in English Canada, associated with the timber and shipbuilding and local industries: a grouping that embodied the interests of an emerging industrial capitalism, as against the old mercantile interest of the fur trade.

It is with the emergence of the first sprouts of "native manufactures," with local capitalist industry seeking to master its own local market, that the rise of national sentiment has tended to be associated. What was happening in British North America was one particular instance of a process that was unfolding in Europe and the Americas. The growth of capitalist industry and pressures for the formation of national states went hand in hand. Both were stimulated by the wars of the 18th and early 19th century. Both led in the direction of bourgeois revolutions: the assumption of power by the capitalist class, displacing the landowner-aristocratic ruling classes of the outlived feudal order.

In Europe, the wars of conquest waged by Napoleonic France called forth movements of national resistance—in Germany, Russia, Spain. The national character of these wars was expressed in various ways. In one case, it was almost wholly a matter of guerrilla warfare; in another the national resistance was primarily the struggle of the organized military forces, supported by the masses of the people. (In Canada, resistance to conquest by the United

States found expression in the regular forces, the militia, and their growing mass popular support.)

Spain's colonial power in the Americas was shaken to its foundations when Napoleon ousted the Spanish Bourbons and their subject peoples in Latin America rose in revolt against the miseries of colonial rule. In 1810 mass demonstrations in Buenos Aires led to the overthrow of the Spanish viceroy; by 1816 Argentina was able to proclaim her independence. In Mexico a war of independence led by Hidalgo began in 1810, involving tens of thousands in large-scale fighting. Struggles led by Miranda, Bolivar, San Martin, O'Higgins, liberated Venezuela and Colombia, Ecuador and Chile. In Haiti during the years of the French Revolution Toussaint l'Ouverture had led a revolutionary uprising of Negro slaves, defying the efforts of the chief West European powers to crush them.

Such was the background of national liberation revolutions in Latin America, which broke the colonial yoke of Portugal and Spain: only to encounter new oppressors with whom the struggle is continuing in our own day.

It was within this setting of wide-ranging national-democratic revolutionary upheavals that the "national war of Canada" took place. As in some other instances, the seed of national sentiment underwent forced growth in the heat of war and invasion, even though a capitalist national economy had not yet developed to the point of posing the issue of independence and national statehood. A special feature of Anglo-Canadian national sentiment was the fact that it was born of resistance to United States expansionism and aggression.

In so far as it was simply anti-American, the sentiment engendered among Canadians by the war tended to buttress British loyalism. But to the extent that it was an actual consciousness of *national identity* (however rudimentary), the new sentiment, once the war was over, led to a more vigorous assertion of a Canadian democratic spirit. National consciousness merged with the radical currents that had appeared in the 1790's and early 1800's. It joined with democratic radicalism in the rising demand for far-reaching reforms in the colonial structure—and eventually for Canadian independence.

The forces making for 1837—and its aftermath in Confederation—were already at work.

POSTSCRIPT

A Note on Marxism and Canadian Historiography

CONTRARY TO AN OFT-REPEATED FALLACY, MARXISM IS not "economic determinism." Marxism holds that it is the people who make history—their labor and their struggles and their dreams; and that these are understandable and have meaning when seen in their real setting: man's progressively extending mastery over the forces of nature, and the succession of social systems that have marked, one after another, the stages of his progression.

This real setting is a universal fact of life. Man in relation to nature; man's society undergoing gradual or revolutionary change: the patterns vary widely as between peoples and countries, but one common denominator underlies them all. "The first premise of all human history," wrote Marx in the *German Ideology*, "is of course the existence of living human individuals . . . Men can be distinguished from animals by consciousness, by religion or what you will. They themselves begin to distinguish themselves from animals as soon as they begin to *produce* their means of subsistence . . ."

Labor, production, the real relationships of living society: this is the point of departure for historical materialism, as it is for every-day life. Thought and feeling, ideas and passion and imagination have their being in a material world, are conditioned by it, work upon it. The struggle and action of millions transform society, as today's world bears witness.

Marx's conception of "the evolution of the economic formation of society . . . viewed as a process of natural history" made possible a science of social development. As Lenin pointed out, in a work that settles accounts with most of the "refutations of Marxism" that are currently in fashion: "Hitherto, sociologists had found it difficult to distinguish the important and the unimportant in the complex network of social phenomena (that is the root of subjectivism in sociology) and had been unable to discover any objective criterion for such a demarcation. Materialism provided an absolutely objective criterion by singling out 'production relations' as the structure of society . . . the analysis of material social relations at once made it possible to observe recurrence and regularity and to generalize the systems of the various countries in the single fundamental concept: *social formation*."

It is this concept, and this approach, that I have sought to apply in the present rough outline of Canada's beginnings. This country's history, in its concrete peculiarities, is unique (as is that of every other country). But its concreteness is understandable, explainable, only to the degree that one can discover within it the general, universal elements of productive forces, relationships of production, classes and class conflict, the state, nation and national aspiration, culture, ideology. The reality is at once particular and general. And the attempt at unravelling it is a matter of more than theoretical urgency.

In Canada today there is a growing concern with questions of national identity and independence, of economic security and control of the economy—and with survival. The recent quickening of interest in our country's past is not unconnected with this quest for a sense of direction in our national life.

Can history help in achieving such a sense of direction? Despite the vast amount that has been done in this field—

and the output is growing steadily—there are many expressions of doubt. Dr. Hilda Neatby, pointing to the dividing line that separates French- and English-speaking historians, cites the "lack of a common philosophy" as an obstacle to "any one general interpretation of Canadian history." Yet in both national communities work now being done on social and economic aspects of our history suggests a common ground of interpretation. (In drawing heavily on this work, as I do, I would hope as well to help bridge the dividing line between the two communities, in however small a measure.)

Yet in the economic and social field, one encounters fresh difficulties. The late H. A. Innis, who made a massive contribution to knowledge of Canada's economic development, wrote: "We have been unable to interpret or predict the lines of Canada's development, either because of its complexity, or the rapidity and magnitude of its changes." As "perhaps the most serious obstacle" he deplored what he called "the lack of a philosophy of economic history applicable to new countries." Prof. Hugh Aitken has recently noted the "critical condition" of economic history on this continent, explaining it by the lack of integration between economic history and economic theory. Prof. S. D. Clark, addressing in 1959 the joint meeting of the Canadian Historical and Political Science Associations, noted the extreme reluctance of sociologists to examine "societies in change" and their avoidance of "the nasty word 'conflict'"; he called for "the development of a sociology of social change."

There is a "sociology of social change." It is Marxism. One need not agree with it, to accept its presence—and growing influence—as a significant fact in today's world. The pretense that it "does not exist" is wearing thin. Noteworthy in this connection is the comment of Harold Innis: "There is much to be said for the Marxian approach to

Canadian history, but not sufficient to support absolute certainty." The possibility that Marxism may provide a new insight into Canadian development surely merits examination.

In the youthful period of Canadian capitalism, a great national-democratic historian like F.-X. Garneau did not shrink from recognizing the existence of classes and fundamental social transformations. Over a century ago he wrote in his *History of Canada*: "The New World was discovered, and began to be colonized, at a time when forms of society unlike those in the old, were in a state of commencing transition; when the great mass of mankind, born to labor and to suffer, — in a word, the people, — were beginning to agitate for obtaining a government suited to public needs; and whose more aspiring members . . . were becoming a middle class, destined soon to take a ruling place in conjunction with, or to the displacement of, the regality of the sword, sustained by a now subordinated aristocracy."

Class relationships today are different. It is labor that is "destined soon to take a ruling place" in Canada, establishing thereby a "form of society" that will replace the rule of capital. The standpoint of labor, not that of capitalist monopoly, makes possible an approach to our history that lays bare the roots of social struggle, the realities of exploitation, the sources of our national dependence: an approach that can shed light on the direction of our national development in a world that is being transformed.

Acknowledgments

SINCE THIS BOOK AND ITS SEQUEL ARE AN EFFORT AT *interpretation* rather than one of search into unexplored areas, I have drawn mainly on already available material: chronicles and journals of participants from the 16th century onward, and the very large body of studies made since Garneau's day. At the same time, in re-evaluating the existing data one is struck by the need for a great deal of further research, particularly into the conditions and struggles of the working people. In this regard I must stress my indebtedness to the authors of recent socio-economic studies in French Canada: such as those on indentured labor and the *engagés* in New France, published in the *Revue d'Histoire de l'Amérique Française,* and on the early bourgeoisie in New France, in the same journal, and in works by MM. Jean Hamelin, Guy Frégault and others; and to the pioneering work of S. D. Clark, *Movements of Political Protest in Canada: 1640-1840.* Among earlier researchers, no one can approach this field without incurring a debt to the immense contributions to Canadian historiography of Dr. Marius Barbeau and the late Professor Harold Innis, in their studies, respectively, of the native peoples and of the early European fishermen and fur traders.

The first major step towards a Marxist interpretation of Canadian development was Gustavus Myers' *History of Canadian Wealth.* It constitutes a landmark; I owe much to it, both in getting my initial bearings in this field over a quarter-century ago, and in projecting some of the lines of search pursued in the present study.

The work of contemporary Marxists abroad has likewise been of very great assistance: A. L. Morton's work, *A People's History of England;* Jean Bruhat's *Histoire du Mouvement Ouvrier français;* Herbert Aptheker's *Colonial Era* and *American Revolution;* and, in the USSR, the work of Julia P. Averkieva and A. G. Mileikovsky.

An initiator of work on a Marxist interpretation of Canadian history was the late J. Francis White. All of us who have worked in this field owe much to him.

In 1946 a Conference on Marxist Studies, held in Toronto, set up a committee to work on a People's History. Its members, and those of the History Group of the recently-formed Marxist Study Centre, have worked on research and prepared valuable material.

To Margaret Fairley, whose writings have made a notable contribution to historical work, I am deeply grateful for both advice and practical assistance.

The fact that persisting McCarthyism makes it injudicious to thank by name some of those who helped greatly in the preparation of the book, is in itself a comment on a state of things that cannot go unchallenged.

For reading the book in proofs and making valuable criticisms and suggestions, I am much indebted to Tim Buck, Leslie Morris and John Weir. Libbie and Frank Park, Robert S. Kenny and others helped at various stages of production. I am grateful to them all. To my wife, who bore a large part of the load, most special thanks are due.

For the maps I am indebted to Avrom Yanovsky.

Omissions, errors and shortcomings are all my own.

THE AUTHOR

Reference Notes

ABBREVIATIONS

Cities of publication: L.: London; Mtl.: Montreal; M.: Moscow;
NY.: New York; O.: Ottawa; Q.: Quebec;
T.: Toronto

Journals, societies, etc.:
AA: *American Antiquity*
ACF: Académie canadienne-française
AS: Academy of Sciences
BRH: *Bulletin de Recherches Historiques*
CHA: Canadian Historical Association
CHR: *Canadian Historical Review*
CJEPS: *Canadian Journal of Economics and Political Science*
MECW: Marx-Engels: Collected Works
OHS: Ontario Historical Society
PAC: Public Archives of Canada
RAPQ: Report of Archivist, Province of Quebec
RHAF: *Revue d'Histoire de l'Amérique Française*
RSC: Royal Society of Canada
TPL: Toronto Public Library

cf.: compare, refer to
cit.: quoted (by, in)
ff.: and following (pages)
fn.: footnote
Fr.: French
Ger.: German
ibid.: same

It.: Italian
loc. cit.: place cited
nd.: no date
op. cit.: work cited
Rn.: Russian
Sp.: Spanish
t.: tome (vol.)

SOURCES OF ILLUSTRATIONS

22 Prévost, *Allgemeine Historie der Reisen,* t. xx, Leipzig, 1771.
25 *Journal of Capt. G. F. Lyon of HMS Hecla,* London, 1824.
76 Herman Moll: *The World Described,* London, 1732.
33, 168 Du Creux, *Historiae Canadensis,* Paris, 1664; courtesy of Baldwin Room, Toronto Public Library.
79, 103 *Recueil de Planches;* courtesy of Baldwin Room TPL.
98, 175, 179 *Encyclopédie*: courtesy of Institute of History, USSR Academy of Sciences.
153, 158, 179 Ibid.; courtesy of University of Toronto Library.
156 J. Bouchette: *British Dominions,* London, 1832.

Page

CHAPTER I

6 F. Engels: *Dialectics of Nature,* M. 1954, pp. 236, 228, 232, 147, 148.

7 A. P. Coleman: "The Geology of Canada." Article, 1930.

OTHER SOURCES (Ch. i):
  E. S. Moore: *Elementary Geology for Canada,* T. 1948.
  M. Nesturkh: *Origin of Man,* M. 1959.
  D. F. Putnam: *Canadian Regions,* L. 1952.

CHAPTER II

12 T. E. Lee: "The First Sheguiandah Expedition." AA vol. xx, p. 101; vol. xxi, p. 179.

12 On Asian-N. American Indian connections: Franz Boas: "Relationships between N. W. America and N. E. Asia" (1933); D. Jenness: "Indian Background of Canadian History" (1937).

13fn C. Winick: *Dictionary of Anthropology,* L. 1957, p. 158.

13-14 On Laurentian, Woodland and prehistoric Iroquoian cultures: P. Sweetman: "Digging up Ontario's History," *New Frontiers,* Winter 1955, p. 31.
  W. A. Ritchie: AA vol. xvii, p. 132; Hurt, AA vol. xviii, pp. 204 ff.

15 On role of women: K. MacGowan: *Early Man in the New World,* NY 1950, pp. 32-3, 200-4.
  Iroquoians: D. Jenness: *Indians of Canada,* O. 1955, p. 137.
  F. Ridley: "The Huron and Lalonde Occupations of Ontario," AA vol. xvii.
      "The Fallis Site," AA vol. xviii.
      "The Frank Bay Site, L. Nipissing, Ont."
      "The Boys and Barrie Sites": Ontario Archaeological Society, 1958.

16 Verrazzano: *Récit du Voyage de la Dauphine.* In Ch. A. Julien, *Les Français en Amérique,* P. 1946, p. 71-72.
  Spelling of Verrazzano: Of several variants, the oldest is used here; cf. H. Deschamps: ed. *Voyages de Champlain,* P. 1951, p. 7.
  M. Bishop cit: *Champlain, The Life of Fortitude,* L. 1949, p. 331.
  La Hontan: *New Voyages to N. America,* 1703, vol. i, p. 420.
  J. P. Baxter: *A Memoir of J. Cartier,* p. 176.

18 Table based on W. A. Ritchie (cited above) and G. I. Quimby: *Indian Life in the Upper Great Lakes,* Chicago 1960.

OTHER SOURCES (Ch. ii):
  F. Engels: *Origin of the Family, Private Property and the State.*
  Institute of Economics, AS, USSR: *Political Economy,* L 1957.
  W. Howells: *Back of History,* NY. 1954.

CHAPTER III

19 G. Heriot: *Through the Canadas,* 1807. p. 11.

21 K. Birket-Smith: *The Eskimos,* L. 1959, p. 70.

22 Quoted in *The Beaver,* March 1954.

23 D. Jenness: *People of the Twilight,* pp. 137, 246-7.
Birket-Smith: pp. 145, 146.
24 Jenness: pp. 165, 159.
Birket-Smith: pp. 144, 152; Jenness: p. 194.
Institute of Ethnography, AS, USSR: *Narodi Ameriki,* M. 1959,
p. 105.

CHAPTER IV

26 Table based on Jenness: *Indians of Canada.*
28 Jenness cit. pp. 56-8.
30 D. W. Prowse: *A History of Newfoundland,* L. 1895, p. 385.
On Algonkian techniques: K. E. Kidd: *Canadians of Long Ago*
(T. 1951).
31 On rock-paintings: Selwyn Dewdney, in *Canadian Art,* Aug. 1959.
D. Thompson: *Narrative*: Jenness cit. p. 43.
32 Jesuit *Relation,* vol. i: Jenness cit. p. 288.
34 J. Collier: *Indians of the Americas,* NY 1947, p. 128.
35 Jenness: p. 134.
36 Collier: pp. 118-119. Jenness: pp. 139, 125.
OTHER SOURCES (Ch. iv):
Lewis H. Morgan: *The League of the Iroquois; Ancient Society.*
D. Leechman: *Native Tribes of Canada,* T. nd.
R. W. Dunning: *Social and Economic Change Among the Northern Ojibwa,* T. 1959.

CHAPTER V

37-8 P. Drucker: *Indians of the Northwest Coast,* NY 1955, pp. 14-15.
H. Griffin: *British Columbia: The People's Story,* Vancouver,
1958.
38-9 On West Coast techniques, D. Jenness, D. Leechman, op cit.
39ff On break-up of primitive communal society: Julia P. Averkieva:
Rabstvo u Indeitsev Severnoi Ameriki (Slavery Among the
Indians of N. America), M. 1941; and by the same author, ch.
iv, *Narodi Ameriki* (Peoples of the Americas) M. 1959.
41 On class-division: Jenness: p. 140; Drucker: pp. 118-119.
Condition of slaves: Jenness: p. 328.
42 T. F. McIlwraith: *The Bella Coola Indians,* T. 1948, vol. i,
p. 158.
Jade tools: Royal Ontario Museum.
Tlinkit and Kwakiutl: Drucker: pp. 122-3.

CHAPTER VI

43 F. Engels: *Ludwig Feuerbach,* part II; in Marx-Engels *Selected
Works,* M. 1951, vol. ii, p. 334.
Bella Coola: McIlwraith, op. cit. vol. i, p. 35.
44 Lalemant: in OHS, *Transactions,* 1908, p. 428.
45 On West Coast myths: Averkieva, op. cit., pp. 88-90.
P. Radin: *The World of Primitive Man,* NY. 1953.

CHAPTER VII

48 Jean Bruhat: *Histoire du Mouvement Ouvrier Français*, P. 1952, t. i., p. 43.
49 R. Bonnycastle: *Newfoundland*, in 1842 L. 1842, vol. ii, p. 303.
M. Dobb: *Studies in Capitalist Development*, L. 1947, p. 15, 142 fn.
50 Florence: In V. Teitelboim: *Amanecer del Capitalismo y Conquista de America*, Santiago de Chile, 1943, p. 83ff.
also F. Antal: *Florentine Painting and its Social Background*, p. 21; and N. Macchiavelli: *Istorie Fiorentine*, pp. 154-5.
On the nation: J. V. Stalin: *Works*, vol. ii, p. 313-14.
53 "New world": R. A. Skelton: *Explorers' Maps*, L. 1958, p. 75.
K. Marx and F. Engels: *The Manifesto of the Communist Party*.
54 K. Marx: *Capital*, M. 1954, vol. i, p. 751.
Thomas More: cit. A. L. Morton: *People's History of England*, L. 1951, p. 170.
55 H. U. Faulkner: *American Economic History*, NY. 1949, p. 39.
A. L. Morton: *The English Utopia*, L. 1952, p. 125.
OTHER SOURCES (Ch. vii):
J. D. Bernal: *Science in History*, L. 1957.
F. Engels: *Anti-Duhring;* Introduction, *Dialectics of Nature.*
P. Boissonade: *Life and Work in Medieval Europe.*
G. & C. Willard: *Formation de la Nation française*, P. 1955.

CHAPTER VIII

56 John Rastell, 1519; and R. Thorne, 1527, cit. J. A. Williamson: *Voyages of the Cabots*, L. 1929, p. 24.
57 cit. Williamson: p. 31. Also L. J. Burpee: *Discovery of Canada*, T. 1944, pp. 13, 14.
59-60 cit. H. Lamb: *New Found World*, NY 1955, p. 232.
60 Williamson: p. 47.
61-2 cit. Ch. A. Julien: *Les Français en Amérique*, pp. 11, 60, 70, 72.
62fn Lamb: p. 79.
63 In J. P. Baxter: *A Memoir of J. Cartier*, NY. 1906; and Burpee: *Discovery of Canada.*
64 Julien: p. 157; Burpee: p. 27.

CHAPTER IX

67 In A. Courtauld: *From the Ends of the Earth*, L. 1958, p. 69.
68 M. Frobisher: in Hakluyt, ed. R. Wilson, L. 1936, p. 37.
Williamson: p. 213.
Courtauld: pp. 55, 56.
69 Ibid.: p. 57.
C. R. Markham: *A Life of John Davis the Navigator*, L. 1885, p. 33.
71 Markham: pp. 52, 61-2.
Courtauld: pp. 78, 80.
Markham: p. 52.
72 S. Purchas: *Hakluyt Posthumus*, vol. xiv, p. 397; in M. Dunbar, K. R. Greenaway: *Arctic Canada from the Air*, O. 1956.

OTHER SOURCES (Ch. ix):
    L. H. Neatby: *In Quest of the North West Passage*, T. 1958.
    V. Stefansson: *The Three Voyages of Martin Frobisher*, L. 1940;
    Great Adventures and Explorations, NY. 1947; *North West to
    Fortune*, NY. 1958.

CHAPTER X

73 H. A. Innis: *The Cod Fisheries*, T. 1954, ch. i.
    Prowse: *History of Newfoundland*, p. 587.
    G. O. Rothney: *Newfoundland*, p. 3.
74 Innis, p. 16. N. Denys: in Champlain, *Works*, vol. ii, pp. 257, 265.
75 cit. Innis, p. 48. Lescarbot: cit. Prowse, p. 20.
76 Prowse, p. 20.
77 Donne: cit. A. L. Rowse: *The Elizabethans and America*, p. 204.
    Gilbert: cit. Lamb: p. 272.
    Gilbert's expedition: Prowse: p. 73; Lamb: ch. vii.
78 Raleigh: cit. Innis: p. 32.
    K. Marx: in Marx-Engels Collected Works, vol. iii, p. 157 (Rn).
    Bacon: cit. Prowse: p. 54.
78-9 Guy's expedition: Prowse: pp. 95-6.
79 Prowse: p. 100.
OTHER SOURCES (Ch. x):
    G. S. Graham: *Empire of the North Atlantic*, T. 1950.
    R. A. MacKay: *Newfoundland*, T. 1946.

CHAPTER XI

80 French finance: *Marx-Engels Archiv*, t. vii, p. 135 (Rn); Breton
    rising: cit. *Istoria Srednikh Vekov* (History of Middle Ages),
    M. 1954, t. ii, pp. 306-7.
81 St. Malo: cit. Baxter: *Memoir of J. Cartier*, p. 388.
83 Master Jacques: *Les Voyages de Champlain*, P. 1613, Livre 1er,
    ch. x, p. 100. Cf M. Bishop: *Champlain*, p. 90.
    On the *Brief Discours*, attributed to Champlain but not published
    in his lifetime: research by C. Bonnault in Seville has cast doubt
    on its origin. Cf. H. Deschamps, ed. *Les Voyages de Samuel
    Champlain*, P. 1951, p. 48fn; and discussion in BRH avril 1954
    and RHAF vol. xi, 163ff; xii, 208; xiii, 544ff (mars 1960).
84 Champlain :cit. L. Groulx: *Histoire du Canada Français*, Mtl.
    1950, t. i, p. 36.
    Opposition to Jesuits: Chrestien LeClercq: *First Establishment
    of the Faith in N. France* (1691), NY. 1881, p. 225; G. Lanctôt:
    Histoire du Canada, Mtl. 1959, p. 164; cf. LeClercq, p. 309,
    Sagard, pp. 862ff.
85 Pamphlet: Du Creux: *Histoire du Canada* (1664) p. 29; Calvin-
    ists, ibid., p. 33.
    "Contemporary": Gabriel Sagard: *Le Grand Voyage au Pays
    des Hurons*, P. 1632: cit. Innis, p. 37.
    1621: C. LeClercq, op. cit., p. 165.

87 cit. Innis: *Fur Trade,* pp. 44, 25, 60.
   G. Raynal: *Histoire Philosophique et Politique des Etablisse-
   ments de Commerce européens dans les deux Indes,* P. 1776, t. vi,
   pp. 21, 64. Innis, p. 34.
88 Innis, p. 16.

CHAPTER XII

90 cit. L. P. Desrosiers: *Iroquoisie,* Mtl. 1947, p. 125; cf. Champlain:
   Oeuvres, t. vi, p. 376 (Fr.).
   La Hontan: *New Voyages,* vol. i, p. 227.
91 *Relation* of 1635; cit. Desrosiers, p. 148.
   G. Sagard: *Le Grand Voyage au Pays des Hurons,* P. 1632; cit.
   Innis, p. 29.
91fn Hunt: p. 70; Frégault: *Civilisation de la Nouvelle France,*
   p. 245.
92 cit. Desrosiers: pp. 276-7, 297, 261-2fn, 286, 250.
93 Ibid. p. 279.
94 La Potherie: cit. in R. Flenley, ed. Dollier de Casson: *Histoire
   de Montréal,* p. 42.
   1650: In P. J. Robinson: Introduction to Du Creux: *Histoire du
   Canada,* T. 1951.
   ambush: Marie de l'Incarnation or Chaumonot: cit. A. Pouliot,
   RHAF, juin 1960, p. 4.
95 cf. Adair, CHR, June 1932.
   cit. G. F. Stanley: *Canada's Soldiers: 1604-1954,* T. 1954, p. 13.
   Dollier de Casson: *History of Montreal,* p. 303.
96 Algonquin-Montagnais: E. Salone: *Colonisation de la Nouvelle
   France,* P. 1906, p. 140.

CHAPTER XIII

97 Lescarbot on Hébert: Salone, p. 29.
   T. Guérin: *Feudal Canada,* Mtl. 1926, p. 27.
97-8 farm implements: R.-L. Séguin: *L'Equipement de la Ferme
   canadienne aux XVIIe et XVIII Siècles,* Mtl. 1959.
99 cit. Séguin, p. 43.
   Champlain: cit. Innis, p. 34.
   Du Creux: *Histoire,* p. 179.
100 "Engagés pour le Canada au 17e Siècle, vus de La Rochelle":
   RHAF, vol. xi, Sept. 1952, p. 185.
   Relation: cit. Salone, p. 127n.
   J. Guérin: cit. W. and E. M. Jury: *Ste. Marie among the Hurons,*
   T. 1954, p. 87.
   Le Jeune: Salone, p. 72.
101 1638-60: "Engagés . . ." RHAF loc. cit., p. 186.
   Montreal: Salone, p. 77; Du Creux, p. 224-5.
   Casson, p. 107.
   Barbier and other workers: E. Z. Massicotte: Transactions RSC
   3rd Series 1914.
   Casson, p. 103.

102 Huronia: Jury, op. cit., pp. 49, 53, 83.
Confrérie of carpenters: D. Levack: *La Confrérie de Ste. Anne à Québec,* Ste. Anne de Beaupré, 1956.

102fn *Confrérie* of metalworkers: P. E. Renaud: *Origines Economiques du Canada,* 1928, p. 389; BRH xxiii, p. 343.

103 Levack, op. cit., p. 63.
"Engagés . . ." RHAF, loc. cit., p. 191.

104 Ibid. pp. 204, 209.
Boucher: Salone, p. 117.

CHAPTER XIV

106-7 Gustavus Myers: *History of Canadian Wealth,* Chicago 1914, pp. 17, 23.

107 K. Marx: Capital, M. 1959, vol. iii, p. 772.

108 Renaud, p. 334; T. Guérin, op. cit., p. 61.

108-9 Guérin, pp. 67, 69.
1707 report: cit. Guy Frégault: *La Civilisation de la Nouvelle France,* Mtl. 1944, p. 212.
"low justice": Guérin, p. 93.

110 Frégault, pp. 184-5.
La Corne: L. Groulx: *Histoire du Canada Français,* Mtl. 1951, t. ii, p. 106.

CHAPTER XV

111 Agriculture: Renaud, pp. 344, 357.

112 lack of mills: J. N. Fauteux: *Essai sur l'Industrie au Canada sous le Régime français,* Q. 1927, t. ii, p. 355.
Montreal bakers: ibid., p. 374.

113 C. A. Julien: *Les Français en Amérique,* t. ii, p. 21.

113fn F. Bacon: cit. E. Roll: *A History of Economic Thought,* L. 1936, p. 75.

114 Colbert: cit. Renaud, p. 396; Talon, ibid., p. 395.

115 cit. Fauteux, t. ii, pp. 450-2.
workshops: Renaud, p. 393fn.
capitalism: ibid., p. 393.
forest resources: Fauteux, t. i, p. 225;
long-saw men: ibid., p. 223.

116 ibid., pp. 232, 234.
iron mines: ibid., p. 39.

117 West Indies: ibid., p. 231; cf also Easterbrook and Aitken: *Canadian Economic History,* pp. 62-3.

118 K. Marx: MECW, t. iv, p. 308 (Rn.)
Louis XIV on trade: cit. Frégault, Brunet, Trudel: *Histoire du Canada par les Textes,* Mtl. 1956, p. 33.
P. Boissonade: *Life and Work in Medieval Europe.*
Marx on Colbert: *Capital,* I, p. 760.

CHAPTER XVI

119 Francis Parkman: *The Old Régime in Canada*, p. 398.
120 Denonville: cit. René Fülop-Miller: *Macht u. Geheimnis der Jesuiten*, Leipzig 1929, p. 313.
Louis XIV: cit. Lanctôt, p. 406.
La Hontan: *New Voyages*, vol. i, p. 381; cit. S. D. Clark: *The Social Development of Canada*, T. 1942, p. 88.
Voil and Laviolette: Salone, p. 135; *Journal des Jésuites*, p. 303; Dupuy: in Parkman: *The Old Régime*, ch. xix.
Intendant de Meulles: cit. Parkman, ibid., ch. xviii.
121 Jesuits: Fülop-Miller; Lanctôt, p. 405.
123 protest movement: Lanctôt, pp. 241-2.
124 R. Bilodeau: RHAF, loc. cit. pp. 50, 52.
125 Talon: cit. *Histoire . . . par les Textes*, p. 42; and in Parkman, *Old Régime*, ch. xviii.
W. B. Munro: *Documents Relating to Seigniorial Tenure in Canada*, p. xvi.
126 "indocility": Hocquart: Frégault: *Civilisation . . .*, p. 165.
Acadians: J. B. Brebner: *New England's Outpost*, p. 47; cit. S. D. Clark: *Movements of Political Protest in Canada*, T. 1960, p. 16.
coureurs de bois: Clark, pp. 18, 21.
Montreal: H. Lorin: *Le Comte de Frontenac*, p. 186.
127 *taille*: E. R. Adair in CHR, Sept. 1954, p. 206.
128 Normandy: G. Willard: *Formation de la Nation française*, P. 1955, p. 61.
USSR: *Vsemirnaia Istoria*, (World History), M. 1958; t. v, pp. 126-7 (chapter by Prof. B. Porshnev).

OTHER SOURCES (Ch. xvi):
F. Parkman: *The Jesuits in North America*, Boston 1895.
W. J. Eccles: *Frontenac: the Courtier Governor*, T. 1959.
W. B. Munro: *The Seigniorial System;* and "The Seigniorial System and the Colony," *Canada and Its Provinces*, vol. ii.

CHAPTER XVII

130 Talon: cit. *Histoire . . . par les Textes*, p. 41.
De Lusson: cit. M. H. Long: *A History of the Canadian People*, 1942, vol. i, p. 312.
131 Marie de l'Incarnation: G. Myers, op. cit., p. 6.
132 Colbert's estimate: A. St. Léger: *La Prépondérance française*, (1661-1715).
134 Marx: cit. A. L. Morton, p. 276.
135 Navigation Acts: cit. H. E. Egerton: *A Short History of British Colonial Policy*, L. 1920, p. 72.
deportations: ibid. p. 66.
navy: Michael Lewis: *History of the British Navy*, L. 1957, ch. 6; and Egerton, op. cit., p. 63; Graham, op. cit., ch. 3.
Monck: Lewis, p. 89.
136 Marx: *Capital*, vol. iii, p. 328.
137 Massachusetts: cit. Egerton, p. 95.

OTHER SOURCES (Ch. xvii):

A. L. Morton: *A People's History of England,* ch. viii.

H. Aptheker: *The Colonial Era,* NY. 1959.

E. A. Kosminsky, Y. A. Levitsky: *Angliiskaia Burzhuaznaia Revoliutsia XVII Veka,* t. i & ii, M. 1954.

CHAPTER XVIII

139-40 W. J. Eccles: *Frontenac, The Courtier Governor,* T. 1959, pp. 95-6.

140 Michigan tribes: La Potherie, cit. E. H. Blair: *Indian Tribes of the Upper Mississippi,* Ohio 1912.

143 Five Nations' spokesman: La Hontan, t. I, p. 83.
Charlevoix, vol. iv, p. 248.
P. Wraxall: *An Abridgement of the Indian Affairs,* 1678-1751. ed. McIlwain, 1915, cit. p. ix.

144 H. Aptheker: *The Colonial Era,* pp. 68, 73.

144-5 S. D. Clark: *Movements of Political Protest in Canada 1640-1840,* pp. 24-5, 30.

146 Pontchartrain: Salone: *La Colonisation française;* pp. 303-4.

OTHER SOURCES (Ch. xviii):

D. MacKay: *The Honorable Company,* NY. 1938.

C. P. Stacey: *Introduction to Study of Military History for Canadian Students,* O. 1955.

R. G. Thwaite: *France in America,* NY. 1905.

CHAPTER XIX

148 Bégon: cf. G. Frégault: *La Société canadienne sous l'ancien Régime,* O. 1954, p. 10.

150 agriculture: Renaud, pp. 344, 357.
Hocquart: cit. *Histoire . . . par les Textes,* p. 67.

151 Dupuy: cit. Fauteux, t. i, pp. 208-9.

152 de Ramezay: Renaud, p. 404.
hydraulic mill: ibid.
Sicard mill: ibid., p. 385n.

154 Hocquart: cit. Fauteux, t. i, p. 244; strike: Frégault: *Civilisation . . .,* p. 179; Raudot: Fauteux, p. 238.

156 ibid., p. 79.

157 Labrèche: ibid. p. 58.

157fn Alice J. Lunn: "Economic Development in New France": McGill Ph.D. thesis, 1942, pp. 327, 329.

157-8 P. Kalm: *Travels in N. America,* in Pinkerton: *General Collection of . . . Travels,* L. 1812, vol. 13, pp. 630-1.

158-9 cit. Lunn, p. 320.

159 Kalm: Fauteux, t. i, p. 121.
Le Page: ibid., p. 242.

160 Easterbrook, op. cit., p. 88.

161 Louis XIV: cit. Renaud, p. 394.
Minister: *Cahiers de l'Académie canadienne française*, No. 2, Histoire, Mtl. 1957, p. 63.
1730: R. Bilodeau, op. cit., p. 65.
162 memorandum: *Cahiers* . . ., p. 76.
163 housewives: cf. Frégault: *Civilisation* . . . p. 69; Vaudreuil: ibid., p. 165.
Bégon: Bilodeau, op. cit.
164 1733: cit. Groulx, t. ii, p. 173.
1737: ibid., p. 172.

CHAPTER XX

166 St. Joachim: *The Arts in Canada*, O. 1957, p. 9; G. Morisset: *La Peinture traditionnelle au Canada français*, O. 1960, p. 26.
Hocquart: cit. *Histoire . . . par les Textes*, p. 71.
166fn L. Groulx: *Histoire du Canada français*, t. ii, p. 143.
166-7 Vaudreuil: ibid.
167fn See page 85, above.
169 theatre: cf. L. Houlé: *L'Histoire du Théâtre au Canada*, Mtl. 1945.
Raudot: Groulx, t. i, p. 211.
169-70 cit. Frégault: *Civilisation* . . ., p. 179.
170 festivities: B. Sulte: Mélanges historiques: *La Saint-Jean-Baptiste*, Mtl. 1929, pp. 24, 28-9.
170fn Sulte, p. 17.
171 Hungarians in New France: I am indebted to S. Szoke of Toronto for research on this question.
German miners: Fauteux and others.
Jews in N. France: B. G. Sack: *History of the Jews in Canada*, Mtl. 1945, pp. 21-5.
1660, Montreal: Massicotte, loc. cit., RSC Series 3, 1913.
172 language: P. Daviault: "La Langue française au Canada," *Royal Commission Studies*, O. 1949-51, pp. 25-32; V. Barbeau: *Le Ramage de mon Pays*, Mtl. 1939, pp. 39-44.
172-3 painting: Morisset, op. cit.
sculpture: *Arts in Canada*, pp. 25-7.
architecture: Alan Gowans: *Looking at Architecture in Canada*, T. 1958, ch. i and ii; on baroque, p. 61.
174-7 A. Vallée: *Un Biologiste canadien: Michel Sarrazin*, Q. 1927.
175 ibid., pp. 84-5.
176 ibid., pp. 123, 216.
177 Gaulthier: cit. R. Lamontagne: "Les Echanges scientifiques entre . . . La Galissonière et les chercheurs contemporains," RHAF juin 1960, p. 30.
178 P. Kalm: *Travels into N. America*, L. 1772; cf. Martti Kerkkonen: *Peter Kalm's North American Journey: Its Ideological Background and Results*. Finnish Historical Society, Studia Historica I, Helsinki 1959.
V. de Forbonnais: "Colonie": *Encyclopédie*, t. viii.

180 Raynal: op. cit., t. iii, p. 331; cit. G. Esquer, *L'Anticolonialisme au XVIIIe Siècle*, P. 1951, p. 37.

CHAPTER XXI

182 fur trade: cf. G. Frégault: *La Guerre de la Conquête*, Mtl. 1955, p. 29, cited hereafter as *La Guerre* . . .
colonists: cit. L. H. Gipson: *The British Empire before the American Revolution*: vol. vi: *The Great War for the Empire*, p. 11.
fears of French: Frégault: *La Guerre* . . ., p. 115.
183 Dupaquai and Louisbourg mutiny: G. Frégault: *François Bigot, Administrateur français*, Mtl. 1948, t. i, pp. 207-211.
186 1710: Col. Nicholson, cit. J. L. Rutledge: *Century of Conflict*, T. 1956, p. 350.
187 cit. Frégault: *La Guerre* . . ., p. 270.

CHAPTER XXII

188 Gipson: op. cit., vol. vii, p. 174.
188-9 Morton: op. cit., p. 296.
coal and iron: F. D. Klingender: *Art in the Industrial Revolution*, L. 1947, pp. 3, 5.
189 observer: Franquet: *Voyages et Mémoires sur le Canada*: 1753, Q. 1889.
190 Doreil, 1755: cit. Frégault: *Bigot*, t. ii, p. 121; ibid. pp. 334, 70; t. i, p. 390.
official: cit. Frégault: *La Guerre* . . ., p. 292.
191 demonstrations: *Bigot*, t. ii, pp. 230, 233, 238.
churchman: Abbé de l'Isle Dieu, 1754: RAPQ 1936-7, p. 358.
on Vaudreuil: RAPQ 1924, p. 115.
Montcalm's lieutenant: cit. Frégault: *La Guerre* . . ., p. 99.
1699: ACF: Cahier No. 2, p. 20.
192 Voltaire: cit. Groulx, t. ii, p. 213.
193 Wolfe: Doughty and Parmelee: *Siege of Quebec*, vol. vi., p. 82.
resistance: ibid., vol. iv, p. 4.
194 Townshend: ibid., vol. v, p. 267.
195fn*** *History of Canada*, vol. ii, p. 43; cf. Doughty, vol. v, pp. 188, 322.
196 Vaudreuil: cit. Frégault: *La Guerre* . . ., pp. 373, 513.
Bordeaux merchants: ibid., p. 436.
197 Pamphlet entitled "Reasons for Keeping Guadeloupe at a Peace": Frégault, p. 418.
Murray: ibid., p. 332.
197fn ibid., p. 420.
198 Pitt: RAPQ 1951-3, p. 433.

CHAPTER XXIII

200fn G. Frégault: *Canadian Society under the French Régime*, p. 4.
201 Murray: cit. A. L. Burt: *The Old Province of Quebec*, p. 17.
203 "Indian Spartacus": cf. G. F. Stanley: *Canada's Soldiers*, p. 99.
Murray: Burt, op. cit., p. 109.

204 petition: ibid., p. 124.

205 Carleton: C. Martin: *Empire and Commonwealth,* p. 119.
seigneurial opposition: Shortt and Doughty: *Documents . . .
Constitutional History of Canada* 1759-91, pp. 493-4.

206 popular resistance: cf. M. Brunet: "Les Canadiens après la Conquête—les Débuts de la Résistance passive": RHAF, Sept. 1958.
Carleton: Shortt & Doughty, pp. 284, 289.

207 Carleton: Burt, op. cit., pp. 158, 162.
North: Cavendish: *Debates ... of the Year 1774,* L. 1839, p. 290.
Carleton: C. Martin, op. cit., p. 114.

208 H. E. Egerton, W. L. Grant: *Canadian Constitutional History,*
T. 1907, p. 34n.
Pitt: G. M. Wrong: *Canada and the American Revolution,* p.
253.
att'y-gen'l: ibid., p. 250.

209 Message: Gustave Lanctôt: *Les Canadiens et leurs Voisins du
Sud,* NY. 1941, p. 98.
correspondent: in Verreau: *L'Invasion du Canada,* Mtl. 1873.
partisans of Congress: Baby: *Journal*; cf. Lanctôt, op. cit. p. 111.

CHAPTER XXIV

210 Washington: cit. M. Trudel: *Louis XVI, le Congrès américain
et le Canada,* Q. 1949, p. 56.
210fn Lenin: *Collected Works,* t. 28, p. 44 (Rn.).
211 resolutions, resistance: Wrong, op. cit., pp. 284, 288; Baby, pp.
19, 22.
212 St. Johns: Lanctôt, op. cit., p. 107.
213 Cramahé: ibid., p. 108.
214 *Works* of Samuel Adams, vol. iii, p. 297.
215 Burgoyne's officer: Trudel, p. 115.
military estimate: G. S. Graham: *Empire of the North Atlantic,*
pp. 195, 209.
216 French opinions: Trudel, pp. 10, 112, 126.
216fn Lenin, *Works,* t. 28, p. 50 (Rn.).
217 Haldimand: Lanctôt, p. 117.
La Fayette: Trudel, p. 173.
Vergennes: ibid., p. 123.

CHAPTER XXV

219 town meetings: K. G. Crawford: *Canadian Municipal Government.* p. 25.
Halifax: T. Raddall: *Halifax, Warden of the North,* pp. 75-6.
220 dockyard workers: cit. G. S. Graham, p. 206.
Washington: Raddall, p. 84.

OTHER SOURCES (Ch. xxv):
S. D. Clark: *Movements of Political Protest in Canada,* ch. 5-6.
224 H. Aptheker: *The American Revolution,* NY. 1960, p. 173.

CHAPTER XXVI

225 agitation: cit. G. Lanctôt: *Les Canadiens Français* . . ., p. 124.
1785: Pitt: Burt, op. cit., p. 427.
1789: PAC Report 1890, p. 10.
227 toasts: R. Christie: *History of Lower Canada,* Mtl. 1866, vol. ii, p. 42.
228 "free speech": cit. L. A. H. Smith, in CHR, June 1957, p. 98.
Pitt: Christie, vol. ii, p. 172.
229 Pitt: ibid., vol. i, p. 73.
230 pamphlet: cit. M. Brunet: "La révolution française sur les rives du Saint-Laurent": RHAF, Sept. 1957, pp. 159-62.
231 Charlesbourg: Christie, vol. ii, p. 114.
bishop: cit. Brunet, loc. cit., p. 156.
McLean: Christie, vol. ii, pp. 113-21.
232 M. Trudel: *L'Influence de Voltaire au Canada,* Mtl. 1945, t. i, pp. 40-2.
cf. R. Flenley: "The French Revolution and French Canada": *Essays in Canadian History,* T. 1939, pp. 54-63.

CHAPTER XXVII

233 1629: Ida Greaves: *The Negro in Canada* (McGill University Economic Studies), p. 9; cf. W. L. Styles: *Unusual Facts of Canadian History,* T. 1947, p. 18; Frégault: *Civilisation* . . ., pp. 83-4.
234 Raudot: Greaves, op. cit., p. 10.
Bégon: Frégault: *Civilisation* . . ., p. 84.
1760: Greaves, p. 10.
1761: A. J. Lunn: "Economic Development of New France", p. 12: cit. H. C. Pentland: "Formation of a Capitalistic Labor Market in Canada," CJEPS, Nov. 1959, p. 451.
235 1765-7: cit. Innis and Lower: *Select Documents in Canadian Economic History* 1497-1783, T. 1929, p. 467.
N.B. historian: Hannay, op. cit., p. 221.
Halifax: articles in *Canadian Negro,* June 1953.
1751: Haliburton, *Historical and Statistical Account of Nova Scotia,* 1829, vol. ii, p. 281.
236 Maroons: ibid., pp. 282-91.
237 Haliburton, ibid., p. 281.
L. Canada: Greaves, pp. 16-17.
U. Canada: ibid., pp. 13-14.
238 Russell: H. Scadding, *Toronto of Old,* T. 1873, p. 293.
Lords Commissioners: in F. Landon: *Lake Huron,* p. 66.
239 authority: Duncan Campbell Scott: "Indian Affairs, 1763-1841," *Canada and Its Provinces,* T. 1913, vol. iv, p. 697.
Johnson: ibid., p. 699.
240 Joseph Brant: ibid., p. 708.
240fn cf. C. C. Royce: "Indian Land Cessions in the U.S." Bureau of American Ethnology, 18th Report, p. 535.
241 John Brant: D. C. Scott, op. cit., p. 721.
Missisauga: ibid., p. 718.
Indian title: ibid., pp. 707, 717

OTHER SOURCES (Ch. xxvii):
H. Chalmers and Ethel Brant Monture: *Joseph Brant, Mohawk*, T. 1955.

CHAPTER XXVIII

242 cit. H. A. Innis, op. cit., p. 190.
243 in W. S. Wallace: *Documents relating to the North West Company*, p. 39; cf. M. W. Campbell: *The North West Company*, ch. i, ii.
244 Wallace, op. cit., pp. 4, 5, 73.
246 Innis, op. cit., pp. 235-6, 272.
247 Alexander Mackenzie: *A General History of the Fur Trade*, L. 1801, pp. 21-2.
Indians: L. Masson: *Les Bourgeois de la Compagnie du Nord-Ouest*, Q. 1889, pp. 17-8; S. Hearne: *Journal*, p. 100; Innis, p. 152.
Mackenzie, p. 51; Campbell, p. 25; Wallace, p. 63.
248 Innis, pp. 214, 223, 241.
249 Mackenzie, p. 53 and fn.; p. 52.
Grace Lee Nute: *The Voyageur*, NY. 1931, p. 50.
Innis, pp. 239, 242.
250 *Journal of Duncan McGillivray*: ed. A. S. Morton, p. 6; cit. Nute, pp. 49-50.

CHAPTER XXIX

253 Leibnitz: V. A. Divin: *K Beregam Ameriki* (To the Shores of America), M. 1956, pp. 8, 9.
254 cartography: L. Breitefuss: *Imago Mundi*, 1939, vol. iii, p. 89.
255 Madrid dispatch: in Rickard, op. cit., p. 121.
257 James Cook: *An Abridgment of Capt. Cook's Last Voyage*, L. 1794, vol. ii, pp. 285, 292.
258 cit. J. B. Brebner: *Explorers of N. America*, p. 332.
Hearne: ibid., p. 368.
259 A. Mackenzie: op. cit., p. 4.
260 McTavish: C. W. Colby, *Introduction* to A. Mackenzie: *Voyages* (1801), T. 1927, p. xxi.
262fn cf. Rickard, op. cit.
263 cf. Howay: "Indian Attacks on Maritime Traders on the NW Coast."
Thompson: cit. M. Ormsby: *British Columbia: a History*, Vancouver 1958, p. 40.
265 1811 pamphlet: in Baldwin Room, TPL: pp. 31-3.
266-7 A. Mackenzie: *Voyages*, pp. 4, 493.
OTHER SOURCES (Ch. xxix):
N. A. Graebner: *Empire on the Pacific*, NY. 1955.

CHAPTER XXX

269-70 cit. T. Mahan: *Sea Power in its Relation to the War of 1812*, Vol. I, p. 65.

270 ibid., p. 71.
　　D. B. Read: *Life and Times of Brock,* p. 102.
　　Mahan: I, p. 194.
271 Grundy etc.: cit. J. W. Pratt: *Expansionists of 1812,* pp. 141, 149.
272 fn V. I. Lenin: *Selected Works* (2 vol. ed.) II, p. 116.
272-3 Morris, Burwell, etc.: Pratt, op. cit., pp. 19, 35, 52, 14, 51.
273 H. L. Keenleyside: *Canada and the United States,* NY. 1929, p. 77.
274 J. B. Brebner: *North Atlantic Triangle,* T. 1945, p. 70fn.
　　Innis & Lower: *Select Economic Documents,* II, p. 21.
275 Imperialist Policy: Of the earlier conflict of 1756-63 Lenin writes: "England and France engaged in a seven years' war for colonies, i.e., they waged an imperialist war (which is as possible on the basis of slavery, or of primitive capitalism, as on the basis of highly developed modern capitalism)." Elsewhere he speaks of "the imperialist wars of Napoleon," adding in a footnote: "I call imperialism, here, the pillaging of other countries in general, and imperialist war, a war among pirates over the division of such spoils." This, in distinction to his use of the term imperialism as monopoly-capitalism, the highest and final stage of capitalist development. (*Collected Works,* vol. xix, "The Pamphlet by Junius," p. 204, Eng. ed.; and vol. xxvii, p. 31, Rn. Cf. Lenin's work: *Imperialism: The Highest Stage of Capitalism.*)

CHAPTER XXXI

275 G. F. Stanley: "Indians in the War of 1812," CHR, June 1950, p. 152-3.
276 M. Edgar: *General Brock,* p. 204.
277 T. C. Haliburton: *Historical and Statistical Account of Nova Scotia,* I, pp. 273-4, 281, 285.
278 cit. G. S. Graham: *Empire of the North Atlantic,* p. 225; Haliburton, pp. 283-4.
279 bishop: M. Trudel, op. cit., p. 77.
280 *Mercury:* Christie: vol. ii, p. 179.
　　Le Canadien: cit. L. A. H. Smith: "*Le Canadien* and the British Constitution, 1806-1810," CHR June 1957, p. 96.
　　N. W. Co.: Christie, vol. ii, p. 183.
　　Wealth of Nations, L. 1799, vol. iii, pp. 80-81; cf. also p. 73.
281 on Locke: L. A. H. Smith, loc. cit., pp. 100, 104.
281-2 Craig: cit. Clark: *Movements . . .,* p. 207.
　　Le Canadien: in *Canada and Its Provinces,* vol. iii, p. 162.
282-3 Craig: cit. M. Wade: *The French Canadians,* T. 1955, p. 111.
283 Act of 1791: Smith, loc. cit., p. 93.
283-4 F. Tupper: *Life of Brock,* pp. 63, 78.
284 Montreal: Clark, op. cit., p. 201.
285-7 Thorpe, Willcocks: J. C. Dent: *Story of the Upper Canadian Rebellion,* T. 1885, vol. i, pp. 85-92.
286 Clark, op. cit. pp. 213-18.
287 A. D. Perlin: *The Newfoundland Story,* St. John's 1958, p. 9.
288-9 Clark, op cit., pp. 133, 137.

290-1 Glenie: ibid., p. 162.
290 Glenie on schools: I am indebted to F. W. Park for this and other material on New Brunswick.
291 William Skirving was secretary of the "British Convention of the Delegates of the People associated to obtain Universal Suffrage and Annual Parliaments"; arrested for sedition 1793, he was deported to Australia. So was Thomas Muir, the eloquent spokesman of the Friends of the People Society, circulator of Tom Paine's writings in Scotland; sentenced to 14 years transportation, he was rescued by a privateer fitted out by U.S. sympathizers, reached France after shipwreck and capture by Spaniards, joining Paine and the Irish patriot Wolfe Tone in Paris.

CHAPTER XXXII

293-4 Edgar, op. cit., p. 21; Read, p. 116; Pratt, p. 40.
294 Brock: Canada, General Staff: *Introduction to Military History* (1952), p. 14.
295 Tecumseh: W. Wood: *Select British Documents of the Canadian War of 1812*, I, p. 508.
295-6 Read, p. 229-30.
296 ibid., p. 252-3.
297 F.-X. Garneau: *History of Canada*, Mtl. 1862, vol. II, p. 278.
    Calhoun: in Mahan, I, p. 303.
298 ibid., p. 390.
298fn ibid., pp. 304, 302.
300 J. M. Smith: *Précis of the Wars in Canada*, L. 1826.
301 cit. G. F. Stanley, op. cit., p. 158.

CHAPTER XXXIII

312 C. Martin: *Foundations of Canadian Nationhood* (1955), p. 70; W. S. Wallace; *The Growth of Canadian National Feeling* (1927), p. 14; Clark: *Movements of Political Protest* (1959), p. 250.
314-5 "Canadian Volunteers": Clark, *op. cit.*, p. 222. Prevost: Lower Lakes Historical Society, *Documents of Campaign of 1812-14* vol. 3, part 3.
315 De Boucherville: ibid, part 4.
    Clark: *op. cit.* p. 222.
    Hull: Lower Lakes Hist. Soc., vol. 3, part 1.
316 Visitor, 1816: cit. F. Landon; *Western Ontario and the American Frontier*, p. 42.
317 Lower: in *Canadian Weekly*, June 23, 1962.
    Garneau: *History of Canada*, vol. II, p. 278.
318 "Answer . . .": L. L. Hist. Soc., vol. 3, part 2.
319 L. L. Hist. Soc., vol. 3, part 1.
320 H. T. Manning: *Revolt of French Canada* (1961), pp. 396-7.
321 Garneau: *Histoire du Canada*, (5e edition), t. 2, p. 543.
    E. Tarlé: *Napoleon's Invasion of Russia*, 1812, p. 275.
322 Molsons: Merrill Denison: *The Barley and the Stream*, p. 86.
    McGillivray: cit. M. W. Campbell: *The North West Company*, p. 275.

OTHER SOURCES (Ch. xxx-xxxiii):

W. Kingsford: *History of Canada*, Vol. VIII.

R. Christie: *History of Lower Canada*, Vol. II.

Henry Adams: *War of 1812*.

F. Beirne: *War of 1812*.

A. L. Burt: *U.S., Great Britain & British N. America.*

Cruikshank: *Documentary History of the War* (9 vols.).

W. Z. Foster: *Political History of the Americas*, NY. 1951.

C. P. Lucas: *The Canadian War of 1812*.

C. P. Stacey: *Military Problems of Canada*, T. 1940.

E. T. Raymond: *Tecumseh*.

C. J. Snider: *In the Wake of the 1812-ers*, T. 1913.

D. G. Creighton: *Commercial Empire of the St. Lawrence*, T. 1937.

A. G. Mileikovsky: *Kanada i Anglo-Amerikanskie Protivorechiia* (Canada and Anglo-American Contradictions), M. 1958, ch. 1-2.

AS, USSR: *Novaya Istoria* (Modern History): *1789-1870*. M. 1958, ch. ii; *Ocherki Novoi i Noveishei Istorii SShA (Essays in Modern and Contemporary History of the USA)*, M. 1960, t. i, ch. 3.

B. Sulte: *La Bataille de Chateauguay* and *Histoire de la Milice Canadienne.*

POSTSCRIPT

K. Marx: *German Ideology*, NY. 1947, p. 7.

K. Marx: Preface to *Capital*, vol. i.

V. I. Lenin: *Collected Works* (Eng. ed.), M. 1960, vol. i, p. 140.

H. Neatby: *Royal Commission Studies: Arts, Letters and Sciences*, O. 1951, p. 211.

H. A. Innis: *Problems of Staple Production*, p. 82; *U. of T. Studies in History and Economics*, vol. ii, p. 61.

Hugh Aitken: "On the Present State of Economic History," CJEPS, Feb. 1960, p. 87ff.

S. D. Clark: "Sociology, History and the Problem of Social Change," CJEPS, Nov. 1959, pp. 395, 399.

D. G. Creighton: *Harold Adams Innis*, T. 1957, p. 93.

F.-X. Garneau: *History of Canada*, Mtl. 1862, vol. ii, p. 277.

Index

Abenaki 19, 19fn, 91fn
Abercrombie 192
Acadia and Acadians 57-8, 62, 75, 82-3, 89, 115, 117, 126, 137, 142, 146-7, 169, 182-3-4, 186-7, 219, 221, 289
Adams, John 269
Adams, Samuel 208, 214
Africa 53-4, 56, 135, 181
Aitken, Hugh 328
Alaska 10, 254
Albany 138, 139, 171, 208, 242
Alberta 3
Aleutians 254, 256
Alexander, Sir Wm. 134
Algonkian 15, 17, 18, 27-32, 44
Algonquin 15, 17, 29, 30, 88, 90, 92, 93, 94, 96
Alien and Sedition Acts 231, 285
Allan, John 221
Allen, Ethan 210
American Fur Company (Astor's) 274
American Revolution, 201, 208-226, 269, 286
Amherst, General 193, 202
Amherstburg 302
Ango, Jean 60
Annapolis 186, 235
Anticosti 201
Aptheker, Herbert 144, 224, 331
Arctic 1, 7, 8, 12, 13, 19, 20, 70, 243, 253, 259-60
Argentine 67, 324
Arnold, Benedict 210, 212-3-4
Asia 5, 9, 10, 11, 49, 53, 67, 135, 253
Assiniboine 147, 247
Astor, John Jacob 245, 264, 274, 276
Astoria 276
Athapaskan Indians 17, 19, 20, 27, 32, 247, 258
Aubert, Thomas 59

Aubery, Father 91fn
Avalon Peninsula 58, 76
Averkieva, Julia P. 46fn
Ayer, Obadiah 221
Ayotte, Pierre 209
Aztec 14fn, 41, 252

Baccalaos 58, 61fn
Bacon, Francis 52, 78, 113fn
Baffin, Wm. 71-2
Baffin I. 71, 257
Bailly, Le 233
Ball, John 55
Baltimore, Lord 134
Bank of Montreal 310
Barbeau, Dr. Marius 46fn, 253fn, 330
Barbier, Gilbert 101
Barlow, Roger 59
Barre, De La 126
Barren Lands 20, 243
Barrieau 259
Basques 56
Batiscan 169
Bay Bulls 223
Bayle, Pierre 174
Beaucourt, Paul 173
Beaucousin, Pierre 115
Beauport 142, 193, 194
Beauséjour 186
Beaver Dam (near St. David's) 300
Bédard, Jérôme 231
Bédard, Pierre 279, 282, 283, 297
Bégon, Intendant 149, 155, 163, 234
Bella Coola 37, 38, 42, 43, 260
Bellin, F. 254fn
Benesteau, Daniel 100
Beothuk 29, 30, 58, 59
Bering, Vitus 253, 254
Bering Strait 9, 11, 253, 260
Berthier (Parish) 211